Contents

iv *Contents*

Acknowledgements

Our thanks are once again due to the many colleagues and friends who have helped us with advice and criticism during the preparation of the third edition of this Reader. The largest debt is still to the members of the Communication Studies course team at Sunderland Polytechnic from 1976 to 1979, the time during which the first edition was planned and prepared. Since then, others have been of assistance in discussing their courses, their teaching and the kinds of material they have found to be most useful. In particular, we would like to thank past members and officers of the Communication and Cultural Studies panel of the Council for National Academic Awards, Sylvia Harvey of Sheffield City Polytechnic and Kay Richardson of the Department of Communication Studies at Liverpool University.

John Corner
Jeremy Hawthorn
August 1988

The publisher wishes to thank the following for permission to use their copyright material:

Addison-Wesley Publishing Company for 'The Issues in Person Perception' from *Person Perception* (© 1970) by A.H. Hastorf, J. Schneider and J. Polefka; George Allen & Unwin, Hemel Hempstead and Basic Books, New York for an extract from *The Interpretation of Dreams*; Edward Arnold for the extract from *Modes of Modern Writing* by David Lodge; Association for Educational Communications and Technology, Washington for George Gerbner's 'Basic Generalized Graphic Model of Communication' from 'On content-analysis and critical research in mass communications' in *Audio-Visual Communication Review* (AVCR) Vol. 6, No. 3, Spring 1958, pp. 85–108; Basil Blackwell for the extract from *The Ethnography of Communication* by Muriel Saville-Troike; The British Film Institute for Richard Paterson's 'The production context of Coronation Street' in R. Dyer *et al* (eds.) *Coronation Street*, Television Monograph 13, British Film Institute, London 1981, pp. 53–66; English Teaching Forum and

Christopher W. Hammonds for 'Language and social behaviour: restrictions and revelations'; Harcourt Brace Jovanovich, A.M. Heath, the estate of the late Sonia Brownell Orwell and Martin Secker & Warburg Ltd for 'A Hanging' by George Orwell from *Adelphi* and *Shooting an Elephant and Other Essays* copyright 1950 by Sonia Brownell Orwell, renewed 1978 by Sonia Pitt-Rivers, reprinted by permission of Harcourt Brace Jovanovich, Inc. and A.M. Heath; Harvard University Press, Cambridge, Mass. for A.R. Luria's 'Education, Generalization and Abstraction' and 'Cultural Factors in Human Perception' from *Cognitive Development* © 1976 by the President and Fellows of Harvard College; Indiana University Press for Bill Nichols's 'Analysis of Representation Images' from *Ideology and the Image* and for the extract from *Towards a Speech Act Theory of Literary Discourse* by Mary Louise Pratt; Michael Lake for the extract 'Michael Lake describes what the executioner actually faces' published in *The Guardian* 9 April 1973; Lexington Books for the extract from *A Perspective on Social Communications* by Stuart J. Sigman, Lexington, Mass.: Lexington Books, D.C. Heath and Company, copyright © 1987, D.C. Heath and Company; Methuen & Co Ltd for the extract from *Watching Dallas: Soap Opera and the Melodramatic Imagination* by Ien Ang; MIT Press, Mass. for Colin Cherry's 'What is Communication?' from *On Human Communication*; Mouton Publishers for David Efron 'Historical Changes in Gestural Behaviour' from *Gesture, Race and Culture*; Trevor Pateman for 'Impossible Discourse' from *Language, Truth and Politics*; Penguin Books Ltd for 'Verbal and Non-Verbal Communication' from Michael Argyle's *The Psychology of Interpersonal Behaviour* (Pelican Original 3/e. 1978) © Michael Argyle, 1967, 1972, 1978; Penguin Books Ltd (Allen Lane, the Penguin Press, 1969 Pelican Books, 1971) © Irving Goffman 1959 and Doubleday & Co. Inc., NY © Irving Goffman 1958 for 'Introduction' from *The Presentation of Self in Everyday Life*; Random House Inc and International Creative Management, Inc. New York for the extract from *Inside Prime Time* by Todd Gitlin, all rights reserved, copyright © 1983, 1985 by Todd Gitlin reprinted by permission of Pantheon Books, a Division of Random House, Inc and International Creative Management, Inc New York; Routledge and Kegan Paul for 'Social Class, Language and Socialization' from Basil Bernstein's *Class, Codes and Control* Vol 1 and for John Ellis 'Broadcast TV as Sound and Image' from *Visible Fictions* and for the extract from *Learning to Write* by Gunther Kress; St Martin's Press, Inc. and Macmillan, London and Basingstoke for 'Beyond Alienation' from *Feminism and Linguistic Theory* by Deborah Cameron; University of Toronto Press and the Open University, Milton Keynes for the extract from *Visualizing Deviance* by Richard Ericson, Patricia Baranek and Janet Chan, 1987 reprinted by permission of University of Toronto Press; Universe Books, New York and Hutchinson (Publishers) Ltd, London for Jean Aitchison's 'Defining Language' from *The Articulate Mammal*.

Introduction

This is the third edition of *Communication Studies*. Like its predecessors, it is addressed to the student reader and primarily designed for use on undergraduate courses in the area. Currently, these courses either form part of degree schemes in Communication or are devised as options within broader, Combined Studies programmes. There is also a strong Communication Studies element emerging in Secondary and Further Education. Here, the book should be of help to teachers preparing a syllabus.

The grouping together of complementary and often convergent lines of enquiry in the humanities and social sciences to make a new category for teaching and research – Communication Studies – is now some fifteen years old as a feature of British Higher Education (it is older still in its separate development within the American system). It thus needs less explanation and defence than it did when the first edition of this book appeared in 1980. Nevertheless, a few brief comments on the character of the field as it has become established and on shifts in its emphases over the last decade might be helpful.

Perhaps it is worth observing first of all that in the opinion of the editors and in the practice of the majority of institutions offering courses, the term Communication Studies does *not indicate a new discipline*. This is not a point about its status but about its character – it is essentially a way of organizing and relating ideas, methods of study and topics drawn from several disciplines and thus might usefully be described as a 'field of study' (Environmental Studies, Urban Studies and Women's Studies are other, cognate examples). Such a gathering and interconnecting activity inevitably produces work of a distinctive character, but the distinctiveness is grounded in a basic familiarity with the relevant sociological, linguistic and psychological literatures and methodologies, to cite three of the more important source-subjects. These circumstances have sometimes led to discussion as to whether Communication Studies is *interdisciplinary* (operating 'across and between' disciplines) or *multidisciplinary* (recognizing a range of distinctive disciplinary inputs). Comment here can quickly become tiresomely low in real substance but it would be appropriate to note that most degree courses in Britain begin with a strongly multidisciplinary programme, offset by various 'integrated study' opportunities, and then move towards a final year in which a more interdisciplinary approach is encouraged, though an option system may also allow for further discipline specialization.

Within this broad pattern of study, the present volume is intended principally to further the 'integrated study' of the earlier part of a programme, the part when introductory specialist studies are concurrently being undertaken but when there is a need for a sequence of reading and discussions which will touch off thinking across a broad range of issues and topics. At its best, such a sequence can light up large areas of the whole field and generate both an early sense of intellectual and substantive interconnections and an informed enthusiasm for the 'communication' focus.

At root, Communication Studies is about how human meanings are made through various types of sign – their production, organization and reception, the visual and verbal systems and technologies used to articulate, record and convey them and the political and social character of signifying activities. Section I of this book explores these matters of definition and approach in detail and the following three sections present the reader with what we hope are clear and stimulating inquiries into the varieties and the social conditions of meaning-making.

Studying communication is vulnerable to two main dangers as an academic enterprise – those of 'bittiness' and of excessive formalism. Bittiness often follows from the desire to make connections just about everywhere on the map of human knowledge ('communication' can be a disastrously capacious category with which to work!). Bits are all that this type of intellectual promiscuity has time to offer. Formalism results from a concern with the nature of signs and sign forms which is so intensive as to obscure from consideration the specific historical and social circumstances within which signification is shaped and has its consequences. There is more about these two problems in Section I but we very much hope to have produced here a collection in which continuities, depth of treatment and a sense of Communication Studies as a kind of *Social Studies,* albeit one with an applied, technologically-aware dimension, are apparent alongside the variety. In practice, most institutions teaching in the area achieve cohesion and an appropriate scholarly thoroughness for their courses by radically selecting from the range of possible topics and approaches in line with staff interests. This book engages with some of the more fundamental and common of the ideas and issues thus addressed, though it often seeks to do so by providing a fresh angle or a pointedly original line of commentary.

In revising the volume we have taken into account certain changes in emphasis which have become apparent since the mid 80s. For instance, it has become increasingly clear that a strand of work developing from structuralist/semiotic perspectives on communication (work associated with writers like Roland Barthes and Umberto Eco as well as the earlier and highly influential figure of Ferdinand de Saussure) has not proved so productive and is therefore no longer as central to developments as once it was. The matter is given proper consideration in the appropriate section introductions but this new edition reflects a growing interest in analytic alternatives to semiotics, whilst nevertheless registering the value of the latter approach in raising pertinent questions about the function and classification of signs in human communication and about the relationship between the political, social and linguistic realms.

There is a related concern, in the pieces new to this edition, with the *pragmatics* of communication, that is to say with the relationships of 'message' structures to addressees and settings. The perspectives of pragmatics press our study of signification firmly into the study of social action and this may lead the inquiry out from the analysis of particular examples of communicative form into the activities of production, understanding and response, into what we can regard as an *ethnography* of communication (the description and analysis of people's routine communicative behaviours).

This re-engagement of theory with empirical detail and the related raising of questions about the *use* of communication has informed our revision throughout. For instance, study of the media has always featured strongly in Communication Studies programmes, due both to the social importance of media institutions and to the engaging variety and sophistication of their communicative procedures. In Section IV, we have attempted to achieve cohesion across a small number of items on the media by giving special emphasis to connected issues concerning intention and interpretation.

Communication Studies as a way of organizing degree-level work has so far been a success. It has attracted able and enthusiastic students and promoted not only topics of study but also forms of study which have often contrasted strongly with the insular, canonical and unreflective teaching in many traditional, single-discipline subjects. It has also informed research, encouraging the emergence of new ideas, methods and topics. We would wish the new edition of the Reader to contribute to the sustaining of this impetus. Many parts of it can be used by the student as unsupervised, independent reading. Elsewhere, lectures and organized discussion are desirable to get the most benefit from the material and many teachers will want to incorporate selected items into schemes of reading drawing on several other sources. We welcome such varied, purposeful use. The book is intended as a set of resources linked by principles of selection and commentary – not as a self-sufficient textbook and least of all as a substitute for good, critical teaching on all the topics it touches on. Although primarily designed for introductory level work, the volume should have its uses well beyond this stage, feeding into later, more specialized treatments.

Apart from the factors of change mentioned above, our selection of items has been guided by three general criteria.

First of all, we have tried to select pieces which raise questions and promote discussion in a clear and accessible way. We have therefore chosen, more than in previous editions, those items which have worked well in teaching (including some which have provoked a usefully critical response).

Secondly, we have favoured items which indicate or explore connections between academic areas and methods rather than those which work exclusively within the terms of one established perspective.

Thirdly, we have included examples of studies widely judged as seminal. Extracts from work by *Bernstein, Goffman* and *Argyle* are indicative of this category.

In preparing a third edition we have revised and substantially rewritten all the editorial material, including the lists of recommended further reading (pruned to give a sharper introductory focus), removed ten items and added ten. We have retained the four-section structure to allow a broad classification of topic without the fragmentation which too many categories can introduce. We think this structure usefully foregrounds connections and contrasts across the items and gives scope for different sequences of reading and use.

Presentation has once again been standardized in accordance with a house-style of punctuation and with the Harvard system of bibliographical reference. On occasion, we have deleted minor references in an item where these were to other parts of the larger work from which the item was taken.

John Corner
Jeremy Hawthorn

Section I

Communication: definitions and approaches

If you were to go out into a busy town centre and to stop passers-by, asking them each to give you an example of something describable as 'communication', you would be sure to collect an interesting variety of responses (and this is to exclude the perhaps less polite ones!). Radio and television would almost certainly be mentioned several times, with newspapers not far behind. Perhaps the telephone might top the list though. Then there would probably be mentions of letter-writing, of conversation, of public speaking and even of your own interview questioning. Less frequently, examples such as advertising hoardings and traffic signals would turn up. A few people might interpret your question in terms of an established plural usage of the word to mean something to do with transport and cite rail or air services as examples. Even with these excluded, it's pretty clear that a long list could be collected quite soon. You will notice too, that some of the suggested examples refer primarily to *means* of communication (e.g. the telephone and radio) while others refer to types of communicative *act* (e.g. letter-writing and public speaking).

Two pertinent questions might then be posed for intending students of communication. First, what is to be gained by grouping together these various message-based systems and activities so as to constitute the subject matter of an identifiable field of study? And then, how on earth is it possible to develop a unitary set of concepts and methods by which to pursue such study?

Briefly, our answer to the first question is that an understanding of the complexity and governing conditions of human communication processes is considerably advanced the more we are aware of the different sign-systems through which they work, the different technologies which can be used in support of them and the different kinds of context in which they occur. It certainly isn't true that everything which we can call 'communication' fits neatly together to make one grand phenomenon, but interconnections across different types of behavioural, verbal and visual processes are both extensive and illuminating. Moreover, as the centrality of meaning-making activities is increasingly recognized in the study of a whole range of political, social and psychological matters, it becomes appropriate to have a formal grouping of studies which can bring connectedness and development to some of the related lines of inquiry. Communication Studies, then, makes sense as a way of organizing and developing knowledge.

Our answer to the second question is that it is *not* possible to get very far in this venture with any single, guaranteed set of concepts and methods. Research and teaching programmes in the area of Communication Studies need to proceed by reference to a *number* of ideas and procedures used in Arts and Social Science disciplines. Since hardly any of these is uncontroversial and many have been the subject of recent academic debate, communications students should quickly acquire a useful critical alertness (and an accompanying sense of challenge) concerning how academic inquiries seek to find things out and explain them.

But don't we need at least a reasonably tight working definition of 'communication' to guide our studies? We think not, although as **Colin Cherry** points out in the first item of this section, attempts at such definitions can promote useful discussion. However, most of the activities and processes we are interested in can be *recognized* according to the kinds of criteria which were used by our hypothetical passers-by. It is only when we have, in a sense, pushed beyond the broad category of 'communication' itself to a *description* and *analysis* of specific communicative practices and interactions that definitional precision becomes essential. Putting theoretical emphasis on the *category*, in a search for a set of universal principles and defining features which will somehow shore it up and convert it into a term fit for precise academic deployment, seems an unpromising venture. It also risks making of 'communication' some rather mystical higher unity, contemplation of whose essential or ideal characteristics is more interesting than looking in detail at examples of what are commonly regarded as communicative systems, activities and, indeed, professions and industries. In fact, over-use of the term can disguise the need for concepts other than 'communication' to be employed in order adequately to tackle this latter kind of investigation.

So we would largely dissociate ourselves from attempts at developing some 'general theory of communication' within whose perspective a comprehensive account would be possible. This is not to deny the value of work which tries to discern general features but to note that a theory so devised would have to operate at such a rarified altitude above actual kinds and means (let alone instances) of human interaction as to severely limit its usefulness. This would be largely confined to the level of broad classification. Secondly, and as a result, a 'general theory' would have to omit virtually all consideration of communicational *contexts* – the actual social settings and relationships (including relationships of inequality and of power). These always serve to shape communicative forms and practices at the same time as such practices are one important way in which social settings and relationships themselves are constituted and, perhaps, changed.

As we suggested in the Introduction, a reduced awareness of communicational contexts due to a desire to achieve the closest possible analysis of communicative forms themselves is already one of the main problems which work in Communication Studies has courted. A consequence of this has perhaps been to give a measure of academic support to the current fashion for talking about the modern world being full of 'problems of communication' (e.g. in industry, in social welfare, in education and in relations with the Third World) as if the circumstances referred to were kinds of technical hitch, resolvable through better (more professional?) kinds of communication, without regard for such factors as material conditions and differing economic interests.

It is important, then, to regard 'contexts' as something other than mere background. Certainly, as Communication Studies students, we have to declare our academic interest in specific kinds of phenomena over and above others, but a recognition of the *fundamental* ways in which, as Cherry puts it, 'communication is a social affair', of the ways in which communicative forms and social circumstances inter-relate, is needed too. In fact, at the end of his piece, Cherry refers to a branch of linguistics known as *pragmatics* which is precisely concerned to relate sign-systems both to users and to contexts of use. Pragmatics approaches are playing an increasingly important function in communication research and further reference to them will appear later in the book.

All the pieces in this section have been chosen because they offer clear, preliminary ideas about the characteristics of communicative behaviour and about the analytic categories through which we can begin to explore it in a controlled and coherent way. For instance, they address questions of communicative *convention* – the codes or rules by which signs are selected and combined in such a way as to be appropriately meaningful to an addressee. These conventions can be as 'tight' as those regulating our word order when writing an English sentence or as relatively 'loose' as those which govern the tones of voice, facial mannerisms and general behaviour associated with 'politeness' in our culture (where a number of options and permutations exist). Or we might contrast the international visual conventions of traffic and road signs with the (again, international, but much looser) conventions at work in television 'soap opera'. Quite frequently, communication analysis involves studying 'tight' and 'loose' conventions in combination since communicated meanings often draw on the broader systems of signification out of which a culture is built as well as on narrower sub-systems.

Successful use of communicative conventions suggests that meaning has effectively been 'transmitted', but this way of putting it radically oversimplifies what is in fact a complex interaction of *intentions, sign-forms* and *interpretive activity*, one which will involve different levels of consciousness. Communication seen as a business of 'sending things' may be an adequate perspective for the postal services but it will serve only to distort the study of most human communication and to mask important variables. To give an example, we might ask how questions of intention figure in respect of what an addressee 'makes of' (a revealing phrase in this context) some remark of ours. If we say we did not intend such a meaning, does that close the matter? Or if the addressee claims in response that, nevertheless, this is what our comment really means, does that close it from the opposite direction? Matters of setting and circumstance may quickly enter here but we can easily imagine situations in which we would accept personal responsibility for an 'unintended meaning' (perhaps regarding it as a result of our careless choice of words) and also situations in which it was seen to be the addressee's problem for 'taking it the wrong way' or 'reading more in to it than was intended' (again, revealing phrases). Were there two addressees, they might well differ in their interpretations as to what was meant, adding a further complication to the communicative act. Straightaway, any direct analogy with the postal system or an electrical circuit looks far too neat to be helpful.

In both this and other sections of the book, the links between communicative conventions, cultural contexts of use and modes of participant understanding will be regularly explored. In examining these links, some writers have made use of the term *ideology* in order to probe the relations between communication, consciousness and power. As noted above, most communication takes place within settings of inequality, quite often framed by the broader patterns of economic inequality. The play of dominant economic and political interests in securing terms of public communication, including the assumptions informing everyday language, which *appear* neutral but which act to reinforce particular prejudices, discriminations and evaluations can be regarded as an ideological dimension to signification. This dimension often becomes 'locked into' the meaning of words and images and, as such, it permeates many aspects of culture. Its presence has given rise to specific charges of 'biased' communication (as in accusations of sexism, racism or of social class partiality). This is particularly so where the media are concerned, though the matter is by no means confined to mass communication and it will be dealt with more thoroughly in all three subsequent sections.

Two other terms which can be helpful right from the start are *denotation* and *connotation*. These will be given more discussion later too but the distinction is essentially between on the one hand, the literal meanings of words or those things which images primarily depict and, on the other hand, the associative meanings which words and images have gathered around them within specific cultural contexts. For instance, 'enterprise', 'gay' and even 'defence' are all words which, in different ways, have generated powerful political associations in the 1980s, taking them well beyond their core meanings (in the case of 'gay', what might have started out as a new connotation has effectively become a new, alternative denotation). Likewise, images of European cities in advertisements for expensive cars are clearly designed to connote cosmopolitanism, sophistication, style and wealth rather than to provide denotative information about, say, Rome or Berlin. Connotative meanings are important in the processes of the ideological dimension referred to above.

Distinguishing between two 'levels' like this is often illuminating (see, for instance, the use made of them in the analysis of television in Section IV, item 25) but you should be wary of assuming a tidy division every time. Indeed, some writers have argued against the terms, finding in the ideas of the 'literal' and 'primary reference' and in the whole notion of 'double-decker' meaning a suspect simplification of the actual relationship between language systems and social values.

Colin Cherry develops a preliminary discussion of aspects of this relationship in his look at the problems of adequately defining communication. In the course of his piece, he attempts to relate a number of the key terms (e.g. code, sign and rule) and to show by examples how their use might help us to think more incisively about the ways in which communication works.

His stress on communication as a 'sharing of rules' keeps our attention on those cultural conventions – the symbol system of a language, for example – which we noted above to be a primary means by which meaning is produced. It is necessary, of course, to see such 'sharing' as always occurring under the terms imposed by the broader schemes of social relationship within which individuals live, feel and think rather than posing it as somehow a natural equality in the human race. Cherry was one of the first British academics to pursue an interest in communication as an organizing concept for research. By citing a number of definitions of both this and related notions, he raises some fundamental points about communication process and signals, too, something of the range of phenomena which communication analysis might find itself considering.

In our second extract, we have reproduced a model of communication devised by **George Gerbner**, a distinguished American media researcher. Again, like Cherry, Gerbner has a basic understanding of general communication processes in mind. The early history of Communication Studies, particularly in the USA, was littered with various diagrammatic representations – most of them failing to make their bold, graphic depictions of process and relationship shed much light on actual, real-world instances. We think that Gerbner's model, though necessarily concentrating on a very few features, has more suggestive power than these and, as our accompanying note indicates, we think it encourages and focuses an investigation of several important features of perception and of signifying activity.

One discipline which has quite a long tradition of examining diverse communicative practices is Anthropology, the study of other cultures. Anthropological inquiry proceeds primarily by 'fieldwork', that is to say by in-depth investigation of people's behaviour and cultural practices. The item by **Saville-Troike** brings out very clearly some of the components and phases of communicative action which the analyst may need to take account of. Starting from a list of categories, it broadens out into numerous examples and gives us a comprehensive sense both of what a 'multi-channel' process human communication is and of its deep embedding within the settings and structures of social life. Many aspects of the 'ethnographic' approach which Saville-Troike is concerned to outline, involving careful observation and description, can usefully inform a communication analysis of systems and activities within our own culture. Indeed, taking 'too much for granted' is always a problem for researching societies and sub-cultures of which the researcher is a member (think of the disadvantages, as well as possible advantages, of conducting a piece of research on student life in your own college). Framing inquiries more in the manner of the anthropologist, naïve to local custom at the outset, can bring freshness to the analysis, although one must be wary of assuming that the 'outside observer's' view is always neutral or that explanations can be satisfactorily offered purely by the accumulation of external data.

Jean Aitchison's piece brings us in closer to the study of that most important element in communication – language. Her main aim is to consider how human language differs from the communicative behaviour of other animals. The discussion is organized around the question 'can animals talk?' and in the course of answering this she lists some of the 'design features' which we might want to use to decide whether a given piece of communication could usefully be said to employ a 'language'. Her comments on certain experiments carried out with bees and with dolphins bring out the importance of *displacement* ('the ability to refer to things far removed in time and place') and of *arbitrariness* (the lack of any necessary connection between conventional signs (e.g. words) and the things they refer to) in human language use. These, together with other characteristics which she mentions, will be treated in more detail in a later section.

The subsequent extract also focuses on a particular aspect of communication, albeit within a broad scheme of classification. It is taken from the work of **Michael Argyle**, a social psychologist with a distinguished record in the researching of interpersonal behaviour. Argyle produces a helpfully illustrated inventory of human communicative actions, one in which a clear account is given of *non-verbal* behaviours. Although the rules at work here are not so precisely listable as are many linguistic ones, Argyle draws our attention to the often highly convention-bound character of what goes on through this important 'channel' of interaction. The treatment is nicely concise, fitting a lot of detail into a tight scheme of description. Rather disappointingly, Argyle seems unwilling to ask *why* the cross-cultural differences which he documents actually occur, perhaps being too prompt in accepting ideas of *innate* rather than culturally formed communicative dispositions and competences. Nevertheless, like all the pieces in the section, the final effect is to provide some basic knowledge and to raise questions and problems in an accessible manner and with plenty of examples to aid discussion and further study.

Our final item, too, concentrates on visual rather than verbal signification, this time raising questions about the use of a *medium* – photography – to *represent* features of the world of appearances. Through photographic representation, meanings are generated which go far beyond the particular features thus depicted (see the discussion of *denotation* and *connotation* earlier). **Nichols** applies the ideas of *semiology* – a theory and method of sign analysis which is particularly concerned with the relations between signs – to a number of photographic examples. His aim is to identify the processes of meaning-making at work. These include matters of perception in response to compositional form right through to questions about the kinds of implicit evaluations and categories of thought – the ideologies – which the images support. Whereas Aitchison talks of the *arbitrary* character of language's *symbolic* signs (no necessary relation between word-forms and things represented), Nichols engages with the *iconic* character of much visual depiction (the image resembles that which it represents). In photography, this iconicity is joined by what has been referred to as an *indexical* factor (the image is actually *caused* by light waves refracted from the represented object entering the camera lens, thus linking object and image in an intimate relationship).* The special communicative power of photography (and of film and video too) stems from this distinctive iconic-indexical mix, which gives evidential values to the image produced. Nichols would not, however, agree with the well-known comment that 'the camera never lies' and he explores the particular configurations of codes (including the verbal codes of captions) which photography can involve at its different levels of communicative address. Here, like Saville-Troike, he refers both to the 'horizontal' axis of sign combination (*syntagmatic* codes) and to the 'vertical' axis of sign selection (*paradigmatic* codes). These terms can more easily be demonstrated in respect of language (where, at the level of the sentence, they roughly equal the rules of syntax and the available options for word choice) but, as Nichols shows, they can be put to revealing use in 'de-naturalizing' the meanings of the photograph, especially of those images which have been produced in order to persuade.

Further reading

The following brief list is of works which continue the definitional and methodological discussions contained in this section of the Reader. For further reading on more specific topics, students are recommended to consult first the appropriate references in the notes to this section and then to look at what is contained elsewhere in the volume.

* The terms 'index', 'icon' and 'symbol' were used by the pioneer theorist Charles S. Peirce (1839–1914) to differentiate sign-types. They have been widely influential though frequently subject to confusion, and even Peirce's own usage was not consistent. There are many secondary expositions; see for instance Fiske, J. 1982 in the Further Reading to this Introduction.

Cashdan, A. and Jordin, M. (eds.) 1987: *Studies in communication*. Oxford: Blackwell.

This collection of articles from one of the foremost centres for Communication Studies in Britain, Sheffield City Polytechnic, is rather uneven in quality and level. Most of the pieces report on current research in the Sheffield department and give the book limited cohesion as an introductory volume. A number of items are clear and stimulating, however, and one or two of these directly address basic concepts and methods from a 'state-of-the-art' understanding.

Dance, F.E. 1970: The concept of communication. *Journal of Communication 20*, 201–10.

A short but helpful discussion of some basic definitional problems.

Fiske, J. 1982: *Introduction to communication studies*. London: Methuen.

A short and well-illustrated introduction both to communication as a topic of study and to the available methods for conducting research and analysis. Fiske believes semiotics to offer a central, unifying perspective in communication research and he gives examples of its application within a number of different kinds of verbal and visual inquiry. Each chapter ends with useful suggestions for further work.

Gerbner, George 1956: Towards a general model of communication. *Audio Visual Communication Review* IV, 3.

A clearly written and very suggestive argument about the general characteristics of communication processes.

Hinde, R.A. (ed.) 1972: *Non-verbal communication*. Cambridge University Press.

A fine book, containing articles which are relevant to several strands of inquiry into communication. It is recommended here because it contains a number of pieces which discuss the principles both of human and animal communication. Other useful articles trace the importance of non-verbal behaviour in children, in the mentally ill, in acting and in the characteristic postures and gestures depicted in Western art.

O'Sullivan, T., Hartley, J., Saunders, D. and Fiske, J. 1983: *Key concepts in communication*. London: Methuen.

A useful guide to the terminology of the area which manages to give potted information without too much superficiality or loss of critical perspective. Well-referenced.

1

What is communication?

Colin Cherry

From Cherry, Colin 1957: *On human communication*. Cambridge, Mass: MIT Press, 3–9.

Communication is essentially a social affair. Man has evolved a host of different systems of communication which render his social life possible – social life not in the sense of living in packs for hunting or for making war, but in a sense unknown to animals. Most prominent among all these systems of communication is, of course, human speech and language. Human language is not to be equated with the sign systems of animals, for man is not restricted to calling his young, or suggesting mating, or shouting cries of danger; he can with his remarkable faculties of speech give utterance to almost any thought. Like animals, we too have our inborn instinctive cries of alarm, pain, etcetera: we say *Oh!, Ah!*; we have smiles, groans, and tears; we blush, shiver, yawn, and frown.[1] A hen can set her chicks scurrying up to her, by clucking – communication established by a releaser mechanism – *but human language is vastly more than a complicated system of clucking.*

The development of language reflects back upon thought; for with language thoughts may become organized, new thoughts evolved. Self-awareness and the sense of social responsibility have arisen as a result of organized thoughts. Systems of ethics and law have been built up. Man has become self-conscious, responsible, a social creature.

Inasmuch as the words we use disclose the true nature of things, as truth is to each one of us, the various words relating to personal communication are most revealing. The very word 'communicate' means 'share', and inasmuch as you and I are communicating at the moment, we are one. Not so much a union as a unity. Inasmuch as we agree, we say that we *are of one mind*, or, again, that we understand *one another*. This one another is the unity. A group of people, a society, a culture, I would define as 'people in communication'. They may be thought of as 'sharing rules' of language, custom, of habit; but who wrote these rules? These have evolved out of those people themselves – rules of conformity. Inasmuch as that conformity is the greater or the less, so is the unity. The degree of communication, the sharing, the conformity, is a measure of one-mindedness. After all, what we share, we cannot each have as our own possession, and no single person in this world has ever been born and bred in utter isolation. 'No man is an island, entire of itself.'[2]

Speech and writing are by no means our only system of communication. Social intercourse is greatly strengthened by habits of gesture – little movements of the hands and face. With nods, smiles, frowns, handshakes, kisses, fist shakes, and other gestures we can convey most subtle understanding.[3] We also have economic systems for trafficking not in ideas but in material goods and services; the tokens of communication are coins, bonds, letters of credit, and so on. We have conventions of dress, rules of the road, social formalities, and good manners; we have rules of membership and function in businesses, institutions, and families. But life in the modern world is coming to depend more and more upon 'technical' means of communication, telephone and telegraph, radio and printing. Without such technical aids the modern city-state could not exist one week, for it is only by means of them that trade and business can proceed; that goods and services can be distributed where needed; that railways can run on a schedule; that law and order are maintained; that education is possible. Communication renders true social life practicable, for communication means organization. Communications have enabled the social unit to grow, from the village to the town, to the modern city-state, until today we see organized systems of mutual dependence grown to cover whole hemispheres (McDougall, 1927).

The development of human language was a tremendous step in evolution; its power for organizing thoughts, and the resulting growth of social organization of all kinds, has given man, wars or no wars, street accidents or no street accidents, vastly increased potential for survival.

As a start, let us now take a few of the concepts and notions to do with communication, and discuss them briefly, not in any formal scientific sense, but in the language of the market place. A few dictionary definitions may serve as a starting point for our discursive approach here; later we shall see that such definitions are not at variance with those more restricted definitions used in scientific analysis. The following have been drawn from the *Concise Oxford English Dictionary*[4]

Communication, n. Act of imparting (esp. news); information given; intercourse; . . . (Military, Pl.) connexion between base and front.

Message, n. Oral or written communication sent by one person to another.

Information, n. Informing, telling; thing told, knowledge, items of knowledge, news, (on, about) . . .

Signal, n., v.t. & i. Preconcerted or intelligible sign conveying information . . . at a distance. . . .

Intelligence, n. . . . understanding, sagacity . . . information, news.

News, n. pl. Tidings, new information. . . .

Knowledge, n. . . . familiarity gained by experience, person's range of information. . . .

Belief, n. Trust or confidence (*in*); . . . acceptance as true or existing (of any fact, statement, etc.; . . .) . . .

Organism, n. Organized body with connected interdependent parts sharing common life . . .; whole with interdependent parts compared to living being.

System, n. Complex whole, set of connected things or parts, organized body of material or immaterial things . . .; method, organization, considered principles of procedure, (principle of) classification; . . .

Such dictionary definitions are the 'common usages' of words; scientific usage frequently needs to be more restricted but should not violate common sense – an accusation often mistakenly levelled against scientific words by the layman.

The most frequent use of the words listed above is in connection with *human* communication, as the dictionary suggests. The word 'communication' calls to mind most readily the sending or receipt of a letter, or a conversation between two friends; some may think of newspapers issued daily from a central office to thousands of subscribers, or of radio broadcasting; others may think of telephones, linking one speaker and one listener. There are systems too which come to mind only to specialists; for instance, ornithologists and entomologists may think of flocking and swarming, or of the incredible precision with which flight manoeuvres are made by certain birds, or the homing of pigeons – problems which have been extensively studied, yet are still so imperfectly understood. Again, physiologists may consider the communicative function of the nervous system, coordinating the actions of all the parts of an integrated animal. At the other end of the scale, the anthropologist and sociologist are greatly interested in the communication between large groups of people, societies and races, by virtue of their cultures, their economic and religious systems, their laws, languages, and ethical codes. Examples of 'communication systems' are endless and varied.

When 'members' or 'elements' are in communication with one another, they are associating, cooperating, forming an 'organization', or sometimes an 'organism'. Communication is a social function. That old cliché, 'a whole is more than the sum of the parts', expresses a truth; the whole, the organization or organism, possesses a structure which is describable as a set of *rules*, and this structure, the rules, may remain unchanged as the individual members or elements are changed. By the possession of this structure the whole organization may be better adapted or better fitted for some goal-seeking activity. Communication means a *sharing* of elements of behaviour or modes of life, by the existence of sets of rules. This word *rule* will be discussed later.

Perhaps we may be permitted to comment upon a definition of communication, as given by a leading psychologist (Stevens, 1950): '*Communication is the discriminatory response of an organism to a stimulus*.[5] The same writer emphasizes that a definition broad enough to embrace all that the word 'communication' means to different people may risk finding itself dissipated in generalities. We would agree; such definitions or descriptions serve as little more than foci for discussion. But there are two points we wish to make concerning this psychologist's definition. First, as we shall view it in our present context, communication is not the response itself but is essentially the *relationship* set up by the transmission of stimuli and the evocation of responses. Second, it will be well to expand somewhat upon the notion of a stimulus; we shall need to distinguish between human language and the communicative signs of animals, between languages, codes, and logical sign systems, at least.

The study of the signs used in communication, and of the rules operating upon them and upon their users, forms the core of the study of communication. There is no communication without a system of signs – but there are many kinds of 'signs'. Let us refer again to the *Concise Oxford English Dictionary*:

> *Sign*, n. . . . written mark conventionally used for word or phrase, symbol, thing used as representation of something . . . presumptive evidence or indication or suggestion or symptom *of* or *that*, distinctive mark, token, guarantee, password . . . portent . . .; natural or conventional motion or gesture used instead of words to convey information. . . .

Language, n. A vocabulary and way of using it . . .

Code, n., and v.t. Systematic collection of statutes, body of laws so arranged as to avoid inconsistency and overlapping; . . . set of rules on any subject; prevalent morality of a society or class . . .; system of mil. or nav. signals. . . .

Symbol, n. . . . Thing regarded by general consent as naturally typifying or representing or recalling something by possession of analogous qualities or by association in fact or thought. . . .

We shall use the word *sign* for any physical event used in communication – human, animal, or machine – avoiding the term *symbol*, which is best reserved for the Crown, the Cross, Uncle Sam, the olive branch, the Devil, Father Time, and others 'naturally typifying or representing or recalling . . . by association in fact or thought', religious and cultural symbols interpretable only in specified historical contexts. The term *language* will be used in the sense of human language, 'a vocabulary [of signs] and way of using it'; as a set of signs and rules such as we use in everyday speech and conversation, in a highly flexible and mostly illogical way. On the other hand, we shall refer to the strictly formalized systems of signs and rules, such as those of mathematics and logic, as *language systems* or *sign-systems.*

The term *code* has a strictly technical usage which we shall adopt here. Messages can be coded *after* they are already expressed by means of signs (e.g. letters of the English alphabet); then a code is an agreed transformation, usually one to one and reversible, by which messages may be converted from one set of signs to another. Morse code, semaphore, and the deaf-and-dumb code represent typical examples. In our terminology then, we distinguish sharply between *language,* which is developed organically over long periods of time, and *codes,* which are invented for some specific purpose and follow explicit rules.

Apart from our natural languages (English, French, Italian, etc.), we have many examples of *systems* of signs and rules, which are mostly of a very inflexible kind. A pack of playing cards represents a set of signs, and the rules of the game ensure communication and patterned behaviour among the players. Every motorist in Britain is given a book of rules of the road called the *Highway Code,* and adherence to these signs and rules is supposed to produce concerted, patterned behaviour on British roads. There are endless examples of such simple sign systems. A society has a structure, definite sets of relationships between individuals, which is not formless and haphazard but organized. Hierarchies may exist and be recognized, in a family, a business, an institution, a factory, or an army – functional relationships which decide to a great extent the patterned flow of communication. The communication and the structure are subject to sets of rules, rules of conduct, authoritarian dictates, systems of law; and the structures may be highly complex and varied in form. A 'code' of ethics is more like a language, having developed organically; it is a set of guiding rules concerning 'ought situations', generally accepted, whereby people in a society associate together and have social coherence. Such codes are different in the various societies of the world, though there is an overlap of varying degrees. When the overlap is small a gulf of misunderstanding may open up. Across such a gulf communication may fail; if it does, the organization breaks down.

The whole broad study of language and sign systems has been called, by Charles Morris, the theory of signs (Morris, 1938, 1946), and owes much to the earlier philosophy of Charles Peirce.[6] Morris distinguishes three types of rule operating upon signs, *(a) syntactic* rules (rules of syntax; relations between signs); *(b) semantic* rules (relations between signs and the things, actions, relationships, qualities – *designata*); *(c) pragmatic* rules (relations between signs and their users).

2

A generalized graphic model of communication

George Gerbner

From Gerbner, George 1956: Towards a general model of communication in *Audio-Visual Communication Review* IV.3, 1956.

Editors' note on Gerbner's model of communication (following page)

Gerbner's model is an attempt to depict diagrammatically some of the issues of perception and representation which must be taken into account in any study of communicational activity as a dynamic, social process.

The flow is from right to left in the diagram.

An event (E) is perceived by someone (M). The event-as-perceived (E^1) is the product of perceptual *activity* and thus the mediations and transformations of particular selective and contextual factors introduce the difference between E and E^1.

The vertical arm of the model shows the *representation* of the event ('statement about event') by the perceiver to be partly a product of the available meaning systems (e.g. print, speech, photograph, film) and of the particular conventions of use of such systems (here it is important to stress the social and historical contingency of these conventions). These formal elements (S) combine with event-related elements (E).

Finally, the lower horizontal arm shows this representation, the statement about the event (SE), being perceived (heard, read, viewed) by a second person (M^2). This perceptual activity will involve, as it did in the earlier case, a transformation such that the difference SE/SE^1 will occur.

Clearly, all academic models must be regarded as depictions of arguments and ideas rather than somehow being straightforward illustrations of the 'way things are'. Indeed, one of the strengths of Gerbner's model is that it draws our attention to just this point. As such, models invite not only our understanding but also our critical assessment of their adequacy.

The processes which Gerbner here treats graphically are nearly all the subject of theoretical debates, some of which you will find discussed elsewhere in this Reader.

The relation of language to reality and to thought, the nature of different forms of representation, the problems which follow from considering 'form' as separate from 'content', the extent to which the perception and representation of events in, say, the natural sciences involve factors fundamentally different from those in, say, sports journalism – questions such as these should be borne in mind when discussing the model.

Finally, it is worth noting that the model carries implications for the study of mass communication, since it suggests the difficulty if not the impossibility of achieving 'neutrality' and 'objectivity' in the relaying of events through the media. By emphasizing the way in which 'messages' are both *selections* from real world events and *constructions* made from the material of whatever medium is used (language, photography, video etc.) Gerbner provides a good base from which to consider the problems of reporting. In fact, the version of the model reprinted here has been used in a brief and helpful article on the professional goals and ethics of journalists (Halloran, 1969).

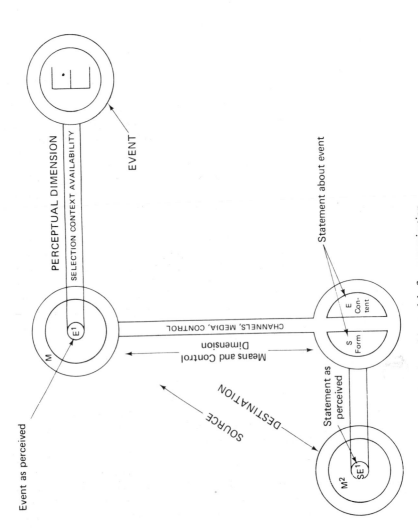

Figure 2.1 Basic generalized graphic model of communication

PERCEPTUAL DIMENSION

SELECTION CONTEXT AVAILABILITY

EVENT

Event as perceived

CHANNELS, MEDIA, CONTROL

Means and Control
Dimension

SOURCE

DESTINATION

Statement about event

Statement as
perceived

E
Content

S
Form

3

The analysis of communicative events

Muriel Saville-Troike

From Saville-Troike, Muriel 1982: *The ethnography of communication*. London: Blackwell, 135–50.

Identification of communicative events

Communication in societies tends to be categorized into different kinds of events rather than an undifferentiated string of discourse, with more or less well defined boundaries between each, and different behavioural norms (often including different varieties of language) appropriate for each kind. Descriptive tasks include enumerating the kinds of events which are recognized or can be inferred in a community, the nature of boundary markers which signal their beginning and end, and the features which distinguish one type from another.

Since a communicative event is a bounded entity of some kind, recognizing what the boundaries are is essential for their identification. A telephone conversation is a communicative event bounded by the ring of the telephone as a 'summons' and hanging up the receiver as a 'close'. Event boundaries may be signalled by ritual phrases, such as *Did you hear this one?* and then laughter to bound a joke; *Once upon a time* and *They lived happily ever after* to bound a story; or *Let us pray* and *Amen* to bound a prayer. Instead of these, or in addition, there may be changes in facial expression, tone of voice, or bodily position between one communicative event and the next, or a period of silence. Erickson and Schultz (1979) also report changes in gaze direction, change of participants' position in relation to one another, and change of rhythm of speech and body movement. Perhaps the surest sign of a change of events is code alternation, or the change from relatively consistent use of one language or variety to another. Boundaries are also likely to coincide with change of participants, change in topical focus, or change in the general purpose of communication. Major junctures in communication are signalled by a combination of verbal and non-verbal cues.

Consecutive events may be distinguished in a single situation. In a trial, for instance, the opening event begins when the bailiff cries *Hear ye, hear ye*, and ends when the judge enters the courtroom and sits down at the bench, and all others are seated. Within the same situation, direct and cross examination of witnesses or the defendant may be identified as separate events because participants are in a different role-relationship, and there is a change in manner of questioning and responding: i.e. different rules for interaction. These events may be bounded by the change in participants, and perhaps by a verbal routine such as *I call____to the stand* to open and *You may stand down* or *Your witness* to close. If a recess is called before a boundary is reached, the interaction can be considered a single discontinuous speech event, even if continued on another day.

Formal ritual events in a speech community have more clearly defined boundaries than informal ones because there is a high degree of predictability in both verbal and non-verbal content of routines on each occasion, and they are frequently set off from events which precede and follow by changes in vocal rhythm, pitch and intonation. Brief interactions between people almost always consist of routines, such as greetings and leavetakings, and the boundaries of longer and most informal communicative events, such as conversations, can be determined because they are preceded and followed by them (Goffman, 1971).

Since the discovery of communicative norms is often most obvious in their breach, examples of boundary violations may highlight what the appropriate boundary behaviour is. Some people are annoyed with what they consider to be premature applause by others at the end of an opera, for instance, which indicates differences in what 'the end' of the event is perceived to be: the end of the singing or the end of all music. Still others may whisper through the overture, since for them the event has not yet begun. Christina Paulston (personal communication) reports the occurrence of a serious misunderstanding between Jewish and Christian parents attending an ecumenical service because the Jewish parents continued conversing after entering the place of worship, while the Christians considered this inappropriate behaviour once the physical boundary into the sanctuary was crossed.

Micro-analysis of boundary signals in less formal situations commonly requires filming a communicative situation, and then asking participants to view the film themselves and to indicate when 'something new is happening'. The researcher then elicits characterizations of the event, and expectations of what may happen next (and what may *not* happen next), in order to determine the nature of the boundary signals, and how the context has changed from the point of view of the participants.

The communicative events selected initially for description and analysis for one learning to use this approach should be brief self-contained sequences which have readily identifiable beginnings and endings. Further, they should be events which recur in similar form and with some frequency, so that regular patterns will be more easily discernible: e.g., greetings, leavetakings, prayers, condolences, jokes, insults, compliments, ordering meals in restaurants. More complex and less regular events yield themselves to analysis more readily after patterns of use and norms of interpretation have already been discovered in relation to simpler and more regular communicative events.

Components of communication

Analysis of a communicative event begins with a description of the components which are likely to be salient (cf. Hymes, 1967; 1972; Friedrich, 1972):

1   The *genre*, or type of event (e.g. joke, story, lecture, greeting, conversation).
2   The *topic*, or referential focus.
3   The *purpose* or *function*, both of the event in general and in terms of the interaction goals of individual participants.

4 The *setting*, including location, time of day, season of year, and physical aspects of the situation (e.g. size of room, arrangement of furniture).
5 The *participants*, including their age, sex, ethnicity, social status, or other relevant categories, and their relationship to one another.
6 The *message form*, including both vocal and non-vocal channels, and the nature of the code which is used (e.g. which language, and which variety).
7 The *message content*, or surface level denotative references; what is communicated about.
8 The *act sequence*, or ordering of communicative/speech acts, including turn taking and overlap phenomena.
9 The *rules of interaction*, or what proprieties should be observed.
10 The *norms of interpretation*, including the common knowledge, the relevant cultural presuppositions, or shared understandings, which allow particular inferences to be drawn about what is to be taken literally, what discounted, etc.

All of these will be discussed in turn below.

Scene (genre, topic, purpose/function, setting)

The first four components comprise the *scene*, or extra-personal *context* of the event. Of these, only the setting may be directly observed, although even for this component researchers might not notice an aspect of the setting which is not salient in their own culture: e.g. the relative elevation of chairs may be very important for understanding the meaning of the event (as in Japanese), and whether chairs in a classroom are arranged in straight rows or a circle may signal the appropriate level of formality (as in English).

The time of day, day of the week, or season of the year often affects choice of language form. This may include whole genres of events designated only for particular times: e.g. in Navajo one cannot talk about hibernating animals except during winter months, so that traditional stories about them may only be told at certain times of the year, and Orthodox Jews are constrained from discussing secular topics on the Sabbath. Routines such as *Merry Christmas, Happy New Year,* and *April Fool* can only be interpreted as joking or sarcastic out of their appropriate temporal or cultural context.

Place and time may affect the meaning of greetings. It is not appropriate for a speaker of the Abbey language to greet everyone in just any location, for instance. Hepié reports on his own usage:

> Suppose I go back to my country [Ivory Coast] and run into a relative in the street. I won't greet him, but quickly let him know that I am on my way to his home to greet him. [This is because] the greeting in such cases shows you care about such people. Therefore it has to be at home, where the relative can at his ease get the news from you.

Nwoye reports that for Igbo, morning greetings are the most significant,

> since the morning is the beginning of the day and it is believed that the sort of person you first encounter in the morning determines your fortune for that day. . . . Therefore people consciously refrain from speaking to those who they know or suspect can bring ill luck and ruin their entire day.

Descriptive questions to be answered regarding the scene are:

- What kind of communicative event is it?
- What is it about?
- Why is it happening?
- Where and when does it occur?
- What does the setting look like?

Additional questions which may prove relevant to understanding the significance of a setting include:

- How do individuals organize themselves spatially in groups for various purposes (e.g. in rows, circles, around tables, on the floor, in the middle of the room, around its circumference)?
- What geospatial concepts, understandings, and beliefs exist in the group or are known to individuals?
- What is the knowledge and significance of cardinal directions (North, South, East, West)?
- What significance is associated with different directions or places (e.g. heaven is up, people are buried with heads to the west, the host at a meal should sit facing the door)?
- What beliefs or values are associated with concepts of time of day or season, and are there particular behavioural prescriptions or taboos associated with them (e.g. not singing certain songs in the summertime lest a snake bite, not telling stories until the sun has set)?

The organization of time and space is of enormous significance in most cultures, and one of the most frequent areas for cross-cultural conflict or misunderstanding, in large part because it is so often unconscious. In particular, ethnographers cannot assume that many of the concepts and attitudes regarding time and space (including personal space) held in their culture will hold for others.

Other components of the scene are not directly observable. The *genre*, or type of event, should be categorized according to indigenous perceptions and divisions. Relevant background questions for both *genre* and *purpose* might include:

- What is considered sacred and what secular?
- What beliefs and practices are associated with natural phenomena (e.g. eclipses and phases of the moon, comets, stars), and who or what is responsible for rain, lightning, thunder, earthquakes, and floods?
- Are particular behavioural prescriptions or taboos associated with natural phenomena?
- What holidays and celebrations are observed by the group and individuals?
- What is their purpose (e.g. political, seasonal, religious, didactic)?
- What range of behaviours is considered 'work' and what 'play'?
- What clothing is 'typical'? What is worn for special occasions?
- Are there any external signs of participation in any ritual events (e.g. ashes, dress, marking of skin)?

Participants

The basic descriptive question to answer about *participants* is:

- Who is taking part in the event?

An adequate description of the participants includes not only observable traits, but background information on the composition and role-relationships within the family and other social institutions, distinguishing features in the life cycle, and differentiation within the group according to sex and social status. Answers to such questions as the following may prove relevant:

- Who is in a 'family'? Who among these (or others) lives in one house?
- What is the hierarchy of authority in the family?
- What are the rights and responsibilities of each family member?
- What are the functions and obligations of the family in the larger social unit?
- What are criteria for the definition of stages, periods, or transitions in life?
- What are attitudes, expectations and behaviours toward individuals at different stages in the life cycle? What stage of life is most valued? What stage of life is most 'difficult'?
- Who has authority over whom? To what extent can one person's will be imposed on another? By what means?
- Do means of social control vary with recognized stages in the life cycle, membership in various social categories, or according to setting or offence?
- What roles within the group are available to whom, and how are they acquired?
- Do particular roles have positive or malevolent characteristics?

Among the questions relating participants to language and culture which will be answered in the process of ethnographic description and analysis are:

- How is language related to the life cycle?
- Is language use important in the definition or social marking of roles?
- What forms of address are used between people in various role-relationships?
- How is deference shown? How are insults expressed?
- Who may disagree with whom? Under what circumstances?
- How do the characteristics of 'speaking well' relate to age, sex or other social factors?
- How does speaking ability, literacy or writing ability relate to achievement of status in the society?
- What roles, attitudes or personality traits are associated with particular ways of speaking?
- Who may talk to whom? When? Where? About what?
- What is the role of language in social control? What variety is used? In multilingual contexts, what is the significance of using the first versus the second language?

The dress of participants may also be relevant to the interpretation of their communicative behaviour, and thus require description: e.g. Arab males may stand closer to females when talking if the woman is wearing a veil.

Belief about who may participate in communicative events is culture-specific, and is often not limited to humans. In the sample analyses below, for instance, Abbey speakers consider the drum and the invisible people who are invoked by the drum participants in condoling events, and the spirit of the deceased is an important participant for Igbo speakers; speakers of English and other European languages often believe they can communicate with pets.

Message form

In studying the various social, cultural and situational constraints on communicative behaviour, both verbal and non-verbal codes are significant in the *message form* and *act sequence* components of communicative events, and each type of code as transmitted by both vocal and non-vocal channels. Code and channel are related as shown in figure 3.1.

CHANNEL

		Vocal	Non-vocal
CODE	Verbal	Spoken language	Written language (Deaf) Sign language Whistle/drum languages Morse code
	Nonverbal	Paralinguistic and prosodic features	Kinesics Proxemics Eye behaviour Pictures and cartoons

Figure 3.1

In describing kinesic behaviour and facial expression, it is important to identify: (1) the part of the body (i.e. what is moving or in a marked position), (2) the directionality of the movement, or how it differs from an unmarked state, and (3) the scope of movement, if any. Several systems for transcribing non-verbal behaviours have been developed (e.g. Birdwhistell, 1952; Hall, 1963; and Ekman, Friesen and Tomkins, 1971) especially for use when this channel is the primary focus of analysis. It is particularly important to correlate verbal and non-verbal transcription, minimally requiring entry of marked non-verbal behaviours at the time they occur in relation to the verbal act sequence.

In most communicative events the message is carried by both verbal and non-verbal codes simultaneously, albeit only one or the other may be involved. Although such forms are universal, the specific value and meanings of each are relevant only in terms of individuals or particular groups.

Message content

Understanding the *message content* requires knowing the meaning of what is unsaid and presupposed by members of the group, as well as what is verbalized. The Japanese term *haragei* 'wordless communication' in part captures this concept, and in that speech community it is valued over eloquence. When silence has an intentional communicative function it may be analysed as one of the forms a 'speech' act may take, and should be considered along with the production of sentence tokens as a basic unit of linguistic communication. Silence may be used to question, promise, deny, warn, insult, request or command, as well as in various kinds of ritual interaction.

Silent communicative acts are to be distinguished from the pauses which may or may not occur in conversational turn-taking, or between questions and responses, but such temporal patterning is also conventional and relevant in ethnographic description. Silent acts are part of the verbal code, and pauses part of the non-verbal. In the sample analyses below, the function and meaning of silence is illustrated by speakers of Japanese, Igbo and Newari.

Some non-verbal behaviours are probably universal, including facial expressions of emotion, but in these cases rules regarding the appropriateness of displaying emotion in particular situations are still culture-specific (Ekman, 1972).

Questions which may be asked about message form and content include:

- What gestures or postures have special significance or may be considered objectionable?
- What meaning is attached to direct eye contact? To eye avoidance?
- What range is considered 'normal' speech behaviour? What is considered a speech defect?
- What language taboos are there? What should not be discussed? What questions should not be asked?

Selection rules govern the use of particular message forms when a choice is made between possible alternatives. An example is provided by the selection of kinship terminology: while ethnographers may collect a single set of static reference terms for people in a particular genealogical relationship, in actual use speakers may select from a great variety of alternatives for the same individual in order to express nuances of feeling, or because of differences in other components in the event.

Once a selection has been made there are restrictions on what other alternative forms may co-occur. The usual distinction is between *paradigmatic constraints* and *syntagmatic constraints* (cf. Ervin-Tripp, 1969; 1972): paradigmatic constraints govern selection of a form from among a possible set of items which might fill the same slot, and syntagmatic constraints govern the sequential selection within the same speech act.

Act sequence

The *act sequence* component includes information about the ordering of communicative acts within an event.

> We deal with the sequencing of action in which the move of one participant is followed by that of another, the first move establishing the environment for the second and the second confirming the meaning of the first. (Goffman, 1971, 149)

Ordering is usually very rigid in ritual events, such as greeting, leavetaking, complimenting and condoling, and less so in conversation.

In describing the sequence, communicative acts may be characterized in terms of their function, with a typical example of the message form and content often also listed. Although description is usually at a level of abstraction which accounts for regular patterns in recurring events, verbatim examples are useful as illustrations. In analysing opening sequences in Japanese door-to-door sales encounters, for instance, Tsuda (1980) bases her generalizations on 23 which she observed and recorded, but includes a verbatim transcript of only one which she considers 'typical'. Her data might be arranged in the following manner:

1   P1 (Salesperson): Greeting
    Gomen kudasai.
    (Excuse me.)
2   P2 (Housewife): Acknowledgement
    P2   *Hai*
    P2   (Yes)
3   P1: Identification
    Shitsurei shimasu. J degozai masu. Hai, J de gozaismasu.
    (Excuse me. I'm from J [company's name].
    Yes, J [company].)
4   P2: Question about purpose
    Nande shō?
    (What do you want of me?)
5   P1: Information about purpose
    Anō, Okusan terebi de senden shite orimasu de sho? Anō, atsumono demo usumono demo neuru to yū.
    (Do you know, *Okusan* [meaning housewife] about television commercial?
    The one we can sew even very thick ones or even very thin ones. . . .)
6   P2: Expression of disinterest/interest
    Un, anō, mishin uchi ni aru wa.
    (Well, a sewing machine. We have one at home.)

This level of abstraction not only allows regular patterns to be displayed, but cross-cultural comparisons to be made. In this case, the act sequence is found to be the same in openings of 'typical' door-to-door sales encounters in the United States, although there are significant differences in the form and content: e.g. American salespeople usually identify themselves first by name rather than by company affiliation, as in Japan.

Rules for interaction

The *rules for interaction* component includes an explanation of the rules for the use of speech which are applicable to the communicative event. By 'rules' in this context, I am referring to prescriptive statements of behaviour, of how people 'should' act, which are tied to the shared values of the speech community. They may additionally be descriptive of typical behaviour, but this is not a necessary criterion for inclusion in this component. How, and the degree to which this 'ideal' is indeed 'real' is part of the information to be collected and analysed, along with positive and negative sanctions which are applied to their observance or violation.

The rules may already be codified in the form of aphorisms, proverbs or even laws, or they may be held unconsciously and require more indirect elicitation and identification. Rules for interaction are often discoverable in reactions to their violation by others, and feelings that contrary behaviour is 'impolite' or 'odd' in some respect.

One example is turn-taking rules in conversation: in English, if one speaker utters a compliment, request or invitation, politeness usually requires the addressee to make an appropriate response on the next turn; in describing communicative patterns of speakers who live on the Warm Springs Indian reservation,

Philips (1976) reports politeness would not require any response, or the response might be given at a later time.

In the sample analyses below,* rules for interaction in a Bambara village meeting require turn-taking based on order of influence or importance in the group, and that each prospective speaker first request permission to speak from the chief. Rules may also prescribe non-verbal behaviour, as in the examples of Abbey condolences, a Japanese marriage proposal, and a Newari prospective bride interview. They may even prescribe silence, as in the Igbo condolence when there had been a 'premature' death.

Norms of interpretation

The *norms of interpretation* component should provide all of the other information about the speech community and its culture which is needed to understand the communicative event. Even the most detailed surface level description is inadequate to allow interpretation of the meaning conveyed. In the sample analyses below,* for instance, a Bambara speaker in a village meeting must know that direct speech is used to defend a point, while riddles or parables are to be interpreted as opposition; an Igbo speaker condoling family members must know that an early death cannot be by natural causes, and that someone who causes another's death cannot stand before the spirit of the deceased without incurring immediate retaliation.

I am calling these 'norms' of interpretation because they constitute a standard shared by members of the speech community; they may also be related to rules of use in the prescriptive sense (cf. Shimanoff, 1980), but the positive or negative valuation and sanctions on use which characterize rules are not a necessary condition for inclusion in this component.

Relationship among components

In addition to identifying the components of a communicative event, it is important to ask questions which relate each component to all of the others. For instance:

- How do the genre and topic influence one another?

There is probably a limited range of subjects which can be prayed about, joked about or gossiped about. Conversely, it may be appropriate to mention a particular topic only in a religious genre, or perhaps only in a joke.

- What is the relationship between genre and purpose?

The primary purpose of myths might be to entertain, to transmit cultural knowledge, or to influence the supernatural; jokes might serve primarily to entertain, or might be a means of social control, or a testing ground for determining hierarchical relationships between speakers in the social structure.

- How are genre or topic and setting related?

Prayers might be said in a particular place, perhaps with altar and specified

* Not included in this extract.

religious paraphernalia, and at certain times of the day or week; particular prayers might be appropriate only for certain holidays or seasons. Topics for stories might be limited by location, with different ones appropriate at the dinner table or in a classroom from those appropriate in a clubroom or a camp in the woods. Often topics are limited by season, as illustrated above.

- What is the relationship between genre, topic, setting, participants and message form?

Some genres will require a more formal variety of language than others, or a different language entirely. In two events of the same genre, such as a greeting, the form might differ depending on season, time of day, whether indoors or outside, or other features in the setting. A lecture on the same topic might be more or less formal depending on the size of the room, the arrangement of furniture, and the number (or identity) of persons in the audience.

The interrelationships of components may be very complex, as when the message form of a greeting is influenced not only by the season, time of day, and physical location, but the age, sex and role-relationship of the participants, and the purpose of the encounter. While not all components will be salient in each event, nor even necessarily in each speech community, they provide one type of *frame* (Bateson, 1955) within which meaningful differences can be discovered and described. The interpretation by the addressee of the utterance 'It's cold in here' as an informative statement, complaint, request or command depends on the scene, participant role-relationships, what precedes and follows in the sequence of communicative acts, and such paralinguistic and prosodic features of speech as pitch, intonation, rhythm and amplitude. These signal what kind of speech event participants are engaged in: i.e. their meta-communicative frame (cf. Gumperz, 1977; Tannen, 1979a).

4

Defining language

Jean Aitchison

From Aitchison, J. 1976: *The articulate mammal*. London: Hutchinson, 36–43.

A useful first step might be to attempt to define 'language'. This is not as easy as it sounds. Most of the definitions found in elementary textbooks are too wide. For example: 'The faculty of language consists in man's ability to make noises with the vocal organs and marks on paper or some other material, by means of which groups of people "speaking the same language" are able to interact and cooperate as a group' (Robins, 1971, 12). This definition, if one ignores the word 'man' and the phrase involving 'marks on paper', might equally well apply to a pack of wolves howling in chorus.

Perhaps the most promising approach is that suggested by the linguist Charles Hockett. In a series of articles stretching over ten years he has attempted to itemize out the various 'design features' which characterize language. For example: '*Interchangeability*: Adult members of any speech community are inter-changeably transmitters and receivers of linguistic signals'; '*Complete Feedback*: The transmitter of a linguistic signal himself receives the message' (Hockett, 1963, 9). Of course, such an approach is not perfect. A list of features may even be misleading, since it represents a random set of observations which do not cohere in any obvious way. To use this list to define language is like trying to define a man by noting that he has two arms, two legs, a head, a belly button, he bleeds if you scratch him, and shrieks if you tread on his toe. But in spite of this, a definition of language based on design features or 'essential characteristics' seems to be the most useful proposed so far.

But how many characteristics should be considered? Two? Ten? A hundred? The number of design features Hockett considers important has changed over the years. The longest list contains sixteen (Hockett, 1963), though perhaps most people would consider that eight features capture the essential nature of language: *use of the vocal-auditory channel, arbitrariness, semanticity, cultural transmission, duality, displacement, structure-dependence* and *creativity*.

Let us discuss each of these features in turn, and see whether it is present in animal communication. If any animal naturally possesses all the design features of human language, then clearly that animal can talk.

The use of the *vocal-auditory channel* is perhaps the most obvious characteristic of language. Sounds are made with the vocal organs, and a hearing mechanism receives them – a phenomenon which is neither rare nor particularly surprising.

The use of sound is widespread as a means of animal communication. One obvious advantage is that messages can be sent or received in the dark or in a dense forest. Not all sound signals are vocal – woodpeckers tap on wood, and rattle-snakes have a rattle apparatus on their tail. But vocal-auditory signals are common and are used by birds, cows, apes and foxes, to name just a few. The advantages of this method of producing the sound are that it leaves the body free to carry on other activities at the same time, and also requires relatively little physical energy. But this design feature is clearly neither unique to humans, nor all-important, since language can be transferred without loss to visual symbols (as in deaf-and-dumb language, or writing) and to tactile symbols (as in Braille). Patients who have had their vocal cords removed, and communicate mainly by writing, have not lost their language ability. It follows that this characteristic is of little use in an attempt to distinguish animal from human communication. So let us proceed to the second feature, arbitrariness.

Arbitrariness means that human languages use neutral symbols. There is no connection between the word 'dog' and the four-legged animal it symbolizes. It can equally be called UN CHIEN (French), EIN HUND (German), or CANIS (Latin). GÜL (Turkish) and RHODON (Greek) are equally satisfactory names for a 'rose'. As Juliet notes:

> What's in a name? that which we call a rose
> By any other name would smell as sweet.
>
> (Shakespeare)

Onomatopoeic words such as CUCKOO, POP, BANG, SLURP and SQUISH are exceptions to this. But there are relatively few of these in any language. On the other hand, it is normal for animals to have a strong link between the message they are sending and the signal they use to convey it. A crab which wishes to convey extreme aggression will extend a large claw. A less angry crab will merely raise a leg: 'Extending a major chaliped is more effective than raising a single ambulatory leg in causing the second crab to retreat or duck back into its shell' (Marshall, 1970). However, arbitrary symbols are not unique to man. Gulls, for example, sometimes indicate aggression by turning away from their opponent and uprooting beakfuls of grass. So we are forced to conclude that arbitrariness cannot be regarded as a critical distinction between human and animal communication.

Semanticity, the third suggested test for language ability, is the use of symbols to 'mean' or refer to objects and actions. To a human, a CHAIR 'means' a four-legged contraption you can sit on. Humans can generalize by applying this name to all types of chair, not just one in particular. Furthermore, semanticity applies to action as well as objects. For example, to JUMP 'means' the act of leaping in the air. Some writers have claimed that semanticity is exclusively human. Animals may only be able to communicate about a total situation. A hen who utters 'danger' cries when a fox is nearby is possibly conveying the message 'Beware! beware! there is terrible danger about!' rather than using the sound to 'mean' FOX. But, as is shown by the call of the vervet monkey who might or might not mean 'snake' when he *chutters*, it is difficult to be certain. We must remain agnostic about whether this feature is present in animal communication.

Cultural transmission or *tradition* indicates that human beings hand their languages down from one generation to another. The role played by teaching in animal communication is unclear and varies from animal to animal – and even within species. Among birds it is claimed that the song-thrush's song is largely innate, but can be slightly modified by learning, whereas the skylark's song is almost wholly learned. Birds such as the chaffinch are particularly interesting: the basic pattern of the song seems to be innate, but all the finer detail and much of the pitch and rhythm have to be acquired by learning (Thorpe, 1961, 1963). However, although the distinction between man and animals is not clear-cut as regards this feature, it seems that a far greater proportion of communication is genetically inbuilt in animals than in man. If a child is brought up in isolation, away from human beings, he does not acquire language. In contrast, birds reared in isolation sing songs that are sometimes recognizable (though almost always abnormal).

The fifth property, *duality* or *double-articulation*, means that language is organized into two 'layers': the basic sound units of speech, such as P, I, G, are normally meaningless by themselves. They only become meaningful when combined into sequences such as P – I – G PIG. This property is sometimes claimed to be unique to humans. But this is not so. Duality is also present in bird song, where each individual note is itself meaningless – it is the combination of notes which convey meaningful messages. So once again we have not found a critical difference between animals and humans in the use of this feature.

A more important characteristic of language is *displacement*, the ability to refer to things far removed in time and place. Humans frequently say things such as 'My Aunt Matilda, who lives in Australia, cracked her knee-cap last week.' It may be impossible for an animal to convey a similar item of information. However, as in the case of other design features, it is sometimes difficult to decide whether displacement is present in an animal's communication system. A bird frequently continues to give alarm cries long after the disappearance of a cat which was stalking it. Is this displacement or not? The answer is unclear. Definite examples of displacement are hard to find. But it is undoubtedly found in bee communication (von Frisch, 1950, 1954, 1967). When a worker bee finds a source of nectar she returns to the hive to perform a complex dance which informs the other bees of its location. She does a 'round dance', which involves turning round in circles if the nectar is close to the hive, and a 'waggle dance' in which she wiggles her tail from side to side if it is far away. The other bees work out the distance by noting the tempo of her waggles, and discover what kind of flower to look for by smelling its scent on her body. After the dance, they unerringly fly to the right place, even if it is several miles away, with a hill intervening.

This is an unusual ability – but even this degree of displacement is considerably less than that found in human speech. The bee cannot inform other bees about anything further removed [in time] than the nectar patch she has just visited. She cannot say 'The day before yesterday we visited a lovely clump of flowers, let's go and see if they are still there' – she can only say, 'Come to the nectar I have just visited.' Nor can she communicate about anything further away in place. She could not say 'I wonder whether there's good nectar in Siberia.' So displacement in bee communication is strictly limited to the number of miles a bee can easily fly, and the time it takes to do this. At last, it seems we may have found a feature which seems to be of importance in human language, and only partially present in non-human communication.

The seventh feature, *structure-dependence*, was discussed [earlier in the book]. Humans do not just apply simple recognition or counting techniques when they speak to one another. They automatically recognize the patterned nature of language, and manipulate 'structured chunks'. For example, they understand that a group of words can sometimes be the structural equivalent of one:

SHE THE OLD LADY WHO WAS WEARING A WHITE BONNET	GAVE THE DONKEY A CARROT

and they can rearrange these chunks according to strict rules:

A CARROT	WAS GIVEN TO THE DONKEY	BY THE OLD LADY WHO WAS WEARING A WHITE BONNET

As far as we know, animals do not use structure-dependent operations. We do not know enough about the communication of all animals to be sure, but no definite example has yet been found.

Finally, there is one feature that seems to be of overwhelming importance, and unique to humans – the ability to produce and understand an indefinite number of novel utterances. This property of language has several different names. Chomsky calls it *creativity*, others calls it *openness* or *productivity*. A human can talk about anything he likes – even a platypus falling backwards downstairs – without causing any linguistic problems to himself or the hearer. He can say *what* he wants *when* he wants. If it thunders, he does not automatically utter a set phrase, such as 'It's thundering, run for cover'. He can say 'Isn't the lightning pretty?' or 'Better get the dog in' or 'Thunder is two dragons colliding in tin tubs, according to a Chinese legend.'

In contrast, most animals have a fixed number of signals which convey a set number of messages, sent in clearly definable circumstances. A North American cicada can give four signals only. It emits a 'disturbance squawk'; when it is seized, picked up or eaten. A 'congregation call' seems to mean 'Let's all get together and sing in chorus!' A preliminary courtship call (an invitation?) is uttered when a female is several inches away. An advanced courtship call (a buzz of triumph?) occurs when the female is almost within grasp (Alexander and Moore, quoted in McNeill, 1966). Even the impressive vervet monkey has only thirty-six distinct vocal sounds in its repertoire. And as this total includes sneezing and vomiting, the actual number used for communication is several fewer. Within this range, choice is limited, since circumstances generally dictate which call to use. An infant separated from its mother gives the lost *rrah* cry. A female who wishes to deter an amorous male gives the 'anti-copulatory squeal-scream' (Struhsaker, 1967).

But perhaps it is unfair to concentrate on cicadas and monkeys. Compared with these, bees and dolphins have extremely sophisticated communication systems.

Yet researchers have reluctantly concluded that even bees and dolphins seem unable to say anything new. The bees were investigated by the famous 'bee-man', Karl von Frisch (1954). He noted that worker bees normally give information about the *horizontal* distance and direction of a source of nectar. If bee communication is in any sense 'open', then a worker bee should be able to inform the other bees about *vertical* distance and direction if necessary. He tested this idea by placing a hive of bees at the foot of a radio beacon, and a supply of sugar water at the top. But the bees who were shown the sugar water were unable to tell the other bees where to find it. They duly performed a 'round dance', indicating that a source of nectar was in the vicinity of the hive – and then for several hours their comrades flew in all directions *except* upwards, looking for the honey source. Eventually, they gave up the search. As von Frisch noted, 'The bees have no word for "up" in their language. There are no flowers in the clouds' (von Frisch, 1954, 139). Failure to communicate this extra item of information means that bee communication cannot be regarded as 'open-ended' in the same way that human language is open-ended.

The dolphin experiments carried out by Dr Jarvis Bastian were considerably more exciting – though in the long run equally disappointing. Bastian tried to teach a male dolphin Buzz and a female dolphin Doris to communicate across an opaque barrier.

First of all, while they were still together, Bastian taught the dolphins to press paddles when they saw a light. If the light was kept steady, they had to press the right paddle first. If it flashed, the left-hand one. When they did this correctly they were rewarded with fish.

As soon as they had learned this manœuvre, he separated them. They could now hear one another, but they could not see one another. The paddles and light were set up in the same way, except that the light which indicated which paddle to press first was seen only by Doris. But in order to get fish both dolphins had to press the levers in the correct order. Doris had to *tell* Buzz which this was, as only she could see the light. Amazingly, the dolphins 'demonstrated essentially perfect success over thousands of trials at this task' (Evans and Bastian, 1969, 432). It

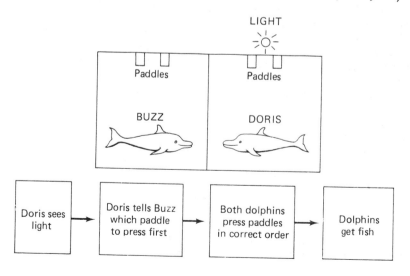

seemed that dolphins could *talk*! Doris was conveying novel information through an opaque barrier! But it later became clear that the achievement was considerably less clever. Even while the dolphins were together Doris had become accustomed to making certain sounds when the light was flashing and different sounds when it was continuous. When the dolphins were separated she continued the habit. And Buzz had, of course, already learnt which sound of Doris's to associate with which light. Doris was therefore not 'talking creatively'.

So not even dolphins have a 'creative' communication system, it seems – though it is always possible that more is known about 'dolphinese' than has been made public. The high intelligence of dolphins has obvious implications for naval warfare, and so has attracted the attention of military authorities, with the result that much research is shrouded in official secrecy. But on the whole it seems unlikely that there exist hidden tanks of 'talking dolphins' (as was suggested in a recent film). Most researchers would agree with the comment of the psychologist John Morton: 'On the question as to whether dolphins have a language, I would like to comment parenthetically from the evidence I have seen, if they do have a language they are going to extraordinary lengths to conceal the fact from us' (Morton, 1971, 83).

It seems, then, that animals cannot send truly novel messages, and that Ogden Nash encapsulates a modicum of truth in his comment:

The song of canaries
Never varies.

And so does Alice in her complaint about kittens:

It is a very inconvenient habit of kittens that, whatever you say to them, they always purr. If they would only purr for 'yes' and mew for 'no', or any rule of that sort, so that one could keep up a conversation! But how *can* you talk with a person if they *always* say the same thing?

(Lewis Carroll)

It is now possible to answer the question, can animals talk? If, in order to qualify as 'talkers' they have to utilize all the design characteristics of human language 'naturally', the answer is clearly 'no'. Some animals possess some of the features. Bird song has duality, and bee dancing has some degree of displacement. But, as far as we know, no animal communication system has duality *and* displacement. No animal system can be proved to have semanticity or to use structure-dependent operations. Above all, no animal can communicate creatively with another animal.

But although animals do not 'naturally' talk, this does not mean that they are *incapable* of talking. Perhaps they have just never had the chance to learn language.

5

Verbal and non-verbal communication

Michael Argyle

From Argyle, M. 1972: *The psychology of interpersonal behaviour*. Harmondsworth: Penguin Books (Pelican Original), 37–50.

2, 7, 10

Different kinds of social act

1. *Bodily contact* is of interest since it is the most primitive kind of social act, and is found in all animals. In addition to aggressive and sexual contacts there are various methods of influence, as when others are pushed, pulled or led. There are symbolic contacts, such as patting on the back, and the various ways of shaking hands. Outside the family, bodily contact is mainly restricted to the hands. Jourard (1966) has surveyed who has been touched by whom and where, and his results for American students are shown in Figure 5.1. It can be seen that there are great differences in who is touched by whom, and on which parts of their anatomy.

There are great cross-cultural differences in bodily contact, and this form of social behaviour is less common in Britain than almost anywhere else. It usually conveys intimacy, and occurs at the beginning and end of encounters. There has been some interest in 'encounter groups' in the USA and Britain during recent years. The greater use of bodily contact here is found to be exciting and disturbing – but it must be remembered that those concerned have been brought up in cultures in which there are strong restraints against bodily contact and will have internalized these restraints.

2. *Physical proximity* is important mainly in relation to intimacy and dominance. It is one of the cues for intimacy, both sexual and between friends of the same sex. The normal degree of proximity varies between cultures and every species of animal has its characteristic social distance. The significance of physical proximity varies with the physical surroundings – proximity to the point of bodily contact in a lift has no affiliative significance, and it is noteworthy that eye-contact and conversation are avoided here. If A sits near B, it makes a difference whether there are other places where A could have sat, whether he is directly facing B or at an angle, and whether there is any physical barrier. Closest distances are adopted for more intimate conversations: at the closer distances different sensory modes are used – touch and smell come into operation, and vision becomes less important (Hall, 1963). It is found that people sit or stand closer to people that they like. There are also large cross-cultural differences – Arabs and

Only of importance where person has choice to stand somewhere else

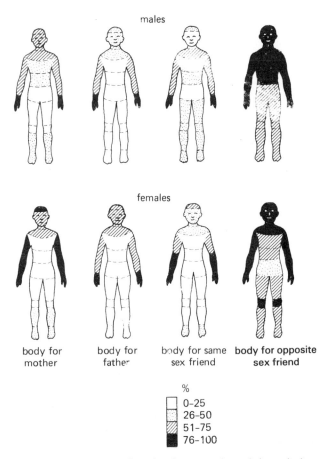

males

females

body for   body for   body for same   body for opposite
mother   father   sex friend   sex friend

%
☐ 0–25
26–50
51–75
■ 76–100

Figure 5.1 Male and female 'bodies-for-others', as experienced through the amount of touching received from others (Jourard, 1966)

Latin Americans stand very close, Swedes and Scots are the most distant (Lott *et al.*, 1969). *Changes* of proximity are of course used to signal the wish to begin or end an encounter, accompanied by other appropriate messages.

3. *Orientation* signals interpersonal attitudes. If person A is sitting at a table, as shown in Fig 5.2, B can sit in several different places. If he is told that the situation is cooperative he will probably sit at B1; if he is told he is to compete, negotiate, sell something or interview A, he will sit at B2; if he is told to have a discussion or conversation he usually chooses B3 (Sommer, 1965). This shows (a) that one can become more sensitive to the cues emitted, often unintentionally, by others, and (b) that one can control non-verbal as well as verbal signals.

If one person is higher up than another – by being on a rostrum, standing, or perhaps simply by being taller, it puts him in a somewhat dominating position – probably because parents are taller than children. On the other hand, there is the curious cultural convention that more important people should sit while others have to stand. Hutte and Cohen in Holland made silent films of managers entering

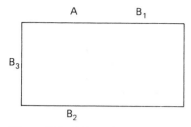

Figure 5.2 Orientation in different relationships

offices of other managers. It was quite clear to subjects who were shown these films which manager was the senior (in a and c), and how friendly they were (in b and d) (Burns, 1964; see also Figure 5.3).

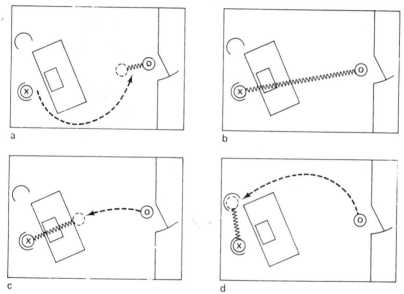

Figure 5.3 Key movements between men in an office indicating their relationship (Burns, 1964)

4. *Bodily posture* is another signal which is largely involuntary, but which can communicate important social signals. There are distinctive 'superior' (or dominant) and 'inferior' (or submissive) postures. The desire or intention to dominate can be signalled by standing erect, with the head tilted back, and with hands on hips, for example. There are also friendly, and hostile postures. (See Figure 5.4.).

By his general bodily posture a person may signal his emotional state, e.g. tense versus relaxed. He can show his attitude to the others present – as when a person sits in a different way from the others, or puts his feet on the table.

People also have general styles of expressive behaviour, as shown in the way they walk, stand, sit and so on. This may reflect past or present roles – as in the case of a person who is or has been a soldier; it also reflects a person's self-image, self-confidence, and emotional state. It is very dependent on cultural fashions:

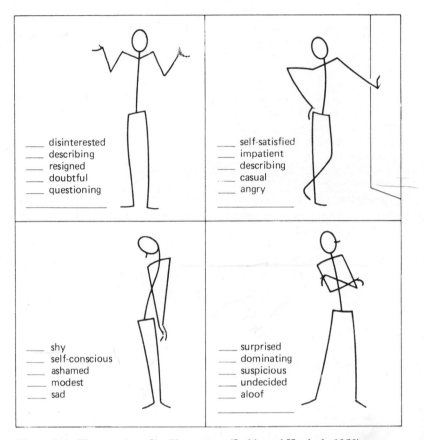

Figure 5.4   The meaning of bodily postures (Sarbin and Hardyck, 1953)

In a street market I watched a working-class mum and her daughter. The mother waddled as if her feet were playing her up. Outside a Knightsbridge hotel I watched an upper-class mum and her daughter come out from a wedding reception and walk towards Hyde Park Corner, the mother on very thin legs slightly bowed as though she had wet herself. She controlled her body as if it might snap if moved too impulsively. Both daughters walked identically (Melly, 1965).

5. *Gestures* are movements of hands, feet or other parts of the body. Some are intended to communicate definite messages; others are involuntary social cues which may or may not be correctly interpreted by others.

Communicating emotional states. When a person is emotionally aroused he produces diffuse, apparently pointless, bodily movements. A nervous lecturer may work as hard as a manual labourer. More specific emotions produce particular gestures – fist-clenching (aggression), face-touching (anxiety), scratching (self-blame), forehead-wiping (tiredness) etc. (Ekman and Friesen 1969).

Completing the meaning of utterances. It has been found that while a person speaks he moves his hands, body and head continuously, that these movements are closely coordinated with speech, and that they form part of the total communication. He may (1) display the structure of the utterance by enumerating elements or showing how they are grouped, (2) point to people or objects, (3) provide emphasis, and (4) give illustrations of shapes, sizes or movements (Scheflen, 1965; Kendon, 1972).

Replacing speech. When speech is impossible for one reason or another, gesture languages develop.

6. *Head-nods* are a rather special kind of gesture, and have two distinctive roles. They act as 'reinforcers', i.e. they reward and encourage what has gone before, and can be used to make another talk more, for example. Head-nods also play an important role in controlling the synchronizing of speech – in Britain a nod gives the other permission to carry on talking, whereas a rapid succession of nods indicates that the nodder wants to speak himself.

7. *Facial expression* can be reduced to changes in eyes, brows, mouth, and so on. The face is an area which is used by animals to communicate emotions and attitudes to others; for humans it does not work so well since we control our facial expression, and may smile sweetly while seething within. Emotions can be recognized to some extent from facial expression alone, as is shown by studies using still photographs of actors. Emotions can be recognized in terms of broad categories – for example, the pleasant and unpleasant ones – but those which are similar are harder to tell apart. The circle below (Figure 5.5) shows which are seen as most similar to one another – those furthest apart are the easiest to distinguish. In addition to these states, it is possible to recognize degrees of emotional tension – by perspiration on the forehead and expansion of the pupils of the eyes.

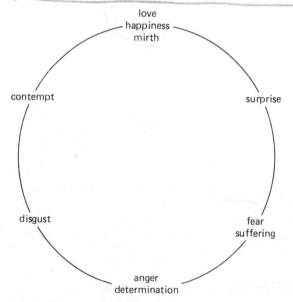

Figure 5.5 The dimensions of facial expression (Schlosberg, 1952)

Facial expression works rather better as a way of providing feedback on what another is saying. The eyebrows provide a continuous running commentary, going from:

fully raised	— disbelief
half raised	— surprise
normal	— no comment
half lowered	— puzzled
fully lowered	— angry.

The area round the mouth adds to the running commentary by varying between being turned up (pleasure) and turned down (displeasure).

8. *Eye movements* have an effect quite out of proportion to the physical effort exerted. When A looks at B, in the region of the eyes, B knows that A is attending primarily to him, and that interaction can proceed. If A gazes for a long time at B, this can have a variety of meanings, depending on A's facial expression and on the situation – it can be an amorous, friendly, aggressive or curious gaze – in each case revealing something of A's feelings towards B. Glances can be long or short, furtive or open, and can combine together to form complex strategies of eye-play. Eye movements play an important part in sustaining the flow of interaction: while A is speaking he looks up to get feedback on how B is responding, and he ends a long utterance with a gaze which tells B that it is his turn to speak. When there is eye-contact between two people this is experienced as a heightening of inter-personal emotions, usually in the sense of greater intimacy.

9. *Appearance*. Many aspects of personal appearance are under voluntary con-trol, and a great deal of effort is put into controlling them – clothes, hair and skin; other aspects can be modified to some extent by clothes and plastic surgery. The main purpose of this manipulation of appearance is self-presentation – signalling how the presenter sees himself and would like to be treated.

10. *Non-linguistic aspects of speech*. The same words may be said in quite different ways, conveying different emotional expressions, and even different meanings, as when 'yes' is used as a polite way of saying 'no'. Davitz (1964) found that when actors read out an emotionally neutral passage to express different emotional states, these were recognizable by judges about 60 to 70 per cent of the time. The emotions in question were: admiration, affection, amusement, anger, boredom, cheerfulness, despair, disgust, dislike, fear, impatience, joy, satisfaction and sur-prise. The author has used this method as a means of sensitivity training. Some people are much better at making such judgements than others. Several aspects of voice quality are involved – loudness, pitch, speed, voice quality (such as breathiness, or breaking into incipient tears), and smoothness. These aspects of speech are correlated, though not perfectly, with emotional states. For example, an anxious person tends to talk faster than normal and at a higher pitch. A depressed person talks slowly, and at a lower pitch; an aggressive person talks loudly.

The pattern of pauses, stress and pitch is really part of the verbal utterance itself. Pauses provide punctuation (instead of saying 'full stop' as when dictating); stress and pitch show whether a question is being asked and provide emphasis, thus showing which of several possible meanings is intended (Crystal, 1969).

There are non-linguistic aspects of the conversation as a whole – the patterns of speech and silence – how much of the time each person talks, how fast, how soon after the other stops, and so on. Chapple (1956) has shown that people have characteristic ways of reacting to interruption and silence on the part of another. In his 'standard interview' the subject is first interviewed in a relaxed manner; later follows a period in which the interviewer fails to respond to twelve successive utterances by the subject, and another period during which the interviewer interrupts twelve successive speeches by the subject. Some people yield at once if interrupted, while others try to talk the interrupter down. Some people cannot tolerate silence, and will speak again if the interviewer is silent.

Another non-verbal aspect of speech is the rate of speech errors. These are of two main kinds – 'ah's and 'er's, and 'non-ah' errors like changes of sentence, repetitions, stutters, etc. 'Non-ah' errors are caused by anxiety; 'ah's and 'er's are not, and seem to be used to create time to think and decide what to say next (Cook, 1969).

11. *Speech* is the most complex, subtle and characteristically human means of communication. Most animal noises simply communicate emotional states. Human speech is different in that it is learned, can convey information about external events, and has a grammatical structure. But it still consists of a set of learned social techniques which are used to influence others. There are great differences in the skill of individuals at using language, mainly associated with intelligence, education and training, and social class. A large part of most social skills lies in putting together utterances which are tactful, persuasive, or whatever is required.

Speech is used to ask questions. These are of interest as they lead to further interaction, and to information about others. Some forms of encounter, such as the interview, consist entirely of questions and the answers to them. Questions vary in the extent to which they are open or closed – an open-ended question requires a lengthy explanation rather than a choice between alternatives; the best way to get someone to talk is to ask this kind of question.

Speech can be used to convey information to others, in answer to questions, as part of the work of committees or work-teams, in lectures, and elsewhere. The speaker may be reporting facts, giving his opinions, or arguing on the basis of these. Such communications are often imperfectly received, because the speaker has not made himself sufficiently clear, or because the hearer attaches different meaning to words or phrases. Ideally, both should speak exactly the same language, i.e. where every sentence carries the identical penumbra of meanings and implications.

Thirdly, speech is used more directly to influence the behaviour of others, by means of instructions or orders, persuasion and propaganda, as well as by aggressive remarks – which may be used when all else fails. Aggressive speech occurs in a variety of forms, of which the milder ones are gentle ridicule and teasing, and the more severe are direct insults.

A lot of speech is not primarily intended to communicate anything very serious, or to solve any problems. Informal speech, as it is called, is more concerned with establishing, sustaining and enjoying social relationships – chat, idle gossip, and joke-telling between friends or family members, or during coffee breaks at work. It has been found that about half of the very expensive conversation over the trans-Atlantic telephone is of this kind. Formal speech, as in a well-delivered lecture, is more concise, conveys information clearly, and is more like written language in structure.

Speech can also be concerned with the process of social interaction itself. This may be acceptable in clinical or training situations, but can be very disturbing in other encounters, when for example someone says 'There's an awkward silence, isn't there.' Words may be used to provide rewards and punishments; in fact this happens continually in the course of interaction, but is largely unintended.

Utterances vary in a number of ways; they can be intimate or impersonal, easy, abstract or technical, interesting or boring to the hearer. In specialized forms of social encounter particular kinds of utterance may be important, like 'interpretation' during psychoanalysis, 'follow-up questions' in an interview, etc. The joke is a special kind of verbal utterance, which has the effect of relieving tension and creating euphoria in social situations. Speeches may have latent meanings, as when the speaker reveals something additional to the main message. This may be unintended, as with the speaker who was asked if he had ever been to Nigeria and replied 'that's a place I've not been to' (Brown, 1965). Or it may be intentional as when a schoolboy says 'Please, Sir, the board's shining' (when it isn't).

Three roles of non-verbal communication

Non-verbal communication (NVC) functions in three rather different ways (Argyle, 1972).

1. *Communicating interpersonal attitudes and emotions.* Animals conduct their entire social life by means of NVC – they make friends, find mates, rear children, establish dominance hierarchies, and cooperate in groups, by means of facial expression, postures, gestures, grunting and barking noises, etc. It looks as if much the same is true of humans too. Argyle *et al.* (1970) carried out an experiment in which superior, equal and inferior verbal messages were delivered in superior, equal and inferior non-verbal styles, nine combinations in all, by speakers recorded on video-tapes. Two of the verbal messages were as follows:

> (1) It is probably quite a good thing for you subjects to come along to help in these experiments because it gives you a small glimpse of what psychological research is about. In fact the whole process is far more complex that you would be able to appreciate without a considerable training in research methods, paralinguistics, kinesic analysis, and so on.
> (2) These experiments must seem rather silly to you and I'm afraid they are not really concerned with anything very interesting and important. We'd be very glad if you could spare us a few moment afterwards to tell us how we could improve the experiment. We feel that we are not making a very good job of it, and feel rather guilty about wasting the time of busy people like yourself.

Some of the results are shown in Figure 5.6 on p. 37.

It can be seen that the non-verbal style had more effect than the verbal contents, in fact about five times as much; when the verbal and non-verbal messages were in conflict, the verbal contents were virtually disregarded. Much the same results were obtained in another experiment on the friendly–hostile dimension.

The explanation of these results is probably that there is an innate biological basis to these NV signals, which evoke an immediate and powerful emotional response – as in animals. In human social behaviour it looks as if the NV channel is used for negotiating interpersonal attitudes, while the verbal channel is used primarily for conveying information.

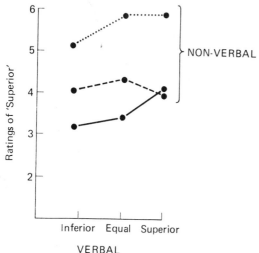

Figure 5.6 Interaction between verbal and non-verbal cues (Argyle *et al.*, 1970) ...., superior; ----, equal; ———, inferior

2. *Supporting verbal communication.* Linguists recognize that timing, pitch and stress are integral to the meaning of utterances, e.g. by providing punctuation. A few linguists recognize that NVC plays a more extensive part – 'We speak with our vocal organs, but we converse with our whole body' (Abercrombie, 1968).

Completing the meaning of utterances. In addition to the *vocal* signals of timing, pitch and stress, *gestural* signals also add to meaning – by illustrating, pointing, displaying structure, etc. Frame-by-frame analysis of conversations has shown that there is a linkage between gesture and speech down to the level of the word, and that there is a hierarchical structure of gesture, where the larger movements correspond to larger verbal units, like paragraphs (Kendon, 1972). These fine movements are unintended, often unseen, and idiosyncratic, so that their full explanation is not known.

Controlling synchronizing. When two or more people are conversing they must take it in turns to speak, and usually achieve a fairly smooth pattern of synchro- nizing. This is done by the use of non-verbal signals such as shifts of gaze, head- nods, and grunts.

Obtaining feedback. When a person is speaking he needs feedback on how the others are responding, so that he can modify his remarks accordingly. He needs to know whether his listeners understand, believe him, are surprised or bored, agree or disagree, are pleased or annoyed. This information could be provided by *sotto voce* muttering, but is in fact obtained from careful study of the other's face, especially his eyebrows and mouth.

Signalling attentiveness. For an encounter to be sustained, those involved must provide intermittent evidence that they are still attending to the others. They should not fall asleep, look out of the window, or read the paper; they should be at the right distance, in the right orientation, look up frequently, nod their heads, adopt an alert, congruent position, and react to the speaker's bodily movements.

3. *Replacing speech.* When speech is impossible, gesture languages develop. This

happens in noisy factories, the army, racecourses, and underwater swimming. Some of these languages are complex and enable elaborate messages to be sent, though rather slowly, as in deaf-and-dumb language, and the sign language used by some Australian aboriginals.

It has been suggested by some psychiatrists that the symptoms of certain mental patients are a kind of NVC used when speech has failed – in pursuit of attention or love.

6

The analysis of representational images

Bill Nichols

From Nichols, Bill 1981: *Ideology and the image.* Bloomington, Indiana University Press: 57–64.
Note: There are two references to colour in the discussion of the examples, though the illustrations in
the original text were, as here, reproduced in monochrome. The extract begins just after a discussion
of the ways in which photographs 'place' viewers in certain viewing relationships to what is in the
image by various devices of framing and composition.

The meaning of images

The photographic image, however, does more than place the viewer; and these
other functions, no less fraught with ideological implications, also need examination. A still image, for example, is a remarkably mute object testifying perhaps
only to a 'having been there' of the image's referent at that single instant in time of
its capture. Meaning, though rich, may be profoundly imprecise, ambiguous,

punch au planteur . . .

Figure 6.1

even deceiving. A large component of the work undertaken in the construction and reading of images becomes directed toward a distillation of that ambiguity of meaning into a more defined, and limited, concentrate. Possible meanings are scattered to the periphery of a solid charge of determined, or overdetermined, meaning pinned down by those nodal points of intersection between signifiers and signifieds, the shadowy trace of a complex *moiré* pattern. The strategies available to the image maker to anchor or secure meaning are numerous and have been frequently catalogued in introductory film texts and in the work of theoretical writers like Rudolf Arnheim or Bela Balazs. Rather than repeat them here, it should be more profitable to trace their application in a number of concrete instances.

We readily recognize Figure 6.1 as a member of the genus *advertising image*. No one cue provides the warranty for identification, but some of the cues intersecting at this point of meaning are (1) the carefully balanced and focused composition, (2) the camera's unprovocative proximity – the privilege accorded it of approaching a man who has receded behind his function as signifier of warmth and pleasure, (3) the finely rendered texture with its attendant spill of gentle light, (4) the pre-eminence of these two additional signifiers of warmth and pleasure – the man's drink and the top of a liquor bottle whose status as commercial merchandise is naturalized by the broad tropical leaves ringing it like a bouquet of floral petals, and (5) the corporate imprimatur (*'punch au planteur ...'*) authorizing the image but incorporated within it, arising from it almost as though (as though!) these very words of authorization had been put into the man's mouth in order to be passed on to us, unmediated by a business world, from one friend to another. . . .

We can go further and tease out those points at which potentially floating signifiers are pinned to the specific signifieds of warmth and pleasure, the dominant association invited between image and product and assured by the image as product, the image as a site readied for and prepared by production, the work of codes. One level of work involves the paradigmatic or metaphoric level: the choice of a specific figure or feature from a repertoire of possibilities, similar to the choice of a specific item from a list of appetizers during a meal. Each choice carries with it a certain meaning – implications or associations that accrue to it on the basis of its difference from other possible choices. Again, this snaring of meaning is overdetermined but would include: (1) the clean (not dirty), frayed-edged (relaxed, not formal) straw hat: (2) the rich brown skin tones (sun-warmed, not etiolated or charred): (3) the white (not stained) regular (not unpleasant) teeth; (4) the slim cigar (neither cigarette – placid and non-aromatic – nor stogy – coarse, acrid); and (5) the flecks of stippled light radiating, improbably, from the man's shaded eyes, rendering them lively (not dull).

Other choices of features could also be identified paradigmatically (in terms of the significance of the actual choice from among possible choices), but it is useful to dwell further on one of the compositional nodal points of the image: the man's mouth. Here the level of work is at a syntagmatic or metonymic level: the actual arrangement of figures of features chosen from a larger repertoire. Our concern is with the spatial (and in film, temporal) relationships between those figures that are present rather than the relationship of figures present to figures absent. The man's mouth is one such figure and its syntagmatic relationships are what might be more traditionally discussed in terms of style.

The mouth occupies a privileged position – centred, one third of the way up from the bottom edge. It is further centred by the shadows de-emphasizing the eyes, nose, and chin, by its location midway between beverage and bottle, by the loosely curled fingers aimed toward it, the cigar extending from it. This carefully orchestrated centre of attention, although consigned to a deeper plane than either drink or bottle, boasts possession of the one object bridging this spatial chasm – the cigar. The cigar, lit but not smoking, provides, like a straw, a bridge from (inflamed) oral cavity to (cool) refreshing drink. Our friend, gazing at us, is drawn via this hypertrophied and tubular tongue into a foreground zone of liquid pleasure. This zone, midway between the two pyramid apexes of vanishing point and camera/viewer, stands ready to sheer or buckle in two directions like a sheet of paper tossed into a fire: the curl of his fingers waits to draw the refreshing drink inwards toward him; the curve of the leaves wait to escort the bottle outwards toward us. Between friends a source of warmth and pleasure is to be exchanged. (Need we add, '. . . for a price'?)

Figure 6.2

Images in combination

The potential ambiguity of the single photographic image can be pinned down by the work of codes internal to that image with or against each other. But, commonly, an image's environment enters into the production of meaning. In film this environment includes the succession of one image, and shot, by another along a diachronic axis and the accompanying sound effects, music, speech, or written words organized in tandem with the image track. With still images combinations of the same possibilities arise (comic books and slide shows, for example), although without the impression of movement peculiar to motion pictures and television. In most instances image-image and images-written-word combinations have the greatest importance. These combinations can be regarded as relationships of context/text or syntagmatic aspects of a text, depending on our point of view and the specifics of the situation. A magazine cover may provide a contextual frame for those images displayed inside the magazine, for example, whereas a combination of images used to produce the cover itself may be more easily seen as a syntagmatic aspect of one text. The emphasis here will once again be on textual analysis and hence syntagmatics.

This image (Figure 6.2) announces its class (advertising image), genus (magazine cover), and species (*Sports Illustrated* cover) quite readily, if we know the codes of magazine merchandising and football. Its combination of images and words is clear testimony to the funnelling of meaning, the reduction of ambiguity, made possible by the interplay of codes. Even though meaning is pinned down, it may not be paraded forthrightly, especially since the relationship of codes such as word to image need not and cannot be one of pure redundancy, guaranteeing already apparent meaning. Much of the meaning continues to originate from the matrix of analog codes that we are hard put to recognize as codes and whose messages are often received at less conscious levels despite being precisely formulated. With this proviso in mind, we can begin an analysis of this cover by noting the complementary relationship between the inset of the coach and the quarterback in the centre of attention. This relationship involves (1) the approximation of an eyeline match (the imaginary meeting of their gazes); (2) the reciprocal pinning down of the quarterback's expression and the coach's gesture from a larger repertoire of possibilities to 'What should I do' and 'Let me help you'; (3) the mutual colour bond of the quarterback's badge of bloodstains and the red border of the inset, which sublimates the brutality of combat from the coach to his frame, to the boundary between brawn and brain; (4) the contrast of scale (looming brawn, diminished brain) rendered ironic by the placement of lettering of the quarterback's jersey (where his own name should be emblazoned, but where the coach's reigns both benevolently – 'divine,' guiding – and oppressively – on his back). This unspoken bond invokes much of the lure football holds for the armchair quarterback – the formulation of strategy, the crossing of the boundary between brain/brawn – and its very invocation upon the magazine's cover carries with it a promise of revelation: within the issue's interior, mysteries of strategy and relationship will be unveiled.

The play on words (Devine/divine), far from diffusing meaning, buttons it still more closely. The coach, Dan Devine, has just come to Notre Dame from the professional ranks: two forms of supremacy (of spiritual being and professional sport) coagulate in the red-framed, free-floating portrait of the coach alongside his team. This meaning, like many others employed in advertising topical commodities like a sports magazine, requires a pre-existing familiarity with current events, with the kind of events the magazine would have covered in a previous issue, for example. Punning here signifies not only the relationship of Devine to Notre Dame and his previous job but also the *au courant* status of the issue itself and its placement in an ongoing series of updates.

(a)

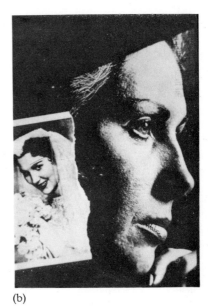

(b)

(c)

Figure 6.3(a), (b), (c) The increments of meaning added to the highly ambiguous image of a woman's face by combination with another image and by yoking both images to a single caption pin down a range of possible interpretations to a far more limited set. This pinning also proposes conceptual constraints around the topic of divorce that are clearly ideological, i.e., sexist.

Images and Ideology

The function of words in relation to images has often been singled out as a factor of singular importance in holding meaning in check. The great precision of a digital code like written language allows a dense mass of meaning to be packed into a relatively small surface area to which the eye is almost inevitably attracted and from which meanings are discharged like a shower of needle points to pin down the ambiguity of images (Figure 6.3). In analysing a widely disseminated photograph of Jane Fonda in North Vietnam (Figure 6.4). Godard and Gorin have this to say about the caption originally printed in *L'Express* (this image forms the basis of their film *Letter to Jane,* 1972).

> The text doesn't mention the Vietnamese people in the photograph. For example, the text doesn't tell us that the Vietnamese who cannot be seen in the background is one of the least known and least moderate of the Vietnamese people. This photograph, like any photograph, is physically mute. It talks through the mouth of the text written beneath it. This text does not emphasize, does not repeat, because a photograph speaks and says things in its own way. The fact that the militant is in the foreground, and Vietnam is in the background. The text says that Jane Fonda is questioning the people of Hanoi. But the magazine does not publish the questions asked, nor the answers given by the representatives of the North Vietnamese people in this photograph. In fact, the text should not describe the photograph as Jane Fonda questioning but as Jane Fonda listening. This much is obvious and perhaps the moment only lasted 1/250th of a second but that is the 1/250th that has been recorded and sent throughout the western world.[1]

Words can indeed lie, and they can lie about images as well as anything else, though the very ambiguity of an image seems to soften these possible lies to helpful notes of emphasis. The play between word and image remains a site for disintegration as well as integration, of non-cooperation as well as incorporation.

Figure 6.4

Section II

The socio-cultural relations of language

In this section we hope to be able to make the reader aware of the limitations of a 'commonsensical' view of language as a sort of neutral medium for the transmission or storing of ideas or thoughts, much as a delivery-van or a warehouse transmits or stores goods. Our aim is to raise some general questions about the role of language in society and culture, and to indicate the extent to which all aspects of social life and cultural interaction are penetrated by language. To do this we need to suggest the many different forms and functions language assumes, but our emphasis will not involve detailed technical analysis of language in terms of, for example, syntax, grammar or phonology.

The extract from Jean Aitchison's book which we included in the previous section compared and contrasted language with the communication systems of animals. We hope that this has enabled readers to appreciate that language does not just enable human beings to *do* certain things (which of course it most definitely does), but that it actually enables us to *be* human. Those studying the emergence of *homo sapiens* have argued that the development and use of tools led not only to a new control over nature, but to new relationships between human beings and to crucial mental changes too. Language is a vital tool for human beings, but it is also radically implicated in micro- and macro-relationships between human beings, and in complexities of human thought and consciousness. Without language, no humanity. Nothing human is untouched by language, and it is this permeation of language into everything that is human that we wish to explore in more detail in the present section.

The very size, complexity and comprehensiveness of language has inevitably led researchers to limit the scope of their enquiry into it. Language can be studied in one of its national–cultural variants (English, Japanese, Swahili) or in a variety such as Black American English vernacular; it can be studied in written rather than spoken form; or the focus of concern can be narrowed down even further by concentrating upon one aspect such as grammar or phonology. In recent years other ways of limiting the scope of enquiry have been influential. Language study has traditionally fallen into one of two dominant approaches: the *synchronic* (language seen as a complete system at a given point in time), and the *diachronic* or historical (language as it evolves over time). Early in the present century the Swiss linguistician Ferdinand de Saussure's use of this division allowed him to make a further important distinction: between *langue* (the overall and abstract system that is language) and *parole* (the individual utterances generated by means of this system). Noam Chomsky's distinction between *competence* and *performance* has something in common with this division of Saussure's.

Such delimitations and distinctions have proved enormously productive in the present century, and without them the study of language would have remained piecemeal and positivistic (that is, concerned only with the accumulation of directly observable facts about language). But in recent years their limitations have been highlighted by researchers concerned both to remind us of the comprehensive presence of language in social and cultural life and to argue against attempts to separate language from human consciousness, activity and history. Earlier this century the pioneer theorist of communication Charles Peirce suggested a tripartite distinction between *syntactics* (or syntax) which would study the formal relation of signs to one another, *semantics* which would study the relations of signs to the phenomena or ideas to which the signs are applicable, and *pragmatics* which would study the relation of signs to interpreters. It is fair to say that within Communication Studies in general, and with regard to the place of language study in Communication Studies in particular, the pragmatic dimension has assumed a position of increasing importance in the last decade, and this shift of emphasis is reflected in the present section. Stephen C. Levinson, in his influential book *Pragmatics*, suggests reasons for this development.

> [This interest in pragmatics] developed in part as a reaction or antidote to Chomsky's treatment of language as an abstract device, or mental ability, dissociable from the uses, users and functions of language.
>
> . . .
>
> Another powerful and general motivation for the interest in pragmatics is the growing realization that there is a very substantial gap between current linguistic theories of language and accounts of linguistic communication. [. . .] For it is becoming increasingly clear that a semantic theory alone can give us only a proportion, and perhaps only a small if essential proportion, of a general account of language understanding.[1]

A similar point was made much earlier this century by the Soviet writer V.N. Vološinov: 'The actual reality of language–speech is not the abstract system of linguistic forms, not the isolated monologic utterance, and not the psychophysiological act of its implementation, but the social event of verbal interaction implemented in an utterance or utterances.'[2] Thus in this section **Gunther Kress**'s approach is representative of a desire to move away from the study of abstract linguistic systems and to get back to a study of language as it is actually used in the primary form of interactive utterances, while recognizing the significant effect that the development of writing systems and the emergence of literacy bring with them – both to society and culture at large as well as to the individual.

Mary Louise Pratt's book *Toward a speech act theory of literary discourse*, as its title suggests, attempts to use the speech act theory associated with the philosophers J.L. Austin and J.R. Searle to bring literary discourse back into closer relationship with the 'ordinary language' of non-literary narratives. Put very briefly, speech act theory investigates the fact that when people utter statements they also often perform *acts* of a variety of kinds: they promise, request, command, apologize, and so on. The development of speech act theory has led other investigators to a concern with the *conditions* for the successful completion of speech acts – otherwise known as 'appropriateness conditions' or 'felicity conditions'. And alongside this concern has developed an increasing interest in the actual pragmatics of human linguistic communication. In the extract we include from her book, Pratt draws on and summarizes the highly influential work of H.P. Grice, a speech act philosopher who attempted (in Pratt's words) 'to clarify and correct the traditional Austinian view of appropriateness conditions by relating the ones which hold for a particular speech act in a particular context to general rules governing all verbal discourse'. The relevance of these 'rules' to the study of actual verbal interaction should be clear, and the extract is further evidence of the growing interest in communicational pragmatics.

Many of the extracts in this section are concerned, albeit in different ways, with the linguistic aspects of power: power over nature, power in society, the power which comes from the ability to distance oneself from concrete experiences, to examine oneself dispassionately and objectively, and to be able to change oneself and, in co-operation with others, one's society. **Deborah Cameron** points out that literacy is related to power; those with it do not just have power over nature, but over those without it (women, for example, in many societies). The extract from Jean Aitchison's book in the previous section showed that the possession of language gave human beings a power over nature that animals lack, and thus it gave, too, power over these animals: even where they were physically much stronger. Aitchison's discussion of *displacement* is particularly important in this context. But while it is true that *any* human speech involves powers of displacement unknown to animals (*all* human beings can talk about things not immediately present, such as 'the things we will do tomorrow'), the extracts from **A.R. Luria, Basil Bernstein** and **Trevor Pateman** in the present section indicate that some human beings possess this ability to a much greater extent than others. There are some things that Luria's subjects are asked about by their interlocutor that *they cannot talk about*. They cannot displace themselves from their immediate life-circumstances sufficiently to imagine certain specific alternative situations or realities.

The subjects about whom both Bernstein and Pateman write, although literate, are claimed not to be able to distance themselves from a different sort of 'immediate life-circumstances'; primarily *ideological* in nature. They cannot, according to Pateman, handle abstractions and counterfactuals in the way that more educated and linguistically sophisticated people can. Bernstein's work is, to a considerable extent, an attempt to find out why, if so, this should be the case. What are the mechanisms which allow an individual to develop more complex and sophisticated powers of reasoning and abstraction? As he phrases it, 'under what conditions does a given speech form free itself sufficiently from its embodiment in the social structure so that the system of meanings it realizes points to alternative realities?' It should be clear that, with a different emphasis, this question lies also behind Cameron's concern with the linguistic aspects of women's oppression. And the argument in the extract included from Pateman's book can be seen as an enquiry into the implications of Bernstein's assertion that 'Historically, and now, only a tiny percentage of the population has been socialized into knowledge at the level of the metalanguages of control and innovation, whereas the mass of the population has been socialized into knowledge at the level of context-tied operations.'

More advanced linguistic abilities give social and cultural power, but social and cultural power provide in their turn access to the opportunity to acquire more advanced linguistic abilities. (Traditionally, one of the first things a newly-rich person would buy would be a more expensive education for his or her children.) As Bernstein puts it: 'It is not only capital, in the strict economic sense, which is subject to appropriation, manipulation and exploitation, but also *cultural capital* in the form of symbolic systems through which man can extend and change the boundaries of his experience.' After reading Cameron's piece we may attach more significance to Bernstein's use of the male gender here than he may have done.

Christopher Hammonds's article works in a rather different direction from the pieces in this section mentioned so far. For if there is a relationship between, on the one hand, individual identity, socio-cultural experience, status and power, and, on the other hand, language, then the language used by an individual or a group might well yield evidence concerning these elements. Hammond's article discloses just how much this sort of 'reading' actually occurs in everyday social intercourse – very often when neither the reader nor the read are conscious of its taking place. This piece can therefore be set alongside the extract from Michael Argyle in the previous section, for just as Argyle showed us how many things can be read off from people's non-verbal behaviour, Hammonds introduces us to the wealth of information which can be read off from their verbal performances. The article reminds us, too, that consciously or unconsciously we *adapt* our language to conform to the requirements of different people, situations and needs – and at a number of varying levels. (Just as we adapt our non-verbal behaviour in response to these same changing requirements.)

This brings us to the topic of *interpretation*, an issue of fundamental importance to the study of communication. Items in the next two sections of this book will explore the issue of interpretation in greater depth, but the present section concludes with a thought-provoking piece giving the literary critic **David Lodge**'s responses to two prose accounts. Although both of these accounts are concerned in a general way with capital punishment, they are very different kinds of written communication. Lodge's commentary demonstrates, we believe, that in our response to written texts we are able (perhaps, in the light of previous discussion we should say 'some of us may be socially enabled') to bring interpretative skills to bear comparable to those which we utilize in our reading of the verbal and non-verbal behaviour of our fellows. Complex issues of *reference* and *truth* are raised by Lodge's discussion, both with regard to the activity of the writer and that of the reader.

The authors of a recent book entitled *Discourse and Social Psychology: Beyond Attitudes and Behaviour*, writing about 'social texts' rather than about written ones, make what is nonetheless an extremely apposite comment in their introductory pages:

> [S]ocial texts do not merely *reflect* or *mirror* objects, events and categories pre-existing in the social and natural world. Rather, they actively *construct* a version of these things. They do not just describe things; they *do* things. And being active, they have social and political implications. We have seen how description is tied to evaluation and how different versions of events can be constructed to justify or blame these events.[3]

In his responses to, and analysis of, the two written texts chosen, Lodge attempts to tease out their manner of 'constructing a version of things,' along with their social, political and also formal implications.

Further reading

All of the pieces in this section except that by Christopher Hammonds come from books, and these contain much additional material of value to the Communication Studies student. In addition to these, the following can all be recommended as accessible to the relatively uninformed reader and relevant to the issues raised in this section.

Bolinger, D. 1980: *Language – the loaded weapon*. London: Longman.
A clear and vigorously-argued book on the 'use and abuse' of language today. Drawing upon contemporary American illustrations, Bolinger discusses the relationships between language and various kinds of social power. His chapters focus, for example, on types of verbal stigma, on sexism, on advertising and on the language of bureaucracies. A close attention to linguistic features is impressively maintained throughout the general, social argument.

Levinson, Stephen C. 1983: *Pragmatics*. Cambridge: CUP.
A splendidly comprehensive and thought-provoking book with a wealth of valuable material for Communication Studies students. The introductory chapters are particularly useful for those wishing to understand in what way pragmatics offers a corrective to previous approaches to the linguistic study of communication.

Montgomery, Martin 1986: *An introduction to language and society*. London and New York: Methuen.
A book which is both introductory but also up-to-date with the latest theoretical developments in this area, moving from language acquisition through linguistic diversity, language and social interaction, and language and representation. The book to start with if you wish to follow up the ideas in this section.

Ong, Walter J. 1982: *Orality and literacy: the technologizing of the word*. London and New York: Methuen.
An engrossing book which investigates the changes in society and the individual which are attendant upon the invention of writing and the attainment of literacy.

Stubbs, Michael 1980: *Language and literacy: the sociolinguistics of reading and writing*. London: Routledge.
A book which aims to provide a sociolinguistic theory of literacy. It contains a persuasive account of the relations between reading and writing which those interested in the issues raised in this section by Gunther Kress should find engaging.

Stubbs, Michael 1983: *Discourse analysis: the sociolinguistic analysis of natural language*. Oxford: Blackwell.
Of many available introductory texts on discourse analysis, this is probably the best. Stubbs is concerned with language in use in social contexts, and with *interaction* or *dialogue* between speakers, but he also provides a very useful chapter on literary competence. The book contains a mass of illuminating analyses, rewarding discussion of key theories, and a full account of problems of practical research.

Trudgill, Peter 1983: *On dialect: social and geographical perspectives*. Oxford: Blackwell/New York: New York UP.

A collection of essays dealing with a range of issues concerned with dialect; all scholarly and readable. The material on the social status accorded to different dialects is very interesting, and there is an amusing chapter on the use of Americanisms by British pop singers. The chapter on 'Linguistic sex differentiation' contains useful material, but may be found lacking in the light of the arguments in Cameron's book (see extract 12 in this section).

Trudgill, Peter 1983: *Sociolinguistics: an introduction to language and society.* Revised ed. Harmondsworth: Penguin.

Perhaps the most accessible introduction to sociolinguistics. A good starting point for those wishing to develop further an interest in this area.

7

Education, generalization and abstraction

A.R. Luria

From Luria, A.R. 1976: *Cognitive development*. Cambridge, Mass., and London: Harvard University Press, 58–60.

Subject: Sher., age sixty, illiterate peasant from the village of Yardan. The task is explained through the example, *shirt – boots – skullcap – mouse,* and subject shown pictures of the following: *hammer – saw – log – hatchet.*

'They all fit here! The saw has to saw the log, the hammer has to hammer it, and the hatchet has to chop it. And if you want to chop the log up really good, you need the hammer. You can't take any of these things away. There isn't any you don't need!'

Replaces abstract classification with situational thinking.

But in the first example I showed you that the mouse didn't fit in.

'The mouse didn't fit in! But here all the things are very much alike *[ukhshaidi].* The saw saws the log, and the hatchet chops it, you just have to hit harder with the hammer.'

But one fellow told me the log didn't belong here.

'Why'd he say that? If we say the log isn't like the other things and put it off to one side, we'd be making a mistake. All these things are needed for the log.'

Considers idea of utility more important than similarity.

But that other fellow said that the saw, hammer, and hatchet are all alike in some way, while the log isn't.

'So what if they're not alike? They all work together and chop the log. Here everything works right, here everything's just fine.'

Look, you can use one word – tools – for these three but not for the log.

'What sense does it make to use one word for them all if they're not going to work together?'

Rejects use of generalizing term.

What word could you use for these things?

'The words people use: saw, hammer, hatchet. You can't use one word for them all!'

Could you call them tools?

'Yes, you could, except a log isn't a tool. Still, the way we look at it, the log has to be here. Otherwise, what good are the others?'

Employs predominantly situational thinking again.

The examples cited indicate that we had no luck getting these subjects to perform the abstract act of classification. Even when they grasped some similarity among various objects, they attached no particular importance to the fact. As a rule, they operated on the basis of 'practical utility', grouping objects in practical schemes rather than categorizing them. When we referred to a generic term we could use to designate a distinct group of objects, they generally disregarded the information or considered it immaterial. Instead, they adhered to the idea that objects should be grouped in practical arrangements. They continued to do so even when we presented objects that, in our view, would be difficult to group together for some genuinely practical scheme. When we clarified the principle of abstract classification, they listened attentively enough to our explanation but failed to take it into account. The following examples illustrate this tendency.

Subject: Abdy-Gap., age sixty-two, illiterate peasant from remote village. After the task is explained, he is given the series: *knife – saw – wheel – hammer*.

> 'They're all needed here. Every one of these things. The saw to chop firewood, the others for other jobs.'

Evaluates objects in terms of 'necessity' instead of classifying them.

No, three of these things belong in one group. You can use one word for them that you can't for the other one.

> 'Maybe it's the hammer? But it's also needed. You can drive nails in with it.'

The principle of classification is explained: three of the objects are 'tools'.

> 'But you can sharpen things with a wheel. If it's a wheel from an *araba* [kind of bullock cart], why'd they put it here?'

Subject's ability to learn the principle of classification is tested through another series: *bayonet – rifle – sword – knife*.

> 'There's nothing you can leave out here! The bayonet is part of the gun.
> A man's got to wear the dagger on his left side and the rifle on the other.'

Again employs idea of necessity to group objects.

The principle of classification is explained: three of the objects can be used to cut but the rifle cannot.

> 'It'll shoot from a distance, but up close it can also cut.'

He is then given the series *finger – mouth – ear – eye* and told that three objects are found on the head, the fourth on the body.

> 'You say the finger isn't needed here. But if a fellow is missing an ear, he can't hear. All these are needed, they all fit in. If a man's missing a finger, he can't do a thing, not even move a bed.'

Applies same principle as in preceding response.

Principle is explained once again.

> 'No, that's not true, you can't do it that way. You have to keep all these things together.'

One could scarcely find a more clear-cut example to prove that for some people abstract classification is a wholly alien procedure. Even when we explained the principle of classification very thoroughly, the subjects persisted in their own approach.

8

Social class, language and socialization

Basil Bernstein

From Bernstein, B., 1971: *Class, codes and control.* Volume I. London: Routledge. This extract taken from the Paladin edition, 193–205.

It may be helpful to make explicit the theoretical origins of the thesis I have been developing over the past decade. Although, initially, the thesis appeared to be concerned with the problem of educability, this problem was embedded in and was stimulated by the wider question of the relationship between symbolic orders and social structure. The basic theoretical question, which dictated the approach to the initially narrow but important empirical problem, was concerned with the fundamental structure and changes in the structure of cultural transmission. Indeed, any detailed examination of what superficially may seem to be a string of somewhat repetitive papers, I think would show three things:

(1) The gradual emergence of the dominance of the major theoretical problem from the local, empirical problem of the social antecedents of the educability of different groups of children.

(2) Attempts to develop both the generality of the thesis and to develop increasing specificity at the contextual level.

(3) Entailed in (2) were attempts to clarify both the logical and empirical status of the basic organizing concept, code. Unfortunately, until recently these attempts were more readily seen in the *planning* and *analysis* of the empirical research than available as formal statements.

Looking back, however, I think I would have created less misunderstanding if I had written about socio-linguistic codes rather than linguistic codes. Through using only the latter concept it gave the impression that I was reifying syntax and at the cost of semantics; or worse, suggesting that there was a one-to-one relation between meaning and a given syntax. Also, by defining the codes in a context-free fashion, I robbed myself of properly understanding, at a theoretical level, their significance. *I should point out that nearly all the empirical planning was directed to trying to find out the code realizations in different contexts.*

The concept of socio-linguistic code points to the social structuring of meanings *and* to their diverse but *related* contextual linguistic realizations. A careful reading of the papers always shows the emphasis given to the form of the social relationship, that is to the structuring of relevant meanings. Indeed, role is defined as a complex coding activity controlling the creation and organization of specific meanings and the conditions for their transmission and reception. The general socio-linguistic thesis attempts to explore how symbolic systems are both realizations and regulators of the structure of social relationships. The particular symbolic system is that of speech *not* language.

It is pertinent, at this point, to make explicit earlier work in the social sciences which formed the implicit starting point of the thesis. It will then be seen, I hope, that the thesis is an integration of different streams of thought. The major starting points are Durkheim and Marx, and a small number of other thinkers have been drawn into the basic matrix. I shall very briefly, and so selectively, outline this matrix and some of the problems to which it gave rise.

Durkheim's work is a truly magnificent insight into the relationships between symbolic orders, social relationships and the structuring of experience. In a sense, if Marx turned Hegel on his head, then Durkheim attempted to turn Kant on his head. For in *Primitive Classification* and in *The Elementary Forms of the Religious Life*, Durkheim attempted to derive the basic categories of thought from the structuring of the social relation. It is beside the point as to his success. He raised the whole question of the relation between the classifications and frames of the symbolic order *and* the structuring of experience. In his study of different forms of social integration he pointed to the implicit, condensed, symbolic structure of mechanical solidarity and the more explicit and differentiated symbolic structures of organic solidarity. Cassirer, the early cultural anthropologists, and, in particular, Sapir (I was not aware of von Humboldt until much later), sensitized me to the cultural properties of speech. Whorf, particularly where he refers to the fashions of speaking, frames of consistency, alerted me to the selective effect of the culture (acting through its patterning of social relationships) upon the *patterning* of grammar *together* with the pattern's semantic and thus cognitive significance. Whorf more than anyone, I think, opened up, at least for me, the question of the deep structure of linguistically regulated communication.

In all the above work I found two difficulties. If we grant the fundamental linkage of symbolic systems, social structure and the shaping of experience it is still unclear *how* such shaping takes place. The *processes* underlying the social structuring of experience are not explicit. The second difficulty is in dealing with the question of change of symbolic systems. Mead is of central importance in the solution of the first difficulty, the HOW. Mead outlined in general terms the relationships between role, reflexiveness and speech and in so doing provided the basis of the solution to the HOW. It is still the case that the Meadian solution does not allow us to deal with the problem of change. For the concept, which enables role to be related to a higher order concept, 'the generalized other', is, itself, not subject to systematic inquiry. Even if 'the generalized other' is placed within a Durkheimian framework, we are still left with the problem of change. Indeed, in Mead change is introduced only at the cost of the re-emergence of a traditional Western dichotomy in the concepts of the 'I' and the 'me'. The 'I' is both the indeterminate response to the 'me' and yet, at the same time, shapes it. The Meadian 'I' points to the voluntarism in the affairs of men, to the fundamental creativity of man, made possible by speech; a little before Chomsky.

Thus Meadian thought helps to solve the puzzle of the HOW but it does not help with the question of change in the structuring of experience; although both Mead implicitly and Durkheim explicitly pointed to the conditions which bring about pathological structuring of experience.

One major theory of the development of and change in symbolic structures is, of course, that of Marx. Although Marx is less concerned with the internal structure and the process of transmission of symbolic systems, he does give us a key to their institutionalization and change. The key is given in terms of the social significance of society's productive system and the power relationships to which the productive system gives rise. Further, access to, control over, orientation of and *change* in critical symbolic systems, according to the theory, is governed by power relationships as these are embodied in the class structure. It is not only capital, in the strict economic sense, which is subject to appropriation, manipulation and exploitation, but also *cultural* capital in the form of the symbolic systems through which man can extend and change the boundaries of his experience.

I am not putting forward a matrix of thought necessary for the study of the basic structure and change in the structure of cultural transmission, *only* the specific matrix which underlies my own approach. Essentially and briefly I have used Durkheim and Marx at the macro-level and Mead at the micro-level to realize a socio-linguistic thesis which could meet with a range of work in anthropology, linguistics, sociology and psychology.

I want first of all to make clear what I am not concerned with. Chomsky, in *Aspects of the Theory of Syntax*, neatly severs the study of the rule system of language from the study of the social rules which determine their contextual use. He does this by making a distinction between competence and performance. Competence refers to the child's tacit understanding of the rule system, performance relates to the essentially social use to which the rule system is put. Competence refers to man abstracted from contextual constraints. Performance refers to man in the grip of the contextual constraints which determine his speech acts. Competence refers to the Ideal, performance refers to the Fall. In this sense Chomsky's notion of competence is Platonic. Competence has its source in the very biology of man. There is no difference between men in terms of their access to the linguistic rule system. Here Chomsky, like many other linguists before him, announces the communality of man; all men have equal access to the creative act which is language. On the other hand, performance is under the control of the social – performances are culturally specific acts, they refer to the choices which are made in specific speech encounters. Thus, according to Hymes, Chomsky indicates the tragedy of man, the potentiality of competence and the degeneration of performance.

Clearly, much is to be gained in rigour and explanatory power through the severing of the relationship between the formal properties of the grammar and the meanings which are realized in its use. But if we are to study speech, *la parole*, we are inevitably involved in a study of a rather different rule system; we are involved in a study of rules, formal and informal, which regulate the options we take up in various contexts in which we find ourselves. This second rule system is the cultural system. This raises immediately the question of the relationship between the linguistic rule system and the cultural system. Clearly, specific linguistic rule systems are part of the cultural system, but it has been argued that the linguistic rule system in various ways shapes the cultural system. This very briefly is the view of those who hold a narrow form of the linguistic relativity hypothesis. I do not intend to get involved in that particular quagmire. Instead, I shall take the view that the code which the linguist invents to explain the formal properties of the grammar is capable of generating any number of speech codes, and there is no reason for believing that any one language code is better than another in this respect. On this argument, language is a set of rules to which all speech codes must comply, but which speech codes are realized is a function of the culture acting through social relationships in specific contexts. Different speech forms or codes symbolize the form of the social relationship, regulate the nature of the speech encounters, and create for the speakers different orders of relevance and relation. The experience of the speakers is then transformed by what is made significant or relevant· by the speech form. This is a sociological argument because the speech form is taken as a consequence of the form of the social relation or, put more generally, is a quality of a social structure. Let me qualify this immediately. Because the speech form is initially a function of a given social arrangement, it does not mean that the speech form does not in turn modify or even change that social structure which initially evolved the speech form. This formulation, indeed, invites the question: under what conditions does a given speech form free itself sufficiently from its embodiment in the social structure so that the system of meanings it realizes points to alternative realities, alternative arrangements in the affairs of men? Here we become concerned immediately with the antecedents and consequences of the boundary-maintaining principles of a culture or subculture. I am here suggesting a relationship between forms of boundary maintenance at the cultural level and forms of speech.

I am required to consider the relationship between the language and socialization. It should be clear from these opening remarks that I am not concerned with language, but with speech, and concerned more specifically with the contextual constraints upon speech. Now what about socialization? I shall take the term to refer to the process whereby a child acquires a specific cultural identity, *and* to his responses to such an identity. Socialization refers to the process whereby the biological is transformed into a specific cultural being. It follows from this that the process of socialization is a complex process of control, whereby a particular moral, cognitive and affective awareness is evoked in the child and given a specific form and content. Socialization sensitizes the child to the various orderings of society as these are made substantive in the various roles he is expected to play. In a sense, then, socialization is a process for making people safe. The process acts selectively on the possibilities of man by creating through time a sense of the inevitability of a given social arrangement, and through limiting the areas of permitted change. The basic agencies of socialization in contemporary societies are the family, the peer group, school and work. It is through these agencies, and in particular through their relationship to each other, that the various orderings of society are made manifest.

Now it is quite clear that given this view of socialization it is necessary to limit the discussion. I shall limit our discussion to socialization within the family, but it should be obvious that the focusing and filtering of the child's experience within the family in a large measure is a microcosm of the macroscopic orderings of society. Our question now becomes: what are the sociological factors which affect linguistic performances within the family critical to the process of socialization?

Without a shadow of doubt the most formative influence upon the procedures of socialization, from a sociological viewpoint, is social class. The class structure influences work and educational roles and brings families into a special relationship with each other and deeply penetrates the structure of life experiences within the family. The class system has deeply marked the distribution of knowledge within society. It has given differential access to the sense that the world is permeable. It has sealed off communities from each other and has ranked these communities on a scale of invidious worth. We have three components: knowledge, possibility and invidious insulation. It would be a little naïve to believe that differences in knowledge, differences in the sense of the possible, combined with invidious insulation, rooted in differential *material* well-being, would not affect the forms of control and innovation in the socializing procedures of different social classes. I shall go on to argue that the deep structure of communication itself is affected, but not in any final or irrevocable way.

As an approach to my argument, let me glance at the social distribution of knowledge. We can see that the class system has affected the distribution of knowledge. Historically, and now, only a tiny percentage of the population has been socialized into knowledge at the level of the meta-languages of control and innovation, whereas the mass of the population has been socialized into knowledge at the level of context-tied operations.

A tiny percentage of the population has been given access to the principles of intellectual change, whereas the rest have been denied such access. This suggests that we might be able to distinguish between two orders of meaning. One we could call universalistic, the other particularistic. Universalistic meanings are those in which principles and operations are made linguistically explicit, whereas particularistic orders of meaning are meanings in which principles and operation are relatively linguistically implicit. If orders of meaning are universalistic, then the meanings are less tied to a given context. The meta-languages of public forms of thought as these apply to objects and persons realize meanings of a universalistic type. Where meanings have this characteristic then individuals have access to the grounds of their experience and can change the grounds. Where orders of meaning are particularistic, where principles are linguistically implicit, then such meanings are less context-independent and *more* context-bound, that is, tied to a local relationship and to a local social structure. Where the meaning system is particularistic, much of the meaning is embedded in the context and may be restricted to those who share a similar contextual history. Where meanings are universalistic, they are in principle available to all because the principles and operations have been made explicit, and so public.

I shall argue that forms of socialization orient the child towards speech codes which control access to relatively context-tied or relatively context-independent meanings. Thus I shall argue that elaborated codes orient their users towards universalistic meanings, whereas restricted codes orient, sensitize, their users to particularistic meanings: that the linguistic realization of the two orders are different, and so are the social relationships which realize them. Elaborated codes are less tied to a given or local structure and thus contain the potentiality of change in principles. In the case of elaborated codes the speech may be freed from its evoking social structure and it can take on an autonomy. A university is a place organized around talk. Restricted codes are more tied to a local social structure and have a reduced potential for change in principles. Where codes are elaborated, the socialized has more access to the grounds of his own socialization, and so can enter into a reflexive relationship to the social order he has taken over. Where codes are restricted, the socialized has less access to the grounds of his socialization, and thus reflexiveness may be limited in range. *One of the effects of the class system is to limit access to elaborated codes.*

I shall go on to suggest that restricted codes have their basis in condensed symbols, whereas elaborated codes have their basis in articulated symbols; that restricted codes draw upon metaphor, whereas elaborated codes draw upon rationality; that these codes constrain the contextual use of language in critical socializing contexts and in this way regulate the orders of relevance and relation which the socialized takes over. From this point of view, change in habitual speech codes involves changes in the means by which object and person relationships are realized.

I want first to start with the notions of elaborated and restricted speech variants. A variant can be considered as the contextual constraints upon grammatical–lexical choices.

Sapir, Malinowski, Firth, Vygotsky and Luria have all pointed out from different points of view that the closer the identifications of speakers the greater the range of shared interests, the more probable that the speech will take a specific form. The range of syntactic alternatives is likely to be reduced and the lexis to be drawn from a narrow range. Thus, the form of these social relations is acting selectively on the meanings to be verbally realized. In these relationships the intent of the other person can be taken for granted as the speech is played out against a backdrop of common assumptions, common history, common interests. As a result, there is less need to raise meanings to the level of explicitness or elaboration. There is a reduced need to make explicit through syntactic choices the logical structure of the communication. Further, if the speaker wishes to individualize his communication, he is likely to do this by varying the expressive associates of the speech. Under these conditions, the speech is likely to have a strong metaphoric element. In these situations the speaker may be more concerned with how something is said, when it is said; silence takes on a variety of meanings. Often in these encounters the speech cannot be understood apart from the context, and the context cannot be read by those who do not share the history of the relationships. Thus the form of the social relationship acts selectively in the meanings to be verbalized, which in turn affect the syntactic and lexical choices. The unspoken assumptions underlying the relationship are not available to those who are outside the relationship. For these are limited, and restricted to the speakers. The symbolic form of the communication is condensed, yet the specific cultural history of the relationship is alive in its form. We can say that the roles of the speakers are communalized roles. Thus, we can make a relationship between restricted social relationships based upon communalized roles and the verbal realization of their meaning. In the language of the earlier part of this paper, restricted social relationships based upon communalized roles evoke particularistic, that is, context-tied, meanings, realized through a restricted speech variant.

Imagine a husband and wife have just come out of the cinema, and are talking about the film: 'What do you think?' 'It had a lot to say.' 'Yes, I thought so too – let's go to the Millers, there may be something going there.' They arrive at the Millers, who ask about the film. An hour is spent in the complex, moral, political, aesthetic subtleties of the film and its place in the contemporary scene. Here we have an elaborated variant; the meanings now have to be made public to others who have not seen the film. The speech shows careful editing, at both the grammatical and lexical levels. It is no longer context-tied. The meanings are explicit, elaborated and individualized. While expressive channels are clearly relevant, the burden of meaning inheres predominantly in the verbal channel. The experience of the listeners cannot be taken for granted. Thus each member of the group is on his own as he offers his interpretation. Elaborated variants of this kind involve the speakers in particular role relationships, and *if you cannot manage the role, you can't produce the appropriate speech*. For as the speaker proceeds to individualize his meanings, he is differentiated from others like a figure from its ground.

The roles receive less support from each other. There is a measure of isolation. *Difference* lies at the basis of the social relationship, and is made verbally active, whereas in the other context it is *consensus*. The insides of the speaker have become psychologically active through the verbal aspect of the communication. Various defensive strategies may be used to decrease potential vulnerability of self and to increase the vulnerability of others. The verbal aspect of the communication becomes a vehicle for the transmission of individuated symbols. The 'I' stands over the 'we'. Meanings which are discrete to the speaker must be offered so that they are intelligible to the listener. Communalized roles have given way to individualized roles, condensed symbols to articulated symbols. Elaborated speech variants of this type realize universalistic meanings in the sense that they are less context-tied. Thus individualized roles are realized through elaborated speech variants which involve complex editing at the grammatical and lexical levels and which point to universalistic meanings.

Let me give another example. Consider the two following stories which Peter Hawkins, Assistant Research Officer in the Sociological Research Unit, University of London Institute of Education, constructed as a result of his analysis of the speech of middle-class and working-class five-year-old children. The children were given a series of four pictures which told a story and they were invited to tell the story. The first picture showed some boys playing football; in the second the ball goes through the window of a house; the third shows a woman looking out of the window and a man making an ominous gesture, and in the fourth the children are moving away.

Here are the two stories:

1. Three boys are playing football and one boy kicks the ball and it goes through the window the ball breaks the window and the boys are looking at it and a man comes out and shouts at them because they've broken the window so they run away and than that lady looks out of her window and she tells the boys off.
2. They're playing football and he kicks it and it goes through there it breaks the window and they're looking at it and he comes out and shouts at them because they've broken it so they run away and then she looks out and she tells them off.

With the first story the reader does not have to have the four pictures which were used as the basis for the story, whereas in the case of the second story the reader would require the initial pictures in order to make sense of the story. The first story is free of the context which generated it, whereas the second story is much more closely tied to its context. As a result the meanings of the second story are implicit, whereas the meanings of the first story are explicit. It is not that the working-class children do not have in their passive vocabulary the vocabulary used by the middle-class children. Nor is it the case that the children differ in their tacit understanding of the linguistic rule system. Rather, what we have here are differences in the use of language arising out of a specific context. One child makes explicit the meanings which he is realizing through language for the person he is telling the story to, whereas the second child does not to the same extent. The first child takes very little for granted, whereas the second child takes a great deal for granted. Thus for the first child the task was seen as a context in which his meanings were required to be made explicit, whereas the task for the second child was not seen as a task which required such explication of meaning. It would not be difficult to imagine a context where the first child would produce speech rather like the second. What we are dealing with here are differences between the children in the way they realize in language-use apparently the same context. We could say that the speech of the first child generated universalistic meanings in the sense that the meanings are freed from the context and so understandable by all, whereas the speech of the second child generated particularistic meanings, in the sense that the meanings are closely tied to the context and would be fully understood by others only if they had access to the context which originally generated the speech.

It is again important to stress that the second child has access to a more differentiated noun phrase, but there is a restriction on its *use*. Geoffrey Turner, Linguist in the Sociological Research Unit, shows that working-class, five-year-old children in the same contexts examined by Hawkins use fewer linguistic expressions of uncertainty when compared with the middle-class children. This does not mean that working-class children do *not* have access to such expressions, but that the eliciting speech context did not provoke them. Telling a story from pictures, talking about scenes on cards, *formally framed* contexts, do not encourage working-class children to consider the possibilities of alternate meanings and so there is a reduction in the linguistic expressions of uncertainty. Again, working-class children have access to a wide range of syntactic choices which involve the use of logical operators, 'because', 'but', 'either', 'or', 'only'. The constraints exist on the conditions for their *use*. Formally framed contexts used for eliciting context-independent universalistic meanings may evoke in the working-class child, relative to the middle-class child, restricted speech variants, because the working-class child has difficulty in managing the role relationships which such contexts require. This problem is further complicated when such contexts carry meanings very much removed from the child's cultural experience. In the same way we can show that there are constraints upon the middle-class child's use of language. Turner found that when middle-class children were asked to role-play in the picture story series, a higher percentage of these children, when compared with working-class children, initially refused. When the middle-class children were asked, 'What is the man saying?' or linguistically equivalent questions, a relatively higher percentage said 'I don't know.' When this question was followed by the hypothetical question, 'What do you think the man might be saying?' they offered their interpretations. The working-class children role-played without difficulty. It seems then that middle-class children at five need to have a very precise instruction to *hypothesize in that particular* context. This may be because they are more concerned here with getting their answers right or correct. When the children were invited to tell a story about some doll-like figures (a little boy, a little girl, a sailor and a dog) the working-class children's stories were freer, longer and more imaginative than the stories of the middle-class children. The latter children's stories were tighter, constrained within a strong narrative frame. It was as if these children were dominated by what they took to be the *form* of a narrative and the content was secondary. This is an example of the concern of the middle-class child with the structure of the contextual frame. It may be worthwhile to amplify this further. A number of studies have shown that when working-class black children are asked to associate to a series of words, their responses show considerable diversity, both from the meaning and form-class of the stimulus word. Our analysis suggests this may be because the children for the following reasons are less constrained. The form-class of the stimulus word may have reduced associative significance and this would less constrain the selection of potential words *or* phrases. With such a weakening of the grammatical frame there is a greater range of alternatives as possible candidates for selection. Further, the closely controlled, middle-class, linguistic socialization of the young child may point the child towards both the grammatical significance of the stimulus word and towards a tight logical ordering of semantic space. Middle-class children may well have access to deep interpretative rules which regulate their linguistic responses in certain formalized contexts. The consequences may limit their imagination through the tightness of the frame which these interpretative rules create. It may even be that with *five*-year-old children, the middle-class child will innovate *more* with the arrangements of objects (i.e. bricks) than in his linguistic usage. His linguistic usage is under close supervision by adults. He has more *autonomy* in his play.

[The final eight pages of this essay, which develop the argument with further examples, are here omitted for reasons of space.]

9

Impossible discourse

Trevor Pateman

From Pateman, T. 1975: *Language, truth and politics*. Newton Poppleford, Devon: Trevor Pateman and Jean Stroud, 70–84.

Note: *Language, truth and politics* was published in a new, revised and enlarged edition in 1980. The extract that follows includes some amendments from this new edition.

Language and logic

I don't understand physics because I don't know the language of physics. This is partly a question of *vocabulary*, partly one of *concepts*, partly one of the mental *organization* of vocabulary – and the last two aspects are interrelated, as I shall try to show. These are some of the obstacles to my understanding physics. Do some people face comparable obstacles to understanding radical or revolutionary politics?

Is it, first of all, that some people lack the *vocabulary* with which they could understand and within which they could think certain thoughts? Though not of central importance, the absence of vocabulary is, I think, of more importance than the logical possibility of paraphrase might make it seem. It is plausible for Orwell in *1984* to attribute considerable significance to the removal of words from the lexicon, for though paraphrase remains logically possible, to actively engage in paraphrase requires a greater commitment to thought than does the simple use of a ready-made word-concept. Words are things to think with, and without them one is obliged to produce the means of thought as well as thought itself.

However, even if a vocabulary is known, the concepts belonging to each word may not be fully or accurately known. 'Trotskyism', 'Anarchism', 'Soviet', 'commune', etc. are known to many people (though how many?), but perhaps in the majority of cases they will be known as the *names* of desirable or undesirable practices. They name objects, institutions and practices and they direct or discharge considerable emotional energy, but their conceptual content in use is small; they are used as *proper names*, which do no more than designate or refer. The words (no more than a proper name) cannot be used to think with about the practices to which they are used to refer. (This is perhaps what people are getting at when they object to *labelling*, that is, the use of an emotionally loaded proper name.) In addition, such words may be used inaccurately to refer, though this is not entailed by their being used as proper names.

The ways in which descriptive words are emptied of their conceptual content, and thereby become purely referential expressions, has been amply commented upon, for example, by Marcuse. I think that Anglo-American philosophers have compounded rather than counteracted this process in their analysis of political terms, since they have taken as the starting point for their analyses the actual occurrence of such words on the surface of discourse, where they are used as mere naming and 'boo' 'hooray' expressions. The results of such analysis are bound to be as disappointing as the discourse being analysed. (On this point, see my 1973a.) The results of such analysis for political philosophy have been disastrous, but no more so than such a use of words has been for the possibility of political thinking among the population at large.

If not by suppression, or emptying of content, then by other means can potentially critical concepts be rendered practically useless for critical thought. Marcuse has commented on such means in *One Dimensional Man* (1964). There he writes of the role of combining contradictory thoughts in a single expression. This occurs, for example, when a policy described in terms which would justify its designation as 'reactionary' is then named as 'revolutionary'. This could be a simple case in which 'revolution' has been emptied of meaning and is used simply to express an attitude or name an object, without giving rise to formally contradictory predication. On the other hand, there do appear to be more subtle cases (and it seems that Marcuse has these in mind) where one can speak of genuine contradiction, since the conceptual content of each of two terms is simultaneously predicated and denied. That is to say, the effectiveness of the statement made by A in persuading B to adopt an attitude towards x involves simultaneously evoking in B his understanding of the conceptual content of (say) 'revolution' whilst describing x in terms which indicate that it does not possess the properties which would justify the predication 'revolution'.

I think I can make this clearer with a concrete example from the sphere of trade names. In one sense, the trade name *Belair* for a brand of cigarette is an arbitrary proper name. If I ask for a packet of *Belair*, I use the name as a proper name and do not think of the name as having a conceptual content. On the other hand, *Belair* contributes to the task of selling the cigarette to the degree that the conceptual meaning (here, the literal meaning) and also the connotations of meaning (such as 'Frenchness') are known to the buyer.

But, with regard to the literal meaning, it might be questioned whether this would work as a selling force if the buyer became explicitly aware of the meaning. For if someone were to become explicitly aware of the literal meaning of *bel air*, would this not equal awareness of a characteristic so 'obviously' the opposite of the real characteristics of the product as to lead the potential buyer to ridicule the product? (In Orwell's *1984*, *Victory* is the brand name for the products with which a defeated population is drugged.)

Against this interpretation, consider what could happen if the potential buyer does not accept as 'obviously' true that 'Smoking can Damage your Health', that is to say, does not accept as obviously true the content of HM Government's Health Warning printed on the side of the packet. In such circumstances, conscious awareness of the meaning of *Belair* would produce a situation which could be characterized as follows: the packet of cigarettes carries, printed on it, two statements which both purport to be true of the contents of the packet. One says that what you inhale when you smoke *can* damage your health; the other says that what you inhale when you smoke is *bel air*, and 'good air' *cannot*, by definition, damage your health. (I am expanding and interpreting the two statements to put them in formally contradictory form, but I don't think that my expansion is far from the truth.) Now, all students of philosophy know that if two statements are formally contradictory, then they cancel each other out. No meaning is 'produced'. Unless the buyer privileges either the Government's statement, or the meaning *Belair*, the formal effect of giving the name *Belair* to the cigarette is to cancel the Government's message. Of course, the meaning of the proposition implied by the name *Belair* is also cancelled. *Belair* remains as a name, and a set of connotations, that is all, though the cigarette manufacturer, like the Government, can try to get the buyer to privilege its statement against that of its opponent, in which case no cancelling of meaning occurs. But, apart from this, the effect of giving the cigarette the name *Belair* is to repulse and reduce the prior critical discourse of the Government.

Marcuse also refers to *telescoping* and *abridgement* of discourse as means by which rational thought with critical concepts is rendered difficult. He writes of this process of telescoping and abridgement that it 'cuts development of meaning by creating fixed images [which "militates against the development and expression of concepts" p. 95] which impose themselves with an overwhelming and petrified concreteness' (1964, 91; compare Barthes, 1972). Perhaps the best example of this process is the photo-journalism in which one is presented with the 'picture which sums it all up'. Of course, the picture is captioned to make sure that there is no misreading of it. But, very literally, meaning is reduced to an *image*. In political thinking, I think that this sort of photo-journalism encourages the reduction of structurally very complex situations to the level of exemplification of very general, a-historical and non-operational concepts, such as 'trouble', 'violence', 'fear', 'hunger', 'bewilderment', etc., all of which have their Faces. Such photo-journalism never improved anyone's understanding of the realities or complexities of political life. Its images fix understanding at the level of surface appearance.

Such practices as those discussed above can become important social phenomena because language, though the socially produced means of thought, is not socially controlled. Increasingly, control over the development of language and its use is held by State institutions, including mass media, and monopolistic private enterprise, as in journalism and advertising. Orwell's *1984* developed the possible consequences of the State's domination over language. The semiologists, who have studied the same kind of linguistic developments as those which interest Marcuse, have sometimes failed to appreciate the possibility and existence of class or other minority control over language, whilst recognizing that minority groups are responsible for the creation of sign systems and fixed combinations of signs in such fields as furniture and clothing. Even Barthes, on whose work Marcuse draws extensively, can write:

> In the linguistic model, nothing enters the language without having been tried in speech, but conversely no speech is possible . . . if it is not drawn from the 'treasure' of the language. . . . But in most *other* semiological systems, the language is elaborated not by the 'speaking mass' but by a deciding group. In this sense, it can be held that in most semiological languages, the sign is really and truly 'arbitrary' since it is founded in artificial fashion by unilateral decision (1967, 31; my italic).[1]

But isn't the situation of 'most other semiological systems' also increasingly true of natural language? Is the language of politics really elaborated by the 'speaking mass'?

Beyond the question of vocabulary, and the effects on it of the way in which it is used, there is the question of how a given vocabulary is organized in the individual's mind, and how this in turn affects the possibilities of thought. What I mean by this can be illustrated by an example from Vygotsky's psychology. In his *Thought and Language*, Vygotsky points out that 'A child learns the word *flower*, and shortly afterwards the word *rose*; for a long time the concept "flower", though more widely applicable than "rose", cannot be said to be more general for the child. It does not include and subordinate "rose" – the two are interchangeable and juxtaposed. When "flower" becomes generalized, the relationship of "flower" and "rose", as well as of "flower" and other subordinate concepts, also changes in the child's mind. A system is taking shape' (1962, 92–3). Vygotsky has already indicated what he takes to be the significance of this development: 'To us it seems obvious that a concept can become subject to consciousness and deliberate control only when it is part of a system. If consciousness means generalization, generalization in turn means the formation of a superordinate concept that includes the given concept as a particular case' (1962, 92).[2] Two further points need to be made before the significance for political thinking of such phenomena can be indicated. First, that relations of superordination and subordination develop as a result of socialization and not as a result of some inner maturation process, proceeding independently of the particular social environment.

Vygotsky himself stresses the significance of formal instruction in school subjects, arguing that through school instruction concepts are learnt from the start in relations of superordination and subordination, and that this catalyses a similar development of the organization of concepts which the child has learnt 'spontaneously': 'It is our contention that the rudiments of systematization first enter the child's mind by way of his contact with scientific concepts and are then transferred to everyday concepts, changing their psychological structure from the top down' (p. 93). This also implies that there is nothing inevitable about the development of conceptual organization.

The second point to be made is that not all the words of a natural language are organizable into the 'trees' which can always be constructed for scientific words, and which – perhaps – makes them scientific. Lyons, who calls subordinate words 'hyponyms' (thus, 'scarlet', 'crimson', 'vermilion' are co-hyponyms of 'red' (1968, 454–5), writes that

> The main point to be made about the relation of hyponymy as it is found in natural languages is that it does not operate as comprehensively or as systematically there as it does in the various systems of scientific taxonomy . . . The vocabularies of natural languages tend to have many gaps, asymmetries and indeterminacies in them' (1968, 456).

– something which is explored at length in Wittgenstein's later writings (1958).

I think that these psychological and linguistic theses are relevant to the question of the possibility of different sorts of political thinking. I think that even if relevant political words are learnt, they need not be organized hierarchically or systematically, even in an adult's mind. In consequence, they can remain wholly or partly a-conceptual. If this is the case, it necessarily affects the possibility of understanding discourse which employs them as concepts. Lyons seems to make a similar point in a 'neutral' context, though it depends on how one reads the 'as for instance':

> It may be impossible to determine and perhaps also to know the meaning of one word without also knowing the meaning of others to which it is 'related' – as for instance, *cow* is to *animal* (1968, 409).

Let me now try to illustrate this line of argument with an example from the realm of political discourse.

Suppose that the concept of *anarchy* or *anarchism*, which would be involved in any proposition about the possibility or features of an anarchist society, is (partly) defined as being a *society without a government*. A verbal or conceptual tree[3] built up from the elements 'anarchy', 'society', 'government' and expanded to include the co-hyponyms of 'government', looks like this:

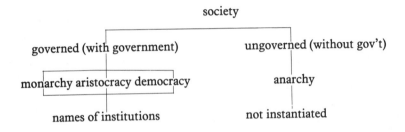

Within the hierarchy presented by the diagram, the higher up the tree you go, the greater the degree of abstraction, though all of the concepts above the level of the names of institutions are abstract ones; they are concepts rather than complexes in Vygotsky's sense of 'complex', which is that a complex word is one for the application of which there is no finite set of necessary or sufficient defining characteristics; in Wittgenstein's terminology, the members of a complex possess no more than a *family resemblance* (1958, paragraphs 66, 67).

Now, I think that though the word 'society' is generally learnt, it is frequently not organized in a person's mind into the kind of tree given in the diagram; it can be and is learnt and retained a-conceptually. The understanding of 'government' which such a person would then have would not be one which related 'government' to 'society' but one where the concepts of types of government or the names of instantiations of governments were used to give it meaning. This would entail that 'government' was understood not as a concept, but as the family name of a collection of particulars. It would be understood as the name of a complex.[4]

Consider now what is required for 'anarchy' to be adequately understood. My theory is that it cannot be adequately understood except when organized within a tree which extends up to and including the level of 'society'. For, first, the concept of 'anarchy' cannot be understood by reference to its own instantiations, since there are none. And, second, the definition of 'anarchy' includes reference to both 'government' and 'society' and it cannot be understood on its own level as a simple *absence* of monarchy, aristocracy, etc. Monarchy, aristocracy, etc., are linguistic co-hyponyms, but I do not see how the concept of 'anarchy' can be produced by opposing these concepts to the word 'anarchy' unless there is already an implied reference to 'society'. In other words, the meaning of 'anarchy' cannot be generated or understood within an opposition to its co-hyponyms. It requires placing in a system which includes not only oppositional features, but super-ordination as well. If this is correct, my understanding (which may be inaccurate) of structuralist theories of meaning leads me to the conclusion that their account of the generation and understanding of meaning requires revision. For, as I understand such theories, their oppositions are made at only *one* level – indeed, the idea of *opposition* implies that of being on the same level (see Saussure, 1966).

But this point is an aside to my main object in this section, which is to suggest a theory of the following sort:

I am suggesting that adults can possess, and some do possess, a vocabulary in a particular area (I am using the case of political vocabulary) without having that vocabulary conceptually organized, with consequences similar to those which psychologists report for the non-conceptual organization of children's vocabularies. Not only would the existence of such non-organization explain failure to understand the meaning of terms, though those terms might be known, and thus explain failure to understand or generate the relevant sorts of discourse, but it would also explain such phenomena as insensitivity to contradiction which has frequently been remarked in adults for specific areas of discourse. Thus, in their case studies, Laing and Esterson remark the insensitivity of schizogenic parents to their own self-contradictions. Studies of the 'authoritarian personality' report the same thing (see Reich 1970, 1971) as do McKenzie and Silver in their study of working-class Conservatism (1969, especially 120, 121). In this last case in particular there are other possible explanations of apparent self-contradiction. Thus, limitations of vocabulary may lead a person to use contradiction as a means of conveying meaning for the explicit conveyance of which he lacks the necessary vocabulary. There is no self-contradiction in the bad sense when I say of a taste difficult to define 'It's sweet and yet it isn't.'

Classical cognitive-defect theories of schizophrenia also comment on insensitivity to contradiction in schizophrenics, and I think these studies are particularly valuable. (See Hanfmann and Kasanin, 1942, and Kasanin, 1944.) For whilst, as Eluned Price told me, these studies have largely been discredited as studies of phenomena specific to *schizophrenic* cognition (see, for example, Wason and Johnson Laird, 1972, chapter 18),[5] this discrediting takes the form of showing that what is allegedly related to schizophrenia is, in fact, related to level of formal education received. It was possible to think that features of schizophrenia were being described simply because most hospitalized schizophrenics have a low level of formal education. Theories about the 'schizophrenization' of culture thus turn out to have a firmer basis than simple analogy. For the features of 'schizophrenia' which originally prompted such analogies turn out to be non-specific to that state; they are features to be found in the thinking of a large proportion of the population.[6]

There may be objections to my procedure of using material from child psychology and psychopathology to understand sane, adult people, who are neither children nor schizophrenics. But there is no reason why they should not share characteristics with children and schizophrenics, and if the latter are better studied than the former (most psychological studies of 'normal adults' in fact use undergraduates as subjects), this is an added reason for using such studies as a jumping-off point. There may be theoretical objections to such a procedure, but this is different from a simple dislike of it, which can only be founded on a contempt for children and 'schizophrenics'. That is simply the chauvinism of the man in the street, defined as sane, adult, white, male and middle class. So I am not too worried by this dislike. I may well be wrong in thinking that some adults, as a result of their socialization, have important characteristics in common with children and schizophrenics. I am bound to think that the theory is at least worth testing.[7]

To return, then, to Vygotsky. In the report of an experiment, Vygotsky tries to show how children regard the name of an object as a property of that object, and thus lack a fully formed appreciation of the nature of symbolism: writers like Cassirer (1944) and Goldstein (1963) would say that the child lacks the *abstract attitude*.[8] To demonstrate his point. Vygotsky confronts the child with a situation in which the name of an object is arbitrarily changed; a dog is henceforth to be called a 'cow'. For most adults, I presume that such an arrangement would produce no substantial difficulties, and about the first thing a Philosophy student learns to recognize explicitly is the arbitrariness of the word-sign. I doubt that an average adult would respond to Vygotsky's questions as does the typical child, who, having been told that a dog is henceforth to be called a 'cow', responds to questions in the following way:

[Experimenter]	– Does a cow have horns?
[Subject]	– Yes
[Experimenter]	– But don't you remember that the cow is really a dog. Come now, does a dog have horns?
[Subject]	– Sure, if it's a cow, if it's called a cow, it has horns. That kind of dog has got to have little horns (1962, 129).

Even if this particular experiment was badly designed and conducted, I don't think it follows that the value of such an experiment is destroyed by the claim (made by objectors to the above argument) that the child is more intellectually sophisticated than the experimenter.[9]

I presume that most adults asked whether a dog, arbitrarily renamed 'cow', would have horns, would reply that it would not (Is that your reply?), but I also presume that it does not follow that they would get the answer right whatever the *kind* of word change involved. I think that the ability to perform this *kind* of intellectual operation could be content-specific. And where the situation is a non-experimental one, from which the motive either to please or displease an experimenter is absent, I think that sane, adult people do sometimes perform operations like those of the child in Vygotsky's experiment. I suggest that in some areas, some adults do treat a word as the property of an object. Aaron Sloman remarked, in comments on draft material for this chapter, that people can be conceptually agile in some domains and strait-jacketed in others. I assume this is so. I shall illustrate the kind of phenomena which the assumption covers, and I shall draw my examples from the realm of political discourse and understanding.

Consider the following case.[10] I come across a person who argues in such a manner that it is clear that he believes that if something is conventionally called a system of Justice, then it must have the property of being Just, again as conventionally defined. This entails such consequences as that, confronted with empirical evidence that an existing institution of Justice contravened in its practice the *conventional* norms of Justice (that is, it is unjust in its own terms), such a person could not admit that such evidence *might be true*. The possibility of empirical evidence being relevant is ruled out *a priori*, and this entails that for this person it is tautologically true that if something is called a system of Justice, then it must be Just. This is not quite the same kind of case as that where the practice of existing institutions, whatever it may be, *defines* what is right, for I am not denying that this person has a concept of Justice defined independently of practice.[11] I am claiming that this person cannot admit that the word 'Justice' could be erroneously applied. This seems to me analysable as a case in which the arbitrariness of the word-sign 'Justice' is not recognized, that is, a case where the word-sign is treated as a property of the object. Hence, any discussion which contrasts Reality with an independently defined Ideal is impossible, which means that any rational discussion is impossible. Though this example, based on a single conversation, may seem extreme (and does leave many questions unanswered), I think there is a widespread tendency to use political concepts in the above fashion. Marcuse sensed it and produced an analysis in terms of one-dimensional thought.

Take another example, a little easier to describe and substantiate from experience. To me it seems that some people are unable to understand, or argue in terms of propositions involving explicit counter-factual conditionals, though again such inability need not be across-the-board; it can be content-specific. What I mean is that some people respond to arguments of the sort which begin 'Suppose you had . . .' with a straightforward 'But I didn't . . .' It has been put to me that this *genre* of response does not show people's cognitive limitations, but rather their cognitive sophistication. They refuse to be drawn into the kind of hypothetical argument in which the most skilled in dialectical debate necessarily wins. Now, whilst I agree that some people use the response 'But I didn't . . .' as a refusal, I don't accept that that this is always the case. My reasons are two-fold. First that one elicits the response 'But I didn't . . .' even in circumstances where the respondent recognizes that it is in his interest to understand the hypothetical argument (as in direction giving: 'Imagine you're standing at the corner of Charing Cross Road and Oxford Street, with Centre Point on your right . . .' Second, that I find it inconsistent that people should be so intellectually sophisticated as my opponents' argument makes out, yet so frequently be taken for a ride by all sorts of con-men, from politicians upwards.

I have produced only two examples, but I am sure others can produce further instances of linguistic or logico-linguistic ways in which adults with little formal education and no experience of other relevant learning situations, can be inhibited or prevented from thinking certain thoughts and understanding certain sorts of discourse or argument. Such incapacities are content-specific and can be given a social explanation. The incapacities may not always be apparent, not least if the person consciously or unconsciously seeks to hide them. Thus, for example, when he does not understand an idea, he may say that it is 'Nonsense'. Roland Barthes has commented on this particular mode of response as a characteristic of petty-bourgeois thinking (Barthes, 1972, especially the essay *Blind and Dumb Criticism*, 34–5). Enoch Powell seems to employ this strategy of labelling as 'Nonsense' that which he does not understand (Wood, 1970, especially *The Enemy Within*, 104–12) though here it is difficult to distinguish the use of 'Nonsense' as an emotive synonym of 'False' from the use of 'Nonsense' to disguise lack of understanding.[12]

The reader could try to add his own examples and analyses to my list. Why is it, for example, that some people reply to Why? questions about causation with restatements of facts?

Theory

Part of my ignorance of physics consists in not knowing the substantive theories of physics. It is out of the question that I should re-invent such theories myself – at least, any but the most elementary ones. Quite aside from the material resources needed to set up and conduct experiments, one person does not have the time or intelligence to re-invent the product of centuries, if not millennia, of collective work. There is no practical alternative to reading other people's books, going to other people's lectures, and using apparatus under other people's supervision.

There are many theories of politics, both scientific and normative. Most people have never had any formal instruction in any of them, let alone the ones, like Marxism, which can help them understand and act upon their own political situation in the world. The *omission* of political education in *theory* from the curriculum of schools is more important, I think, than any substantive instruction they administer to their pupils, such as 'British Constitution', the ideology of which seems to consist in presenting the abstract formal description of institutions as a model of their actual functioning. Again, such political theories as the media present seem to me either to be of too high a level of abstractness, or to be trapped in the concrete example. It is the middle range of the theoretical concepts which is *missing*, and this quite aside from any overt *bias*. The abstractness of media concepts consists in the use of reified 'forces' such as 'progress', 'reaction', 'order', 'disorder', etc., as explanatory concepts; the concreteness of the media consists in the description of social reality at the level of isolated *events*. Of course, it is at the most abstract and most concrete levels that there is least disagreement (at least overtly so) and the resort to abstract and concrete may be the means whereby they discharge their obligation to be overtly unbiased. The middle range of concepts (which includes sociological concepts like 'class', 'status', etc.) is the area of greatest overt controversy and it is therefore *excluded*. (The exclusion of substantive *contents*, perhaps the most important way in which bias operates, is a different issue.)

Professional politicians are possibly even worse as sources of theoretical understanding of political reality. Their position depends on limiting understanding of politics and their own role within it. The fact that the speeches of very few politicians bear reprinting is some indication of the absence of theoretical (even informational) content from what they say. The reading public has nothing to learn from them, only about them: the Collected Speeches of Edward Heath or Harold Wilson could be used only to damn.

To the degree that people feel the need for explicit political theories, I think they are left very much to their own devices. The vocabulary of politics is determined externally, and certain ideologies of voting are propagated, but for the rest, politics, far from being the field *par excellence* of deliberately propagated ideology, is left to a great degree to be occupied by *spontaneous ideologies*.

These spontaneous ideologies reflect closely the immediate circumstances of daily life and do not transcend them; they take appearance for reality and concrete incident for theory. They reify the existing order of things. Thus, racism and working-class conservatism. Reification involves at least three processes absent from radical and revolutionary theories. First, there is no theoretical recognition of the historical character of the present social order. Even if there is an awareness of the historical emergence of the present system, that system is seen as the culminating goal of the historical process beyond which no substantial change is possible. Second, there is no conscious awareness of the dependence of social change on human action, whether collective or individual. This is true of religious conceptions in which 'God has his plan', of technocratic conceptions in which technology has its own immanent plan, and in deference views in which 'You've got to have the people with money' – where a contingent feature of society, that wealth is the dominant source of power, is reified into a necessary feature of social existence. Third, the needs, wants or interests which might stimulate action to change the social order are repressed and sublimated. Wilhelm Reich theorizes in detail about the mechanisms by which this is accomplished (1970, 1971).

The argument of this chapter has been that many people are linguistically inhibited from thinking theoretically about politics, and if this is correct it helps explain the weakness of spontaneous ideologies. For essential to theory (which is what such ideologies aspire to) is the employment of elaborate causal and functional concepts and the corresponding vocabulary. In my teaching, I noticed that when asked for explanations of social phenomena, apprentices often redescribed the phenomena or restated the question minus the interrogative (e.g., Why is there a housing shortage? There aren't enough houses. Compare Halliday, 1969, 35). There was, at least, a lack of readiness to volunteer causal explanations, though no lack of readiness to offer answers. In terms of theory, I have read and been influenced by the work of Basil Bernstein, but I do not think that my arguments depend for their validity on acceptance of his theory of restricted and elaborated linguistic *codes*. For Bernstein, it is a defining feature of a restricted code, to which the lower working class (at least) is allegedly confined that it lacks 'elaborate causal conceptions' (1971, 47). I agree that elaborate causal conceptions are lacking, but doubt that the lack is necessarily or empirically systematic enough to merit the use of the concept of 'code'.

If there is such a thing as a restricted code, lacking in elaborate causal concepts, then I think its existence would have to be explained by reference to the fact that some people think they have no *use* for elaborate causal conceptions. They may have reconciled themselves, for example, to their real exclusion from politics (see section following). Such privatization would explain the use of a restricted code, as Bernstein himself indicates (1971, 147), though I would expect a dialectical relationship between code and circumstances: that is to say, that whilst the circumstances produce the code, the code strengthens the grip of circumstances.

Practice

I don't think explanations are needed of people's conceptual limitations. What is needed is an explanation of how such limitations are ever broken out of. Aaron Sloman, in remarks on draft material for this book. (Compare Wertheimer, 1961.)

If I were to make the attempt to learn physics, I should need a motive (and a pretty strong one) if I were to make any progress in the subject. I might be driven by ambition, pure or idle curiosity, or necessity. It is unlikely that I shall ever be strongly enough 'motivated' to learn physics.

Could the relation of people to the understanding of politics be similar? A motive is needed equally for someone to set out to understand politics, but it would seem, at first glance, that such a motive is always and universally present. For the life of every person is inescapably a political life, and chances of being happy and free depend in direct and important ways on the form of society within which a person lives. Failure to 'recognize' such facts is precisely what constitutes the psychological side of real alienation and political exclusion (see my 1973b).

Because of real and psychological alienation, the ever-present motive for understanding politics does not 'surface' in the form of an interest in politics, whilst alienation does surface in the flight[13] from politics into 'private' modes of existence, doomed to defeat because based on belief in a non-existent possibility of privacy. Rather than challenge a real state of affairs, or the psychological states which it generates, people try to escape them both. Perhaps they can conceive of no other way out. Certainly, their attempted solutions only compound their powerlessness and sense of powerlessness; but why might they not be able to conceive of any other way out?

On the one hand, I am sure that some people make a rational calculation and conclude that change is practically impossible. On the other, I am sure – as indicated in previous sections – that there are people who can't or don't envisage radically different situations, let along believe that it is possible to bring them about. The non-existence of fully acceptable alternatives elsewhere in the world is a potent factor in confirming both these perspectives, which is why it is far from irrelevant for left-wing organizations to devote a great deal of intellectual effort to analysing the structure of the Soviet Union, China, Cuba, etc.

Again, it is not as if the work or the family situation provides alternative experience which might be applied critically to the political realm from the point of view of changing it. If anything, work and family are less democratic situations than is politics, though, interestingly, the family situation at least produces reactions in children structurally very similar to the reactions of adults to the political situation in which they find themselves. For example, in their studies of the families of schizophrenics (many of the characteristics of which must be regarded as typical rather than deviant, at least of practice if not of ideological norms), Laing and Esterson (1970) show how children respond to denial or prohibition of their practice, or invalidation or negation of their own self-definitions, by *withdrawal* (which becomes catatonia in the clinical stage). When there is no way out through the door, or there seems no way out, or where they lack the means to fight back (including the cognitive means), children may withdraw as the only alternative to complete submission. It resembles political apathy or privatization in being a fugitive practice in response to a denial of the *need* for self-determination.[14]

Last but not least, changing the world demands a great deal of time, effort, strength and courage. Serious efforts to change society frequently encounter severe repression. Who'd be a revolutionary?

The powerful, over-determined character of the obstacles to political action and knowledge does illustrate the meaning and realism of the Marxist perspective which emphasizes not an abstract political-educational effort as that which generates a political movement, but, rather, the force of economic circumstances, and the needs and interests which economic developments simultaneously generate and frustrate. But if this is so, then the greatest of the obstacles to political action would then appear to be those practices which encourage people to accept frustration, or make them fearful of fighting for their needs, or lead them to repress their self-knowledge of their own frustrations. In chapter I, section 6,* I discussed and criticized the established assumption that men *will* act to satisfy their needs and further their interests. The most difficult problem facing radicals and revolutionaries is that where men do not or will not act to satisfy their needs, where they accept frustration or repress their knowledge of it.[15]

This is why I think the writings of Wilhelm Reich deserve such careful study, and also why I think that any political movement today must itself be a source of satisfaction to its members and not purely a sacrifice. There should be nothing 'religious' about a political movement.[16] Activities like theatre, film and music should be neither decorative features of a political movement or narrowly instrumental. For in them people may come to know their own desires and become willing to act collectively to satisfy them.[17]

Conclusions

I have compared politics to physics, but I do not wish to encourage the scientization of politics in the sense that that phrase is understood by writers like Habermas. That is, I do not wish to regard politics as a sphere in which exclusively instrumental problems arise; nor do I wish that political control should be vested in 'experts'. On the other hand, I do believe that theory is needed to understand what is going on in political society, and I come reluctantly to the conclusion that people will always remain unequal in the level of their theoretical sophistication, and that, in consequence, there will be theoretical leaders. But they need not be leaders in everything else as well; and if they claim to be, and enforce their claim, the effects are often enough disastrous. Leaders can also be subject to greater control and enjoy less permanence than they now do.[18] Yet it still remains true, I think, that people cannot spontaneously generate the range and depth of political knowledge required for them to function effectively as political agents. In this sense, I think my heuristic analogy between physics and politics is not so misleading, and I have to come down, against some of the anarchists, on the side of Lenin.

My ignorance of physics is historically explicable and of no importance. Comparable ignorance about politics is common, explicable and important. I think that the theories I have sketched in this chapter are relevant to political activists in their daily work, and that the effort to confirm or refute them would be worthwhile. This book would more than have achieved its purpose if some of its remarks were found useful by those engaged in the nitty-gritty work of achieving radical social change.

* Not included in this extract.

10

The co-operative principle and the rules for conversation

Mary Louise Pratt

From Pratt, Mary Louise 1977: *Toward a speech act theory of literary discourse*. Bloomington: Indiana UP, 125–32.

The processes of pre-paration and pre-selection that the literary speech situation presupposes have important consequences for the next set of 'ordinary language' rules whose applicability to literature I propose to explore. I refer to H.P. Grice's concepts of the Co-operative Principle and conversational implicature, as outlined in his 1967 William James lectures titled *Logic and Conversation*. Like Searle and Austin, Grice is primarily a speech act philosopher rather than a linguist; however, his work, too, has great implications for linguistics, and his lectures have had an enormous impact in linguistic circles. Grice attempts to clarify and correct the traditional Austinian view of appropriateness conditions by relating the ones which hold for a particular speech act in a particular context to general rules governing all verbal discourse and indeed all goal-directed co-operative human behaviour. Because of its generality, I believe Grice's approach to discourse holds promise for those of us interested in making a space for literature inside the theory of language use. I shall outline Grice's theory in the next few pages and then* discuss the extent to which his model of conversation works for literature as well.

As his title suggests, Grice uses the term *conversation* to mean, roughly, 'ordinary language' or 'talk' as opposed in this case to formal logic. Grice is mainly concerned in *Logic and Conversation* with clarifying the distinction between meaning and use of utterances. In particular, he calls into question a tendency among speech act analysts to account for the inappropriateness of a given word or phrase in a given context by attaching appropriateness conditions to that word or phrase as aspects of its meaning or 'sense'. Grice aims to show that many cases of inappropriateness which have previously been analysed as violations of conditions governing the applicability of a particular word or expression in question are actually best viewed as violations of other more general rules governing all discourse. Once these general rules are specified, he argues, many of the appropriateness conditions previously attached to individual words or phrases – as semantic features of the expression itself – will become unnecessary, and a simpler and more powerful grammar will result. Here is an example. It is true but inappropriate to say 'it looks like a car to me' when 'it' obviously *is* a car and I obviously know it. Pre-Griceans would account for this inappropriateness by stating an appropriateness condition to the effect that the expression 'X looks like

---

* Not included in this extract.

a Y' presupposes either that X is not a Y or that the speaker does not know whether X is a Y. Grice argues that the inappropriateness can actually be accounted for by a much more general rule of language use which requires that wherever possible one should give as much information as is required by the purposes of the talk exchange in which one is participating. Thus, if X *is* in fact a Y, then to say merely that it *looks like* a Y is to say too little – less than I know and less than I am required to say by the rules of conversation. It is important to note that such a rule would apply to all conversation regardless of its subject matter and consequently would apply independently of the specific word or phrase in question.

Similarly, it is true but usually inappropriate to say 'Bill is in Oxford or in London' when I know for certain that Bill is in London. This fact, says Grice, 'has led to the idea that it is part of the meaning of "or" . . . to convey that the speaker is ignorant of the truth-values of the particular disjuncts' (I, 10).[1] Rather, argues Grice, this inappropriateness, too, is accounted for by the general rule requiring that one give all the relevant information one has. If I knew where Bill was, I would say so unless, say, I had promised not to tell, in which case I must explain this fact or take responsibility for misleading my addressee. When I say 'Bill is in Oxford or in London', my addressee understands that I am ignorant of Bill's whereabouts, but he understands that not because of something he knows about the *meaning* of 'or' but because of something he knows about language *use*, namely, the 'all-the-relevant-facts' rule. The same rule explains the inappropriateness of saying 'X tried to turn on the lights' when X in fact succeeded in doing so and there was no reason to think he would not succeed. There is then no need to attach to the word 'try' an appropriateness condition saying that 'try' presupposes failure or difficulty.

The example with 'or' that I have just quoted is an important one to Grice, for one of his particular interests in *Logic and Conversation* is to show that the divergence in meaning which philosophers have commonly believed to exist between ordinary language expressions like 'not', 'if . . . then', 'either . . . or', and their counterparts in formal logic, ' $\sim$ ', ' $\supset$ ', ' $\lor$ ', are not really differences in meaning but in use. Once the rules for the use of ordinary language are isolatd, Grice contends, the devices of formal logic and of ordinary language can be seen to have the same meaning. Obviously, his argument is intended to refute the philosophical position (commonly associated with Bertrand Russell) that ordinary language is loose, imperfect, metaphysically loaded, and altogether inadequate to philosophy and science, a position which holds that 'the proper course is to conceive and begin to construct an ideal language, incorporating the formal devices [of logic], the sentences of which will be clear, determinate in truth-value and certifiably free from metaphysical implications; the foundations of science will now be philosophically secure, since the statements of the scientist will be expressible (though not necessarily expressed) within this language' (Grice, II, 2).

Grice's polemical interest – stating the case for ordinary language *vis-à-vis* the so-called 'language of science' (formal logic) – seems curiously related to my present interest in stating the case for ordinary language *vis-à-vis* the so-called 'language of poetry'. It is worth noting that the idea of an 'ordinary language' that was alien to the purposes of science achieved prominence about the same time as did the idea of an 'ordinary language' alien to the purposes of literature – in the first three decades of this century. 'Ordinary language', it seems, was too poetic for the scientists and too scientific for the poets. It is probably not a coincidence that 'ordinary language' became the whipping boy of two apparently opposed factions at once.

In any quarter, scepticism about 'ordinary language' (the term was used until recently only by the sceptical) is in the end scepticism about ordinary people, be they non-scientists or non-poets. In both the new, improved 'poetic language' of the futurists and the new, improved scientific language of the logicians we witness a movement toward increased artificiality and, more importantly, toward unrecognizability. Both the science and the literature of the academy become increasingly inaccessible linguistically to the speaker lacking special training, and this inaccessibility becomes the sign of their value. 'Specialized' comes to equal 'special'; the scientist's ideal audience is scientists, the poet's poets. The connection between this tendency toward specialization and the advent of mass literacy, mass education and mass printing has often been pointed out. It would also be worth investigating the hypothesis that the 'ordinary language' concept arose as a kind of residue left over from the seventeenth-century poetry–science split which reached an extreme at the beginning of this century. At any rate, it does seem that the fault Grice finds with the 'scientific language' doctrine is the same one I have been finding with the 'poetic language' doctrine, namely the mistake of positing a contrast based on intrinsic features of expressions when in fact the contrast, to the extent that it exists, is based on meaning-independent contextual features, that is, use. Grice aims to show how the rules for language use mediate between logic and conversation; I am concerned with examining the extent to which the same rules can mediate between literature and conversation, bringing to light the similarities and differences of the two verbal activities.

The all-the-relevant-facts rule I mentioned earlier is one of a set of exceedingly general rules Grice proposes as a framework for a theory of language use. I will outline the rest of his schema here. According to Grice, the fact that conversation normally exhibits some degree of coherence and continuity suggests that our conversational behaviour is governed by 'a rough general principle which participants will be expected (*ceteris paribus*) to observe, viz: 'Make your conversational contribution such as is required, at the stage at which it occurs, by the accepted purpose or direction of the talk exchange in which you are engaged.'" (II, 7) Grice calls this the *Co-operative Principle.* He then proposes four sets of conversational 'maxims' that we observe in observing the Co-operative Principle:

I Maxims of Quantity
1 'Make your contribution as informative as is required (for the current purposes of the exchange).'
2 'Do not make your contribution more informative than is required.' (Grice expresses some doubt about whether this maxim is needed.)

II Maxims of Quality
Supermaxim: 'Make your contribution one that is true.'
Maxims
1 'Do not say what you believe to be false.'
2 'Do not say that for which you lack adequate evidence.'

III Maxim of Relation
  1 'Be relevant'

> Grice's note: 'Though the maxim itself is terse, its formulation conceals a number of problems which exercise me a good deal; questions about what different kinds of foci or relevance there may be, how these shift in the course of a talk-exchange, how to allow for the fact that subjects of conversation are legitimately changed, and so on.' (II, 8)

IV Maxims of Manner
Supermaxim: 'Be perspicuous.'
Maxims:
  1 'Avoid obscurity of expression.'
  2 'Avoid ambiguity.'
  3 'Be brief (avoid unnecessary prolixity).'
  4 'Be orderly.'
There are possibly others.

The rules can be understood as large, very general appropriateness conditions that participants in a speech exchange normally assume to be in force. A participant in a speech exchange normally takes it for granted that his interlocutor shares a knowledge of the rules, is trying to observe them, and expects the same of him. I say 'normally' because of course there are speech situations where participants will not assume the Co-operative Principle and maxims to be in effect. A soldier captured by the enemy, for example, will be expected to co-operate to the extent of giving his name, rank and serial number, but beyond that he can be expected to try *not* to observe any of the conversational maxims. This kind of exception helps to prove Grice's rules. The soldier does not co-operate because he would much rather not be engaged in the speech situation at all.

Grice appends two important qualifications to the rule schema outlined above. First, like the turn-taking procedures discussed earlier, the maxims he is proposing can be seen to govern not just conversation but also any co-operative, rational human activity (two people fixing a car is his example). This fact suggests to Grice that talking is 'a special case or variety of purposive, indeed rational behaviour' (II, 9), the implication being, apparently, that the Co-operative Principle may have a cognitive basis. Second, the list of maxims he offers is not intended to be complete:

> There are of course all sorts of other maxims (aesthetic, social or moral in character) such as 'Be polite', which are also normally observed by participants in talk-exchanges.... The conversational maxims, however, and the conversational implicatures connected with them are specially connected (I hope) with the particular purposes which talk (and so talk-exchange) is adapted to serve and is primarily employed to serve. I have stated my maxims as if this purpose were a maximally effective exchange of information; this specification is of course too narrow, and the scheme needs to be generalized to allow for such general purposes as influencing or directing the actions of others. (II, 9)

This caveat is important, clearly, if we are to make room within Grice's model for the full range of illocutionary acts[2] possible in a given language. Obviously, there are a great many types, including natural narrative and literature, whose purpose is not a maximally effective exchange of information in the Gricean sense.

Indeed, as the maxims stand, they represent those aspects of discourse which literature has often been felt to subvert. Finally, the maxims are anything but iron-clad. In fact, they are honoured as often in the breach as in the observance. One of the main virtues of Grice's model is that it offers a way of describing the breaches as well, a matter of no small importance to the present undertaking.

11

The structures of speech and writing

Gunther Kress

From Kress, Gunther 1982: *Learning to write*. London: Routledge, 22–33.

The immediate presence of the audience in the case of spoken language is reflected in one of its most significant structural characteristics. Superimposed on the clausal structure of speech (which will be discussed below) is a structure determined by the speaker's wish to present information in the form most accessible to the hearer. Consequently the speaker parcels up by intonational means the information which he or she wishes to present to the hearer in what the speaker regards as the relevant chunks or units of information. This structure of *information units* derives from the interactional nature of speech, and encodes some of its major features, namely the exchange of information from one participant to the other, the mutual construction of meaning, and the mutual development of a topic. It also takes account of the transient nature of speech. A hearer cannot usually pause or check back over the message to make sure that he or she has understood it. The structure of speech makes major allowances for this factor by structuring information, providing sound cues which highlight the relevant informational structuring.

This structure is expressed through intonation. The speaker uses intonation to bracket together segments of his utterance which he regards as constituting one relevant parcel or unit of information. The function of intonation in providing clearly marked structures in speech has been the subject of research by a number of linguists, foremost among them Michael Halliday, whose innovative work has in turn been taken up and furthered in important directions by David Brazil. Halliday calls the basic unit of the spoken language the *information unit*. It is expressed intonationally in the *tone group*, a phonological entity. It encodes what the speaker wishes to present as one segment or unit of information. It is marked off in speech by a single unified intonation contour, and above all, by containing one major pitch-movement. The unit has no previously determined length. It may correspond to a clause but need not do so at all. For instance, in the following text, clausal structure and information structure coincide partially. (The speaker is a six-year-old child.)

> //let's have a look in your mouth to make sure// no//like that//no//none// . . . put the bottom lip down// . . . no//it's not your teeth//

(The double oblique strokes are used to mark the boundaries of information units.) The clauses in this brief text are *let's have a look in your mouth, to make sure, like that, put the bottom lip down, it's not your teeth.* That is, there are five clauses, but eight information units. A clausal analysis inevitably strikes problems with items like *no none*, which either have to be treated as clauses by some theoretical contortion, or else fall uncomfortably outside the description. In terms of informational structure there is no problem of description. It is clear from this example that the information units need not coincide with the clauses or the clause-boundaries; for instance, the first information unit contains two clauses.

The information units are motivated directly by the interaction between the speaker and the other participant. Some response on the addressee's part causes both the specific content and the structure in which it is presented. The speaker can monitor the hearer's reaction from moment to moment, and adjust the informational structure accordingly.

The information units are, as mentioned, segments of speech which have (are spoken with) one unified intonational 'tune'. Each unit has an internal two-term structure, of 'known' and 'unknown' information. That is, within each unit the speaker represents some part of the information contained in the unit as being unknown to the hearer, the other part by implication as being already known to the hearer. The unknown part is marked by intonational prominence, in that the greatest and most pronounced pitch-movement occurs at the beginning of the unknown segment. So in the example just given

//let's have a look in your mouth to make sure//

sure receives intonational prominence with a noticeable fall in pitch, thus marking it as informationally unknown. The whole of this text has a known/unknown structure as shown here (with the unknown segment underlined).

//let's have a look in your mouth to make sure//no//like that//no//none// . . . put the bottom lip down// . . . no//it's not your teeth//

It can be seen from this that the unknown segment tends to occur at the end of the information unit. An exception is the last information unit, where the second from last segment is prominent. Where the intonation prominence falls other than on the last word, the prominence is noted by the hearer as unusual or marked, and is interpreted as being special in some sense. In this example a contrast is established between *your* teeth and *other* teeth (in this case, the speaker's teeth). From this text it is also clear that information units need not include anything other than unknown information. The known, by definition, can be left unsaid.

The two-part structure implies that there is always some common ground, some known information, between speaker and hearer. The unknown must be said, the known may be said or it may be left unsaid and implicit. It is, of course, the speaker's judgement which determines that something is shared knowledge, and what that shared knowledge is. It is also not clear from the speaker's decision to treat some information as known just how well known this may be to the hearer. David Brazil makes a similar point in *Discourse Intonation*:

> Another way of expressing the same distinction is to say that some parts of what a speaker says merely *make reference* to features which he takes to be already present in the interpenetrating worlds of speaker and hearer. Others have the status of *information* in that they are presented as if likely to change the world of the hearer. (p. 6)

Brazil is here introducing a twofold distinction into the element which Halliday regards as unknown. In doing so he draws attention to the fact that it is the speaker's decision to present content either as though it belonged to the shared knowledge of speaker and hearer, or was drawn from outside that area.

In this example the *known* is (among other, much more taken for granted information) that the previous conversation has been about losing teeth, and about whose teeth may have been replaced with a coin by the fairies. *Mouth, looking in one's mouth, your*, etc., are all assumed to be known to the hearer as they have been the topic of the preceding conversation and the shared experience of speaker and hearer. What is new, and hence 'unknown' to the hearer, is the suggestion to make *sure*. Of course, the speaker may be wrong in his assumptions about what is and what is not known to the hearer. In that case there will be some perplexity on the hearer's part, a momentary check in the flow of the interaction. Also, the speaker may be deliberately misconstruing and misrepresenting the hearer's knowledge, and by presenting information as known may attempt to coerce the hearer into accepting this insinuated assumption.

In this extract there are a number of information units which consist only of unknown information. That is not unusual. An information unit must consist of an unknown item of information, and it normally includes a known segment of information as well. To some extent the known segment is redundant, by definition. However, in interactional terms the *known* is not redundant, it serves as a link between the two participants: it provides them with common ground and shared knowledge, which serves as a starting point, a bridge almost, for each speaker in turn. (That is, making reference to 'the interpenetrating worlds of speaker and hearer'.) Thus while the known segment is informationally redundant, it is most important from an interactional point of view. Features of this structure of speech have been regarded as faults in speaking. Some parents and teachers have a habit of correcting children who give 'monosyllabic' answers, insisting that children should always speak, and in particular answer, in full sentences. This clearly rests on a misunderstanding of interactive language, as well as on the assumption that sentences are the basic units of spoken language so that any utterance which is not a sentence is defective. That assumption is incorrect, and the view could only persist because of the absence of research and hence understanding of the structure of spoken language.

Many of the interactional aspects reflected in the structure of spoken language are clearly absent from the context in which written language occurs, so that there is no need for linguistic forms to express them. However, written language does have a need for emphasizing particular items; equally, it must have the means for indicating the writer's topical and thematic organization of his material. The written language does not, of course, have intonation available for these purposes (other than parasitically by getting the reader to superimpose intonation – on italicized, underlined items, or words and phrases in inverted commas, or by the use of exclamation marks, etc.). Instead, written syntax uses sequential ordering of items or more thoroughgoing restructurings to express these meanings. Emphasis may be expressed by placing an item out of the normal syntactic order: *John she couldn't stand*, or *couldn't stand John, could Mary* (from *Mary couldn't stand John*). The writer may restructure the sentence more thoroughly: *It was John whom Mary couldn't stand*. These reorderings and restructurings still employ intonation indirectly, in the sense that these forms invite or even deter-

mine a particular reading which involves a more or less silent intonational implementation and actualization of the reading. However, even less drastically
reordered or restructured sentences allow the writer to organize his material in a
manner which presents his content in a particular fashion. All sentences display a
two-part structure. One part, the theme, announces what the writer has chosen to
make the topic of the sentence; the other part, the rheme, consists of material
pertaining to that theme, furthering and developing it in some sense. In the
sentence above, *All sentences display a two-part structure, all sentences* is the theme
and *display a two-part structure* is the rheme. That is, the first syntactic constituent of a sentence is always theme, the rest rheme. Consequently theme is not
another label for subject; frequently the two will coincide, but often they will not.
In the preceding sentence *consequently* is the theme, and *theme is not another label
for subject* is rheme.

Hence the textual structuring of speech and that of writing proceed from two
distinctly different starting points. The structure of speech starts from the question: 'What can I assume as common and shared knowledge for my addressee and
myself?' This question, and its answer, are at the basis of the structure of speech.
Writing starts with the question: 'What is most important, topically, to me, in this
sentence which I am about to write?' This question, and its answer, are at the
basis of the structure of writing. The cohesive and continuous development of a
topic is thus paramount in writing, while the construction of a world of shared
meaning is paramount in speaking.

The immediacy of the interaction and the speaker's awareness of the hearer
lead to another major structural difference between speech and writing, a clausal
structure which is both evidence of immediate thinking, in that the speaker does
not have time to assemble complex structures, and evidence of the needs of the
hearer as the recipient of information. Speech is structured by sequences or
'chains' of clauses, which are, generally speaking, co-ordinated, or else adjoined
without any co-ordinating particles (rather than subordinated or embedded). An
example of a co-ordinated structure is *let's have a look in your mouth and make
sure*, where the two clauses have equal status, and are joined by a conjunction. An
example of an adjoined structure is *let's have a look in your mouth(,) make sure,*
where the two clauses have equal status, and are adjacent but without a conjunction. A subordinating construction would be *when we look in your mouth we'll
make sure*, where there is a main clause, *we'll make sure*, and a subordinate
when-clause. In the text from which the example is taken the structure is an
embedding one, *let's have a look in your mouth to make sure*, where *to make sure* is
syntactically integrated into the main clause *let's have a look in your mouth* and
forms a syntactic constituent of it. 'Adjoined' is, however, open to a misinterpre-
tation, namely that it means 'simply adjoined, adjoined without indication of the
structural and semantic relationship of the clauses'. Such an interpretation is
incorrect. The absence of a co-ordinating particle is possible because of the use of
intonation to provide the structural connections. The pitch movement and the
pitch height at the information unit/clause boundaries give a precise indication of
how the following clause connects both structurally and semantically with the
preceding clause. The direction of the intonation contour in the new clause makes
this structural connection, and further develops it. The pitch movements
involved in this are minute but absolutely clear indications of the structure.
Taking a further extract from the text already discussed as an example

(numbering the information units)

// No^1 // we got them separate^2 // see^3 // the big^4 one //
we got him from my //$_5$,. . . uh . . . // we got him from my^6
brother's friend // my oldest brother //

1 would have a falling intonation to a medium low position with a slight rising
'hook'; 2 would begin at that level, rise slightly, fall on *separate* to a medium low
position; 3 would be level, at that height; 4 would start at a medium high position,
fall on *big*, continue to fall on the first part of *one*, with a slight rising hook at the
end; 5 would start at that level, continue to rise slightly to medium level on *my; uh*
would be on that level; 6 would continue at that level, rise steadily to the end of
brother's, at a medium level, and fall on *friend*, to a medium low level; 7 would start
at the same height as *friend* and fall on *oldest*, to a full low position (without final
rising hook) on *brother*. This over-arching link is not broken until an information
unit ends in a high rise without any downturn, or in a full fall without any
upturning hook, and where the following information unit is not an exact
intonational copy of its preceding unit. For instance, the fact that 7 starts at the
same height as the highest point of 6 is interpreted by the hearer as indicating that
7 is a gloss on the item which had the same height in 6, that is, that it is offering
further information and elaboration on aspects of one element of 6, namely that
with the intonation (and information) focus.

Consequently, far from the linking structure being missing or weakly articulated, the structure and the meaning of clausal connections in speech are highly
articulated and capable of the finest nuance. In writing, this structure is mirrored
to some extent in the system of punctuation, which is not, however, capable of
expressing the same detail and precision. In *Discourse Intonation*, Brazil discusses
a related feature, namely the semantic connectedness of tone-groups (that is,
information units) in discourse. He points out that tone-groups are spoken in one
of three *keys*, that is, relative pitch-levels: mid, high, or low.

> Any occurrence of a high-key tone group can be thought of as being phonetically bound
> to a succeeding tone-group; any low-key tone group as bound to the preceding one. The
> former carries the implication, 'There is more to follow'; the latter 'This is said in a
> situation created by something that went immediately before'. In discourse we can say
> that one sets up expectations, the other has prerequisites. (p. 10)

This suggests that in addition to the linking discussed above, there exists another,
superimposed level of intonationally expressed linking, relating the content of
tone-groups in the way indicated by Brazil.

Topic development in speech, within this clausal structure, is by sequence,
restatement, elaboration and intonational articulation. The evidence of 'thinking
on your feet' is everywhere evident in speech. This is in contrast to writing, where
there are, typically, no traces of immediate thinking. Writing is the domain of
circumspection, of (self-)censorship, reworking, editing. The development of the
topic in writing is by another order: not by sequence but by hierarchy. That which
is more important is given structural prominence, the less important is structurally subordinated. Consequently writing is the domain of a more complex syntax,
typified by the sentence, by subordination and embedding of various types, by
syntactic and conceptual integration. Speech is typified by the syntax of

sequence, of the clausal chain, of addition and accretion. To the extent that there is circumspection and self-censorship in speech, it emerges in the form of hesitation phenomena. The greater the need for circumspection, the more prominent hesitation phenomena are likely to be; the less need for care, the less likely hesitation phenomena are to occur. Bernstein and others have noted that hesitation phenomena are more common with middle-class than with working-class speakers.

Perhaps the most obvious and most characteristic unit of the written language is the sentence. It features prominently in linguistic theory (it also features quite prominently in folk linguistics), and we tend to assume that we know what a sentence is. In fact, and this is also well known, there is no agreement in linguistic theory on the definition of sentence. I wish to say that the sentence (whatever its definition) is not a unit of informal spoken language, but that it is the basic textual unit of the written language. Because of the influence of writing on speaking and because of its higher status, the assumption is that speech is also organized by the sentence as its basic linguistic unit. I think that is not correct. There is much evidence, for instance from the description of Australian Aboriginal languages, which seems to suggest that, in some of these languages at least, there are chains of clauses and paragraphs but there are no sentences. One of the problems in attempting to write these languages down, to make them literate languages and to give them a 'literature', is precisely this absence of the sentence, so that in transcribing narratives and myths the transcriber wants to impose a sentence structure on the narrative; this falsifies the narrative, because in its spoken form it is not structured in sentences. The interesting point is that after a while the original tellers of the myth also want to organize the written versions of the narratives in sentence form. There seems to be something about writing which demands a different syntactic and textual organization from that of speech.

To show the difference between these two forms of the language, here is an example of the same adult (myself) speaking and writing. The spoken text is from the transcript of a lecture given without notes; the written text was prepared from the transcript, for publication. I deliberately kept reasonably close to the spoken style of the lecture; a fully fledged translation into writing would have been very different.

Text 1

Spoken text

Now of course an exhortation to be open in the way we look at things is easier said than done *because* we have all finished I suppose much of our learning *with* most, I think all of us have finished probably all of our significant learning *and* learning has of course positive aspects it has the posi-
5   tive aspect of enabling us to live in the culture that we are born into *but* learning also has um I feel quite negative aspects um the positive ones as I say are clear enough they enable us to function. In our world the negative ones have also been pointed to um frequently enough, I'll just er perhaps talk about them very briefly in relation to language um the negative
10 aspects of learning I think are concerned with a kind of reduction that goes on with a kind limiting that goes on when we learn cultural things. We

come to learn things *and* once we have learned them they seem to be the only way to do things um the way we say things seems to be the natural way to say things *and* so forth.

Text 2

Written text

Now of course, an exhortation to be open in the way we look at things is easier said than done *because* we have all finished most of our significant learning. Learning has positive aspects, enabling us to live in the culture that we are born into; *but* learning also has quite negative aspects. These
5 are concerned with a kind of reduction, a kind of limiting that goes on when we learn cultural things. We come to learn things *and* once we have learned them they seem to be the only way to do a thing; the way we say things seems to be the natural way to say things *and* so forth.

I had asked a typist to transcribe the tape, which she kindly did. The 'punctuation' of the spoken text is therefore as the typist heard it. Clearly, the main organizing unit of the spoken text is not the sentence. Though it may be unusual to find the structure of speech in the formal register of 'lecture', the structure itself is not at all untypical of speech. It consists of clauses of equal or near equal syntactic status 'chained' together in sequence. This chaining may take the form of co-ordinated clauses, or of main and subordinated clauses, linked by conjunctions such as *and, but, or, if, so, because, though*. That is, the structure of speech is characterized by 'chains' of syntactically relatively complete and independent clauses. For instance, Text 1, lines 3-6: *I think all of us have finished probably all of our significant learning and learning has of course positive aspects it has the positive aspect . . .* - here three syntactically complete clauses are in the chain. Where a clause is significantly changed syntactically in order to make it part of another clause we have examples of either subordinating or embedding constructions; these are less typical of speech. For instance, in Text 1, lines 6-7; *it has the positive aspect of enabling us to live in the culture, enabling us* is a clause which is heavily modified to fit syntactically into its syntactic unit: *to live in the culture* is, similarly, a clause which has been significantly modified to fit into its matrix clause. In Text 1 the chaining syntax predominates, though it is clearly a mixture of chaining and embedding syntax. Examples of the latter are *an exhortation to be open, the way we look at things, enabling us to live, the culture that we are born into*. Informal speech tends to have even fewer instances of embedding than this text.

The written text by contrast is not only much shorter (eight lines compared to fourteen), it has more sentences (four compared to two) and the number of co-ordinated and adjoined clauses is significantly lower. Proportionately, full subordination and embedding is more prominent in the written text (twenty-one clauses, five-co-ordinated or adjoined clauses, a ratio of 3.2:1) than in the spoken (thirty-four clauses, thirteen co-ordinated or adjoined clauses, a ratio of 1.6:1). It is worth bearing in mind that this spoken text was a relatively formal one, so that it contains a higher proportion of subordinated and embedded clauses than informal speech. Also, as the written text derives from the spoken one, it preserves some of the latter's informality. A formal written text would show a higher degree of subordination and embedding.

To summarize: speech, typically, consists of chains of co-ordinated, weakly subordinated and adjoined clauses; writing by contrast is marked by full subordi -nation and embedding. There are other characteristics too. The spoken text is longer, to make allowances for the different mode of reception, it shows repeti- tion, allowing the hearer time to assimilate information. It also contains many features of an interpersonal kind, referring to the interrelation of speaker and audience.

The discussion so far suggests that for our society linguistic competence includes a number of things over and above those which are normally assumed to be included in competence. The traditional Chomskyan version of competence assumes that a speaker of a language has internalized the rules of sentence forma- tion and transformation of that language and uses them as a basis for the produc- tion of an infinite set of sentences. There is also a sociolinguist's definition of competence, for instance that of Dell Hymes (1972), who talks about the rules we use in correctly applying these sentences in given situations. I would like to extend this notion of competence, and speak about differentiated competences for speaking and writing. These would include at least two additional types of rule. One would indicate how the structure-forming rules are to be applied in either speaking or writing. Further, if *sentence* is not a linguistic category of speech, then the competence for writing would include rules of sentence-formation, and the competence for speaking would not. In either case the competencies for speech and writing would include knowledge about strategies of conjunction – predominantly chaining for speech and embedding for writing. However, beyond these, the competence for writing would need to include a second type of rule, which indicates the knowledge of those syntactic structures which occur only in the written mode of language; and similarly for speaking. For instance, if a speaker said *Mary was supposed to do the trifle* with intonational prominence on *Mary*, then the most likely form of this in writing is *It was Mary who was supposed to do the trifle*. This structure belongs to writing; when it occurs in speech it is there as an importation, much like a loan-word from another language. Lastly, there would need to be a differentiated textual competence, as textual structures and processes differ significantly from one mode to the other, in areas such as cohesion, topic development, staging. In speaking, the text is usually constructed in interaction with another participant, whereas typically in writing that is not the case.

In the discussion so far I have proceeded as though all speakers and writers were identical. That is not the case. I mentioned above that access to writing is unevenly distributed in Western technological societies. Some members of these societies have no competence at all in writing (or reading) – the figure for countries such as Britain or Australia is between 10 and 15 per cent. Full compe- tence in writing may be restricted to as few as 10 per cent of the population. Obviously there are strong links between the structures of those societies and this uneven distribution of written competence. Speakers too are differentiated according to regional and social dialects. For certain social groups – the profes- sional classes, for instance – the structure of the spoken form of their dialects is very strongly influenced by the structures of writing. As a result, the difference between the syntax of speech and that of writing is far less for such groups than it is for groups whose dialects are little if at all influenced by the structure of writing. This factor has important implications for children learning to write. For some children the syntax of writing will be more familiar than for others, to whom it may be totally unfamiliar. Hence in a group of children some may start with knowledge which others have yet to acquire. This difference in knowledge is unacknowledged, because the fundamental differences between the two forms of language is not a well understood and widely known fact. Teachers are likely to attribute this difference in the performance of children to differences in intelligence. There exists therefore an initial unnoticed hurdle in the learning of writing on which many children stumble and never recover. They will not be fully competent writers and will be regarded as failures in the eyes of our literate society and in terms of our educational system.

12

Beyond alienation: an integrational approach to women and language

Deborah Cameron

From Cameron, Deborah 1985: *Feminism and linguistic theory*. London: Macmillan, 141–6, 149–61.
Note: Omitted from this extract are some introductory comments on what is meant by 'language' and 'meaning,' and a section on 'Women and literacy' in which it is pointed out that the majority of illiterates in the world today are women, and that even where women are literate they are often denied access to particular language registers.

Meaning, understanding and alienation

We may now return to the experience described by Simone de Beauvoir: 'I saw greys and half-tones everywhere. Only as soon as I tried to define their muted shades, I had to use words, and I found myself in a world of bony-structured concepts.'[1] This frustration at being unable to make language express the exact nuances of experience is something we have already encountered in women's own testimony: 'Sometimes when I am talking to people I really feel at a loss for words. . . . A vast number of the words I use all the time to describe my experience are not really describing it at all.'[2] Audre Lorde, a poet, notes that we speak of our experience only 'at the risk of having it bruised and misunderstood'.[3] Difficulty in finding words and difficulty in being understood are often spoken of by women as signs of their alienation, the proof that 'this is the oppressors' language' with meanings and limits defined by men. The solution is to create a new language in which women can express their meanings and be understood.

But if we accept the idea that meaning is complex, plural and ultimately perhaps impossible to pin down, the new language solution appears utopian. There will never be a perfect fit between private experience and linguistic expression, and there will never be perfect mutual understanding. Sociologists of language have long been familiar with the idea that participants in any kind of talk take for granted a degree of comprehension which, when you look more closely at the interaction, cannot ever be quite justified. Thus the problems of expressing oneself and being understood are not exclusively women's problems. They are built into all interaction and affect all speakers. Which is not to say that women do not suffer to a greater degree than men: for the causes of their particular problems, however, I think it is necessary to consider the whole social situation of women and men, and not just their relative positions in an abstract symbolic order.

The notion that perfect mutual understanding – telepathy – is not the normal or the ideal outcome of speaking, frightens and confuses many people. It is clear that without the indeterminacy that stops us communicating telepathically we would not be able to adapt our language to the novel situations we need it for; imperfect communication is the price we pay for a creative and flexible symbolic system. But this important insight frequently meets with a great deal of resistance. If we cannot ever really understand each other, are we not trapped in our own private worlds with no hope of making contact? And is this not the ultimate nightmare of alienation?

This fear, and the comforting certainty that perfect understanding *is* possible, goes very deep. For instance, a well-known myth of human prehistory refers to a time when humans did understand each other perfectly, and this understanding conferred enormous power on them. God not unnaturally saw that power as a threat and destroyed it by destroying the unity of human language.

> And the Lord said, Behold, the people is one, and they have all one language; and this they begin to do: and now nothing will be restrained from them, which they have imagined to do. Go to, let us go down, and there confound their language, that they may not understand each other's speech. So the Lord scattered them abroad from thence upon the face of all the earth.[4]

The perfect understanding which supposedly results from 'speaking the same language' is seen here as an essential prerequisite for any kind of collective action. God, in replacing linguistic unity with linguistic diversity, undermined the power of the builders. Feminists have their own version of the Tower of Babel story. They feel that men have undermined women by confounding their language, the language of their bodies, their unconscious, their desire or their experience. In order to act together, an authentic language of women must be forged. If there is no common language, there can be no true collective action.

I do not feel, however, that the view of meaning I have put forward excludes the possibility of collective action, nor does it negate the communication that obviously *does* occur between individuals. Rather, it says that if we are ever to understand the nature of collective action and interpersonal communication, we must first acknowledge its inherent difficulties and limitations. Until we do acknowledge that communication is to some extent an everyday triumph, until we get rid of our fantasies of what it never can be, we can hardly study it at all, but will be content either to avoid the issue or to take it for granted.

Where does this leave the feminist theories of language and oppression we have discussed in this book? I suggest that it leaves us with three propositions corresponding to the three feminist axioms of linguistic determinism, male control and female alienation.

1 Linguistic determinism is a myth. Where there is no determinacy, there can be no determinism. In a system where language and linguistic acts are integrated with non-linguistic acts and social life generally, language can be only one of the multiple determinants of any individual's perceptions and experience. An important determinant it may be, but it cannot be privileged to the extent that both Saussurean and Whorfian[5] theories privilege it.
2 Male control over meaning is an impossibility. No group has it in their power to fix what expressions of a language will mean, because meanings cannot be fixed, and interpretation will be dependent not on the authority of some vast internal dictionary, but on the creative and ultimately idiosyncratic use of past experience and present context.

Learning to communicate and to participate in social life is something which both male and female children do. They do it by actively interacting with their environment and the people in it, and thus they construct – rather than learn –

meanings that are highly contextualized, dependent on that environment and those people, subject (as the environment is) to variation and to change.

It would be very surprising if this learning process did not exhibit sex-linked differences. Girls and boys, after all, are very specifically socialized into female and male gender roles; one would expect them to construct meanings which were different not only idiosyncratically, because each individual has a different experience, but more generally, because in patriarchal societies males and females are allowed a different range of experiences. Perhaps, then, we may talk to some extent of male and female meanings. But we cannot speak of women being socialized into male meanings, or of both sexes being socialized into patriarchal meanings (except in the sense that their experience is one of living under patriarchy). Meanings have to be constructed by the individual language user (in this way language is radically unlike, say, folk tales or table manners) and any child who does not learn to construct meanings out of her own interaction with the world cannot be said to possess language at all.

3 Female alienation from language does not exist in the form postulated by the theories we have considered (it should not be denied either in theory or in practice that many women do feel extremely alienated in some modes of language use). Since language is a flexible and renewable resource, and since girls must come to grips with it as their socialization proceeds, there is no reason in principle why language cannot express the experience of women to the same extent that it expresses the experience of men.

In saying this, however, I do not wish to deny that women have real problems in speaking and being heard. Although I reject the usual explanations of them, I believe that the means do exist for men to oppress, silence and marginalize women through language. The sources of silence and oppression are what I want to turn to now.

Linguistic oppression: what it is that men control

One consequence of the integrational approach to language is that the linguist has to take seriously the fact that languages are not used in a social and political vacuum, i.e. she must recognize the institutional aspects of language I have already mentioned in this chapter.

In every society, one finds law, rituals and institutions which regulate language (especially its more public modes) in particular ways. As we saw in Chapter 3,* it is not always easy to separate these 'metalinguistic' or 'discursive' practices from language proper, since there is a constant interaction between the two. From an integrational standpoint it is not even worth trying to exclude the metalinguistic: institutional phenomena are part of what the linguist must be concerned with.

If we look closely at the regulatory mechanisms which grow up around languages, it is clear that they are rather closely connected with the power structures of their society. The institutions that regulate language use in our own society, and indeed those of most societies, are deliberately oppressive to women. Men control them, not in the rather mystical sense that they are said to control meaning, by making esoteric semantic rules or possessing the vital signifier, but

* Not included in this extract.

simply because it is the prerogative of those with economic and political power to set up and regulate important social institutions.

Language, the human faculty and communication channel, may belong to everyone; because of the crucial part it plays in human cognition and development, it cannot be appropriated. But *the* language, the institution, the apparatus of ritual, value judgement and so on, does not belong to everyone equally. It can be controlled by a small elite. As Trevor Pateman remarks,

> Language, though the socially produced means of thought, is not socially controlled. Increasingly control over the development of language and its use is held by state institutions, including mass-media and monopolistic private enterprise, as in journalism and advertising.... The semiologists have sometimes failed to appreciate the possibility and existence of class or other minority control over language.[6]

If we acknowledge the importance of institutional control, the crucial question is: how is male control over metalinguistic processes manifested, and what effects does it have on women? I want to consider this now, and true to my integrational aims I shall not be limiting my remarks to linguistic phenomena alone. It is impossible to understand the practices that regulate women's relation to language except with reference to gender roles and regulatory mechanisms in general.

High language and women's silence

Cora Kaplan, in a short but influential essay, makes a point that has since become the received view about women's oppression by linguistic institutions; the point is that women are denied access to the most influential and prestigious registers of language in a particular culture.[7] That is to say, everything defined as 'high' language (for instance, political and literary registers, the register of public speaking and especially ritual – religious, legal or social) is also defined as *male* language. Kaplan observes,

> The prejudice seems persistent and irrational unless we acknowledge that control of high language is a crucial part of the power of dominant groups, and understand the refusal of access to public language is one of the major forms of the oppression of women within a social class as well as in trans-class situations.[8]

If it is in their relation to high language that women are linguistically disadvantaged, it seems that we must ask three questions: *what* are the registers that men control, *how* do they gain and keep control of those registers, and *why* does male control constitute a disadvantage for women? I propose to explore these questions by focusing on particular areas of language use and linguistic control. First there is the area of written language and women's relation to it. An investigation of this shows how a denial of language can constitute a denial of knowledge and of certain kinds of consciousness. Then, there is the problem of bureaucratic/-institutional language. Recent work on interethnic communication demonstrates how very tightly controlled norms are used to define subordinate groups as inadequate communicators (and thus to *make* them inadequate). Finally, we must examine the exclusion of women from public and ritual speech, investigating the extent to which femininity has been produced as incompatible with the sphere of rhetoric.

[A section 'Women and Literacy' is omitted at this point]

Institutional language: communicating in urban societies

If literacy is a problem for the underprivileged in less developed countries, bureaucracy is a major linguistic headache for the underprivileged of modern western cities. In two recent books advocating a new approach to communication ('interactional sociolinguistics')[9] the linguist John Gumperz points out how important 'communicative skills' have become with the growth of state and other bureaucracies (health, education, employment and tax services, for instance) in modern industrial society. More and more frequently, individuals in their everyday lives are having to negotiate linguistic interactions with these bureaucracies, and the result is that

> The ability to manage or adapt to diverse communicative situations has become essential and the ability to interact with people with whom one has no personal acquaintance is crucial to acquiring even a small measure of personal and social control. We have to talk in order to establish our rights and entitlements. . . . Communicational resources thus form an integral part of an individual's symbolic and social capital.[10]

The individual needs to be able to interact effectively with institutions and their representatives. Since it is the individual, for the most part, who wants something from the encounter, 'effectively' will mean 'in conformity with the norms of the institution'. Those who cannot express themselves in a way the bureaucracy finds acceptable (or minimally, comprehensible) will be disadvantaged.

Gumperz and his associates have produced a good deal of work on 'crosstalk' or, in plain language, *misunderstanding* between individuals whose norms of interaction are different. Their work has focused mainly on interactions between bureaucrats of various kinds (social workers, clerks, personnel managers) and Asian speakers of English, but the two main points that emerge from it are equally applicable to other ethnic minorities, working-class speakers in certain situations and, of course, women talking to men.

The first point is simply that socially distant individuals (especially those differentiated by ethnicity) do not share rather subtle strategies for structuring and interpreting talk, and this results in misunderstanding which can be frustrating for both parties and seriously disadvantageous for the Asian trying to get a job or a Social Security cheque. The second point, which is rather less explicit in Gumperz's books, is that bureaucracies use their experience of inter-ethnic misunderstanding to generate representations of Asians as defective or inadequate communicators – representations which derive from racist stereotypes and reinforce racism. It is important to note that the right to represent and stereotype is not mutual, and that the power asymmetry here has serious consequences. Undoubtedly the Asians have their own less than complimentary ideas about the *gore* (white people), but these are the ideas of people without power. They do not serve as a base for administrative procedures and decisions, nor do they get expressed routinely in mass media: whereas institutional stereotypes of Asians *do* inform procedures, decisions and media representations. If Asians are defined as inadequate language users, they become *de facto* inadequate (crudely, no one listens any more to what they are actually saying, simply filtering it through the negative stereotype) and as Gumperz points out, in a modern industrial society this can have disastrous consequences.

It is important for feminists to ask whether women have the same ability as men to interact with people 'with whom one has no personal acquaintance' and 'adapt to diverse communicational situations'. If not, why not? Are women routinely misunderstood by men who have power over them, with disadvantageous results? Do men represent women as inadequate communicators, thus reducing their precious 'symbolic and social capital'? The question of misunderstanding between women and men has been addressed by two of Gumperz's associates, Daniel Maltz and Ruth Borker, and they believe that the subcultural differences between Asian and white speakers are paralleled by male/female differences.[11] Using the available literature on children's talk and play patterns they argue that females and males in western culture do in fact form separate subcultures, and that this significantly affects male/female interaction. Women and men do not attempt to do the same things in the same way when they talk, and thus there is likely to be a rather poor fit between what the speaker intends and what an opposite-sex hearer picks up.

It seems likely that there is a good deal in this idea, though Maltz and Borker do depend heavily on the competition versus co-operation stereotype which I have criticized [earlier] and which is itself inspired by a lot of rather dubious literature. My main reservation is that the sociolinguistic analysis of subcultural differences ought to include far more discussion about the political structure superimposed on these differences. In other words, Maltz and Borker say very little about the power of male *definitions* of female speakers, the use of such definitions to exclude women from certain registers and devalue their contribution to others. This omission is what I shall try to make good in the remainder of the chapter.

Discourses and registers

I have already discussed the exclusion of women from written and learned 'registers' (i.e. kinds of language appropriate in content, style and tone to a particular domain of use, say 'scholarship' or 'legal documents' or 'religion') and pointed out that whereas it makes no sense at all to speak of women not possessing 'language' it is quite in order to say that, for historically specific reasons, they may be forbidden to use certain registers at particular times and in particular places. Registers of language historically created by men very often represent women as marginal or inferior, and may well continue to do so even after women have begun to use them (in this book we have already looked at the registers of news reporting and lexicography, and while these practices were undoubtedly masculine originally, they have long been open to women without any noticeable diminution in their sexism). Partly this conservatism reflects the importance of tradition, 'custom and practice' in institutions. The conventions codified in style-books, rule-books, standing orders, editing and sub-editing manuals are quite literally handed down from generation to generation of professionals. They are part of a professional mystique, sanctified by history and enforced very often by the authoritarian training and advancement procedures of hierarchical organizations (the Civil Service and political parties, for instance). Partly, however, it reflects more general ideological matters. This point has been made very forcefully by semiologists like Roland Barthes (whose work on the ideological determinants of literary style in France remains a classic demonstration), Michel Foucault, Michel Pêcheux, Colin MacCabe, Maria Black and Rosalind Coward.

Semiologists refer to what I have been calling 'registers' as *discourses* (MacCabe representatively defines a discourse as a set of statements formulated on 'particu-lar institutional sites of language use').[12] Each discourse needs to be understood in relation to its own conventions (thus TV chat shows and court cases exemplify different linguistic norms) and its functions in society.

Maria Black and Rosalind Coward, in the article on Dale Spender I have already discussed,* explicitly say that discourse and not language (by which they mean *langue*) is the proper place for feminists to concentrate their efforts.

> Linguistic systems ... serve as the basis for the production and interpretation of related utterances – discourses – which effect and sustain the different categorizations and positions of women and men. It is on these discourses and not on language in general or linguistic systems, that feminist analyses have to focus.[13]

By concentrating on discursive regularities (for instance, the use of generic masculine pronouns or the linguistic representation of women in the reporting of rape trials) we will discover more about the relation between language use and patriarchal ideology to which not only men but a great many women also subscribe.

What is stressed both in the semiologists' approach and in my own register-based approach is the *materiality* of the practices in question. Thus rather than posit, as Dale Spender does, a historically ubiquitous and unobservable operation by which males regulate meaning through an underlying semantic rule pejorating words for women, linguistic materialists look for the historical moment and circumstances in which a particular practice arose and the specific group who initiated it or whose authority and interests maintain it. We rarely find that a practice is initiated/maintained by all men (an exception might be the practice of pornoglossic intimidation discussed in Chapter 4)* or that extends into every linguistic register. The negative relation of women not to 'language' or 'meaning' but to various discourses is a variable and piecemeal affair.

Nevertheless, it seems to me that ultimately this piecemeal linguistic dis-advantage must be related to the general roles and representations of women in their various cultures. Not every area of language use is regulated by obvious and consciously invoked conventions, and we must now turn to the part played be folklinguistic value judgements and gender-role expectations in silencing women and representing their speech as inadequate. We must consider in particular the Dalston Study Group's assertion that women's day-to-day language is under-valued even by women themselves, and that the disadvantaged 'doubt the strength and potential of their own language'.[14] Is women's language in fact strong and full of potential, or is it repressed/suppressed, impoverished and inauthentic? How could women be persuaded to suppress or undervalue their own speech? To answer these questions we will need to look at the creation and regulation of femininity itself.

Silence: a woman's glory?

Some very obviously male-dominated metalinguistic practices are the customs and traditions of public speaking, which normally require women to be silent in

---

* Not included in this extract.

public gatherings and on formal occasions. The key to this cross-culturally widespread phenomenon is, as Jenkins and Kramarae observe, the boundary between the private or familial, and the public or rhetorical. 'We find that women's sphere includes the interpersonal but seldom the rhetorical.'[15] In many societies different linguistic registers, dialects or even languages are used to mark the private/rhetorical boundary. And it is part of women's role generally, not just linguistically, to symbolize the private as opposed to the public. When this split is important in organizing a society (as in most capitalist societies) women are important in defining the boundaries of the private.

An illustration of female marginality in the public and ritual speech of our own culture is provided by the etiquette of the wedding reception. Here we have a number of visible roles distributed between males and females equally: bride and groom, mothers and fathers, bridesmaids and best man, etc. Yet the women are ritually silent. The bride's father proposes a toast to the happy couple; the groom replies, proposing a toast to the bridesmaids which is replied to by the best man. Men speak, women are spoken for: here we have an epitome of women's position as 'seen and not heard'.

Is this the same as children being 'seen and not heard?' Cora Kaplan, in her essay 'Language and Gender', argues that it is.[16] Children are subject to restrictions on their speech in adult company, but whereas boys are eventually admitted to public speaking rights (Kaplan fixes this at puberty, the onset of adulthood and symbolically the beginning of manhood) girls are never allowed to grow up in the same way. Their participation in political, literary, formal, ritual and public discourse is not tolerated in the same way that children's participation is not. This view seems to me to be open to a number of objections, the main one being that restrictions on women speaking are often far stricter than those affecting children, and appear to be linked with explicitly *sexual* rites of passage. I am thinking here of the many taboos on women's speech discussed by Ardener and Smith.[17] It is not uncommon to find women being forbidden to speak for a set period after marriage, or to find men censuring the conduct of married women who allow their voices to be heard outside the private house.[18] Books of etiquette and advice to brides also warn that a married woman must underline her wifely deference with wifely silence. In other words, silence is part of femininity, rather than being an absence of male privilege.

Unaccustomed as I am . . .

Women as public speakers suffer not only from the customs that silence them, but also from negative value-judgements on their ability to speak effectively at all. Whatever style a culture deems appropriate to the public arena, women are said to be less skilled at using; whatever style is considered natural in women is deemed unsuitable for rhetorical use. So, for example, Jespersen thinks indirectness typical of women's style, mentioning 'their instinctive shrinking from coarse and gross expressions and their preference for refined and . . . veiled and indirect expressions'.[19] This lack of 'vigour and vividness' is what makes women unfit to be great orators. Among the Malagasy, however, things are rather different. Here the favoured style for ritual speech or *Kabary* is indirect and allusive. Women's speech is thought to be direct and vigorous, and thus women are once again debarred from public speaking.[20]

It is necessary, as always, to treat the interaction between actual usage and folklinguistic stereotype with the utmost care. The excessively ladylike style 'described' by Jespersen is unlikely ever to have been used consistently by women: it is the usual idealization based on the usual mixture of prejudice and wishful thinking. But folklinguistic beliefs are never without significance, and certainly this kind of belief, expressed in a score of passages masquerading as description in anti-feminist tracts, etiquette books, grammars and even feminist writings, have an effect on how women think they speak and how they think they ought to speak. In formal situations where speech is monitored closely, women may indeed converge toward the norms of the mythology, obeying the traditional feminine commandments (silence, not interrupting, not swearing and not telling jokes).

Value

Folklinguistics inculcates an important set of value judgements on the speech and writing of the two sexes. A whole vocabulary exists denigrating the talk of women who do not conform to male ideas of femininity: nag, bitch, strident. More terms trivialize interaction between women: girls' talk, gossip, chitchat, mothers' meeting. This double standard of judgement is by no means peculiar to linguistic matters. It follows the general rule that 'if in anti-feminist discourse women are often inferior to men, nothing in this same discourse is more ridiculous than a woman who imitates a male activity and is therefore no longer a woman'.[21] This can apply not only to speaking or writing, but also to the way a woman looks, the job she does, the way she behaves sexually, the leisure pursuits she engages in, the intellectual activities she prefers and so on *ad infinitum*. Sex differentiation must be rigidly upheld by whatever means are available, for men can be men only if women are unambiguously women.

This imperative leads to an attitude toward the upbringing of women summed up in 1762 by Jean-Jacques Rousseau:

> In order for [women] to have what they need . . . we must give it to them, we must want to give it to them, we must consider them deserving of it. They are dependent on our feelings, on the price we put on their merits, on the value we set on their attractions and on their virtues . . . Thus women's entire education should be planned in relation to men. To please men, to be useful to them, to win their love and respect, to raise them as children, care for them as adults, counsel and console them, make their lives sweet and pleasant: these are women's duties in all ages and these are what they should be taught from childhood on.[22]

In this notorious passage Rousseau gives us an account of why this sort of femininity must be constructed (to make men's lives 'sweet and pleasant'), how it is constructed (by indoctrination from childhood) and why women conform (because they are entirely dependent on men for the things they need).

Language, like every other aspect of female behaviour, has to be produced and regulated with this male-defined femininity in mind. Parental strictures, classroom practices and so on are designed to make the girl aware of her responsibility, and failure to conform may be punished with ridicule, loss of affection, economic and physical hardship. In short, then, we must treat the restrictions on women's language as part of a more general restricted feminine role. We cannot understand women's relation to language or to any other cultural phenomenon, unless we examine how in different societies those with power have tailored customs and institutions so they fit Rousseau's analysis and obey his prescription.

The limits of control

This model of male dominance locates the linguistic mechanisms of control both in explicit rules and well-known customs restricting women's speech, and in the 'voluntary' constraints women place on themselves to be feminine, mindful of the real disadvantages attendant on failure. Since these mechanisms are not located in immutable mental or unconscious structures, control can only be partial, and even women's silence has its limits.

The more radical feminist theorists have often been unduly pessimistic because they did not acknowledge the limits of control and silence. When Dale Spender claims,

> One simple . . . means of curtailing the dangerous talk of women is to restrict their opportunities for talk. . . . Traditionally, for women there have been no comparable locations to the pub which can encourage woman talk; there have been no opportunities for talk like those provided by football or the union meeting. Because women have been without the space and the place to talk they have been deprived of access to discourse *with each other*.[23]

she is simply wrong. If Spender is thinking here of the captive wife's alone with small children in an isolated flat, this is a relatively recent and restricted phenomenon. Even in middle-class Anglophone culture women's talk with each other is an important part of social organization:[24] in other cultures, where segregation is often the norm both occupationally and socially, women's lives revolve around interaction with each other.

Spender is trying to make a case for the subversive nature of women's talk with each other, but by ignoring the age-old oral culture of women (as she must, to argue this case convincingly) she misleads us into accepting what is only a half-truth. Women's talk is not subversive per se: it becomes subversive when women begin to attach importance to it and to privilege it over their interactions with men (as in the case of consciousness-raising). Men trivialize the talk of women not because they are afraid of any such talk, but in order to make women themselves downgrade it. If women feel that all interaction with other women is a poor substitute for mixed interaction, and trivial compared with the profundities of men's talk, their conversations will indeed be harmless.

Women's talk: the myth of impoverishment

Recently, feminists have begun to research women's talk. The picture that emerges from their studies is not one of silent or inarticulate women who struggle to express their experiences and feelings. On the contrary, it is of a rich verbal culture.[25] Moreover, that culture has a long history (if obscure: male metalinguistic practices strike again, this time by omission). It may be appropriate to see early women poets breaking through silence and absence, working in a genre where they were insecure and had no rights, but the ordinary women speaker in her peer group cannot be adequately treated in this way.

To sociolinguists this story will have a familiar ring to it. One of the most celebrated achievements of sociolinguistics in the 1960s and early 1970s was to put working-class black American speech on the map through painstaking study of the vernacular black speakers used amongst themselves. Before the sociolinguist Labov and his associates undertook this research, using a methodology specifically designed to win the informants' co-operation (see Chapter 3),* conventional wisdom among commentators on black language was that its speakers developed silent and inarticulate because they grew up in a linguistically deprived culture, were seldom addressed by their parents and not encouraged to speak themselves. The dialect they came to school speaking was labelled 'a basically non-logical form of expressive behaviour' or, in the terms of Bernstein a *restricted code*.[26]

Bernstein's code theory (which was developed with the English class structure, rather than American ethnic differences, in mind) holds that the two types of socialization typical of the middle and working classes respectively, give rise to differing relations to language. The middle-class child controls both a restricted code (roughly emotional, illogical, inexplicit and incorrect, useful for expressing group solidarity and feeling) and an elaborated code (which facilitates higher cognitive operations through its logic and explicitness). The working-class child controls only restricted code, and thus her ability to perform the sort of intellectual tasks expected at school is limited.

The claim that black children were restricted code only speakers, therefore, was an attempt to explain why they failed, or underachieved relative to white children, at school. It led to a compensatory education project in which children were taught the appropriate elaborated code (i.e. white middle-class English). The sociolinguist Labov showed that this project, and the premises underlying it, were fundamentally misguided.[27] For one thing, the linguistic features defining elaborated code turned out to be nothing more than an amalgam of middle-class habits (like use of the passive and the pronoun *one*): it was hard to argue they had any inherent value. The features stigmatized in black English were not failed attempts at standard English, but systematic variations, or more accurately, parts of a related but different dialect. In other words, it was (and is) fundamentally unclear whether there is such a thing as a restricted code which is unable to express complex ideas, logical relationships and so on.

In the second place, Labov demonstrated that black children grow up in an extremely stimulating verbal culture with its own rituals. Individuals who at school were silent or inarticulate were very likely to metamorphose, within their peer group, into skilled verbal performers. To unearth the rich verbal culture of black adolescents, Labov had to go to a great deal of trouble, for they did not willingly display it to white outsiders – which was why successive experiments had failed to elicit anything but silence and inarticulacy. Labov used a young black fieldworker to elicit a wide range of data, and in analysing it he deliberately abandoned his educated middle-class notions of correctness and formality. Labov concluded that black children failed in school mainly because they had no motivation to succeed. They defined themselves in opposition to dominant white values, and to be fully integrated members of their peer group they had to express disdain for formal education.

Other studies of nonstandard language users (to use the term *restricted code*

* Not included in this extract.

would be to beg the question linguistically, as I have already pointed out) stress that there is a linguistic problem, but not in the language itself so much as in the stigma people attach to it. In other words, the theory of codes could be boiled down to an essentially political truism: those who do not speak the language of the dominant elite will find it difficult to get on.

I have dealt with Bernstein's code theory in detail because I think there are parallels in it with the case of women, and that feminists could learn a number of lessons from the controversy it provoked.

Women are not in quite the same position as working-class and black speakers. Their language is less obviously different from men's than working-class from middle-class or black from white varieties, and the differences are much more often below the level of speakers' consciousness. Nor has anyone yet suggested that women's speech variety is responsible for massive educational under-achievement. In many respects, however, women's language has been treated as if it were a type of restricted code. And this evaluation has come both from feminists (who speak of the silence and inarticulacy of women and their culture, and of the inauthenticity with which they have been forced to express themselves) and by old fashioned gallants and chauvinists. Jespersen, for instance, presents the features which typify female speech as products of an impoverished cognitive apparatus whose shortcomings are surprisingly similar to those detailed by Bernstein in his descriptions of restricted-code speakers. Even the linguistic hallmarks of restricted code and women's language are the same: a preference for conjoining over the more complex embedding, unfinished sentences, and a heavy reliance on intonation rather than more 'explicit' syntactic devices.[28] Writers agree, in short, that there are various things women's language is inadequate to express.

Except in so far as it applies to all communication, this strikes me as a false and dangerous belief. Perhaps research now being done on women in small groups, on female folklore and culture, will break it down, both by showing that women have rich and complex verbal resources, and by proving that the folklinguistic consensus on women's speech style is inaccurate. Researchers in this latter area should focus, as I have tried to do in this book, on the connections and similarities between feminist and anti-feminist folklinguistic beliefs, and on the importance of value judgements in producing what disadvantage women do suffer as speakers and writers.

It is also important to make explicitly the connection between *women* as disadvantaged speakers and the disadvantaging of other subordinate groups such as ethnic minorities and the working class. Such groups could certainly learn from the WLM's* refusal to ignore questions of language and politics; on the other hand, the WLM in making those links might be moved to revalue certain theoretical excesses.

As the Dalston Study Group observe, 'Immigrants and working-class people too have a negative point of entry into our culture, something no one has yet explained with reference to the penis/phallus.'[29] If language is an important political and personal resource, feminism cannot afford a theory that tells women only how they are oppressed as speakers: it must convince them also of 'the strength and potential of their own language'.

Although the nature of communication is such that men cannot appropriate

* Women's Liberation Movement

meaning nor completely control women's use of language, they (or a subset of them) control important institutions and practices. The effect of that control is to give men certain rights over women and to hedge women around with restrictions and myths. Its mechanisms range from explicit rules against women speaking in public or on ritual occasions to folk-linguistic beliefs and values denigrating women's language and obscuring female verbal culture. These rules, prescriptions and beliefs can be related on the one hand to femininity in general, and on the other, to the linguistic and cultural subordination of other oppressed groups.

Whereas the current feminist belief in determinism, male control and female alienation offers very little prospect of struggle and liberation, we get a more hopeful picture when we concentrate on metalinguistic and discursive processes linked to women's identity and role in particular societies. These processes can be challenged much more easily and effectively than *langue*, meaning, alienation and other such abstractions.

13

Language and social behaviour: restrictions and revelations

Christopher Hammonds

From Hammonds, Christopher W. 1980: Language and social behaviour: restrictions and revelations. *English Teaching Forum* 18 (1), 15–24. [Introductory and concluding paragraphs omitted, and extract slightly revised by the author.]

In the first part of this article, I shall examine some of the linguistic and communicative restrictions within the English language. The second part looks briefly at the way our speech reveals to our hearers what kind of people we are.

Restrictions at various levels

As is the case with all other languages, English operates on a number of levels. Each level is a system with its own rules, and a proper use of the language implies correct application of these rules at each level. In this way our usage may be termed 'acceptable,' that is, acceptable according to the norms tacitly agreed on by native speakers of the language. The existence of rules, and the necessity of adhering to them, implies restriction, and since the system at each level of the language has its own rules, we find restrictions at each of these levels.

At the *phonological level* English cannot, for example, accept certain consonant clusters, even though they may be perfectly pronounceable and acceptable in other languages. For example, */fst/or */ʃtʃ/ in word-initial position. (Both of these clusters occur in Polish.)

At the *syntactic level* Standard English cannot accept a sentence such as *I is seen him. However, within the grammatical system of nonstandard Black English of the United States (Black English vernacular) such a sentence, as an emphatic statement, is quite acceptable. Standard English would here require the use of the verb HAVE instead of BE, and the Standard English first-person form would be different from the third-person form.

At the *semantic level* the American linguistician Chomsky's well-known example *Colourless green ideas sleep furiously* rather dramatically illustrates how a sentence may fulfill all the phonological and syntactic requirements for acceptability as a piece of English, yet still fall very short when semantic criteria are applied.

At the *suprasegmental level* English would reject the sentence *ˇ *The sunset is beautiful* with an intonation pattern consisting of a fall-rise nucleus on the first word.

---

* In writing on Linguistics an asterisk preceding a phrase or sentence conventionally means that it is unacceptable – either in terms of syntax, or semantics, or on occasions in terms of pragmatics.

At the *paralinguistic level* it would be strictly against the rules of the language for a speaker to wear a broad, sincere smile while uttering the words *Come over here for a minute and I'll kick your teeth down your throat!*

At the *contextual level* we find that any utterance is governed by what came before it and governs what will follow it. Equally, it is governed by what did not come before it and it prohibits certain utterances from following it. To the question *Excuse me, could you tell me the time, please?* the following phrase would not be an acceptable answer: *The Romanian Orthodox Church.* However, care must be taken when judging acceptability at the contextual level. We must examine as broad a context as possible, not just the immediate surroundings. For example, the question and answer *Do you admit that? Yes, of course it was* appear to be quite unacceptable as a sequence until we learn that the sentence which preceded them was *A revolver was found in your hand-luggage.* [Heard on a BBC World Service play for radio, 1976.]

At the *sociocultural level* the rules are just as binding and the restrictions just as limiting as at the other language levels. They are, however, more subtle, less easily examinable, and consequently more problematic for the foreign learner of the language.

It is, for example, totally unacceptable in most parts of the world to say to a woman within days of her husband's death: *I'm terribly sorry to hear your husband has just died, but don't let it upset you too much. You're an attractive woman, I'm sure you'll find someone else soon.* The sentiments expressed here may be very well intentioned and genuinely sympathetic, but if they are uttered at all, the rules of acceptable language usage demand that they be uttered to a third person about the bereaved, and not to the bereaved person herself.

Just as there are times when silence is considered appropriate in our society and culture, there are other times when prolonged silence embarrasses us. 'Neutral' topics, such as the weather, are useful fillers on such occasions. However, to the neighbour or stranger who happens to be standing waiting at the same bus stop and who avoids silence by making a comment such as *Ooh, isn't it windy this morning?* the following reply would be not only unacceptable but even absurd, irrespective of the accuracy of its content: *Yes, it's from the north-northwest, force 5, and causing a certain amount of rain to fall on the high ground about 35 miles west of here.* Equally unacceptable, in most cases, would be a long, detailed list of maladies as a reply to the question *How are you?* even if the list was an accurate description of the speaker's state of health.

The roles played by sarcasm or understatement are sometimes particularly difficult for the foreign learner to grasp, and failure to detect their use or significance might result in quite serious misunderstanding. The recently publicized case of an immigrant trying to adapt to a new country's conventions provides us with a useful – and true – example.

The individual concerned habitually arrived late for his work at the factory and on the day in question was greeted by his English boss with the words: *I'm so glad to see you actually managed to make the effort to come to work in time for the morning tea break, Mr. S!* The person addressed was not aware of the sarcasm intended, and so did not interpret the comment as a reprimand, but felt genuinely happy at having pleased his boss. His reply, reflecting his own lack of a perception that something was amiss, was not only quite inappropriate, but actually served to inflame an already explosive situation.

What our speech reveals about us

Having described the levels of English and having briefly illustrated some of the restrictions that apply at each of those levels, let us now examine the ways in which our speech is a revelation of ourselves and of our backgrounds.

Perhaps the most obvious revelatory aspect of our speech is in terms of our *geographical origin* or background. Most native speakers of English are able, with a fair degree of accuracy, to detect from a person's accent (that is, mode of pronunciation) whether he is also a native speaker, and, if so, from which part of the English-speaking world he originates. Most Britons have difficulty in distinguishing between the accents of Canada and the United States, and also between Australian and New Zealand accents of English, but it is probably true to say that within their own country most native speakers are able to recognize several broad categories of accents on a North/South/East/West basis and even, in many cases, on an urban-versus-rural basis. Dialect (that is, a variety of the language which differs to some extent in syntax and lexis from the standard variety), in addition to accent, may be a significant factor in enabling us to identify each other's geographical backgrounds, especially within the boundaries of our own country.

A second revelation from our speech concerns our *educational background*. Generally speaking, the greater the extent of our formal education the more likely we are habitually to use the standard variety of the language rather than a nonstandard dialect.

In Britain, prior to the days of universally available free state education, it was possible to discern whether a person was educated not only from his dialect (that is, standard versus nonstandard) but also from his accent. Since almost all organized secondary education was conducted by the so-called public schools (that is, the elitist, prestigious, old established schools such as Eton, Harrow, and Winchester, which were in private hands and which demanded considerable fees or aristocratic connections from their pupils), and since the predominant accent in these residential establishments was RP (Received Pronunciation, meaning that it was the pronunciation received [that is, accepted] in the best social circles), it followed that anyone speaking RP was educated, at least to secondary, and possibly to tertiary level. Conversely, anyone speaking with a broad regional accent of English was unlikely to have received more than a rudimentary education.

Nowadays, with the vast majority of the population obtaining their education through the state system rather than through the public schools, RP is no longer the indicator it used to be. Today, the use of RP generally points to the kind, and not the degree, of education which a person has received, so we can say that only a small proportion of the well-educated classes are RP speakers.

Quite apart from dialect and accent, our speech is likely to reveal something of our educational background through the sophistication, or otherwise, of our language. This will involve such things as range of vocabulary and the number and kinds of registers (that is, varieties of the language according to subject matter) in which we are able to operate competently and efficiently.

Our *social background* may also be revealed by our speech. In Britain this will be reflected to some extent in our particular accent and probably also in our choice of lexical items. Certain words tend to be used by, and associated with, certain social classes at particular periods of time. For example, in Britain during the last twenty-five years the individual person's use of the word *sweet* rather than the roughly synonymous *dessert* or *pudding*, or of *lavatory* rather than *toilet* or *loo* ('polite' slang), or of *napkin* rather than *serviette* has often been a fairly accurate indicator of the social class to which he belongs or to which he aspires. This last point is particularly important and relevant. It is a well-established fact that one of the major forces behind language change and development and the adoption or abandoning of particular items of vocabulary is mere fashion. A certain social class adopts or encourages the use of a particular phrase or word, and by its use the individual establishes or asserts his membership in that social class. (The same process is at work with the phenomenon of slang, where a subgroup [for example, jazz musicians, sailors, drug addicts, college students, prostitutes] uses particular words or phrases as badges of membership in the group.)

However, once the phrase or word becomes generally associated with a social group with which others wish to be identified, the language item gains wider currency and may eventually come to be replaced by a new (or old) item by the social group which originally fostered its use. Since words and phrases go in and out of fashion in this way, we are often able, at a particular point in time, to make fairly accurate statements about an individual's social background from his use of such items.

'Situation' – which will be specifically discussed below – along with the formality or informality of an occasion, is a significant factor in determining language use. But in addition to these factors, social class, status, and prestige often have a very direct influence on the words different people will use in comparable situations. It used to be remarked, semi-humorously, that 'men sweat, gentlemen perspire, and ladies glow.' Humour apart, if we imagine three different people in an unpleasantly hot situation: a working-class labourer digging a hole in the road on a hot day, a business executive playing squash energetically, and a society debutante dancing in a crowded room, we can without too much difficulty imagine that each would use very different expressions to indicate that he or she was uncomfortably hot. As we rise in the social scale we are more likely to avoid direct reference to bodily functions, euphemism or indirect reference apparently being considered more appropriate. (The use of understatement, particularly in Britain, is also more often associated with the higher social groups.) It is possible, of course, that linguistic differences of this kind may, to some extent at least, be a reflection of the fact that upper-class people tend to be exposed to formal situations to a greater extent than people from the lower strata of society.

'*Intelligence*' and '*personality*' are problematic concepts, but they figure importantly in our assessment of others, and the way a person uses language (spoken and written) causes us to infer facts about both. The greater the mental powers, the more likely a person is to use language creatively and inventively, to control and manipulate speech with precision and dexterity, to display mental agility, and to demonstrate wit through linguistic subtlety. Similarly, it is normally assumed that the ability to present one's thoughts clearly and logically in speech betokens intelligence.

In the same manner, personality traits such as sycophancy, aggression, and dogmatism will be detectable (or thought to be detectable!) to a fellow native-speaker in a person's use of the spoken language. We can easily tell from a person's speech whether or not they are sympathetic to us. At each level of the language the speaker offers clues: his tone of voice, loudness of delivery, typical stress patterns and sentence rhythm, predominant intonation tunes, facial expression and gesture, in addition to actual choice of words (that is, the content of the speech) – all of these will provide information about his personality.

Our *mood*, though relatively transitory, will be displayed by much the same linguistic means as our personality. For example, tone of voice and rate of delivery will convey a speaker's boredom, laziness, or sleepiness to the ear of the listener, and we are all able to whine or laugh in our speech, according to the mood or whim of the moment.

Role relationships and kinship – often very complicated in themselves – are paralleled in complexity in our linguistic means of dealing with them. A grand-father, for example, speaks differently to his son than to his grandson. The grandson, in his turn, speaks differently to his grandfather than to his school-mates. He will, possibly, also vary his mode of speech to his grandfather according to whether they are alone or in the company of others (for example, the boy's mother). Forms of address (for example, use of surname, or first name, or title plus surname) reflect the roles and status of the interlocutors in relation to each other. A trade union representative, or shop steward, will probably address his fellow workers differently when acting in his capacity as a union representa-tive (for example, at a strike meeting) than when working alongside them on the production line. Similarly, though a man might be in a position of authority over a colleague at work, either through seniority or skill, when the two men meet as ordinary members of a religious congregation their status will be equal in that situation. This temporary change of status may well be paralleled in the way they speak to each other, though the different environment and probable difference in topic must, of course, be partly responsible for any such change in speech behaviour.

Our *age and sex* tend also to be revealed in our spoken use of the language. (In some non-English-speaking societies any such differences are not mere tendencies. There may be strict, inviolable rules governing speech usage according to the sex or age of the individual.) A child's speech will not be the same as the speech of an old person. Generally speaking, the older we become the more conservative we are in our speech habits. An adolescent's speech will differ from that of his parents. (One obvious difference is in the fairly widespread use of rapidly changing slang forms among school and college students.)

Since society and language are so intimately bound together, it follows that change in the one will normally imply some changes in the other. With women's liberation movements bringing about some quite radical changes in women's attitudes and behaviour, particularly in the United States, it is hardly surprising that women's use of language is also undergoing many changes. Until fairly recent times the use of swear words (especially the 'stronger' ones) has been a predominantly male activity, but there are significant indications of rapidly increasing usage by women of all classes and ages, though, as one might expect, the tendency is stronger among the younger age groups.

Many men tend to avoid using words, expressions, and even pronunciations that they feel are weak-sounding or have feminine connotations. They prefer to use words such as *knives, forks, and spoons* rather than the collective (and perhaps more refined) term *cutlery*; or *cups and saucers* rather than *china*, for example. *Crystal* sounds more delicate than *glassware*, and to a specialist would almost certainly signify a difference in quality, but many men would hesitate to use the word, preferring instead to use the more mundane *glasses*, even if the vessels in question were of the finest quality.

With regard to pronunciation there is strong evidence to show that women in general (lower-middle-class women in particular) in the United States and Great Britain are much more conscious of accents than are men. As a rule women tend to use a pronunciation phonetically nearer to the generally accepted 'prestige' pronunciation than do men of equivalent social class. Furthermore, their pronunciation changes much more drastically than men's in the direction of the prestige pronunciation when they are in formal situations. This tendency indicates considerably more linguistic insecurity on the part of women (especially lower-middle-class women) and a much greater awareness of the prestige forms and desire to approximate to them than is the case with men. There is evidence, too, than many men associate strong regional or urban accents with roughness and masculinity, and in England probably a majority of working men living in the Midlands and North consider that certain southern English vowels sound affected or even effeminate. It is, of course, fairly obvious that such judgments are not based on any inherent qualities of the vowels themselves. Since the life-style in south-east England is, for the most part, more luxurious and 'softer' than life in the industrial Midlands and North, the speech of southerners is felt to reflect their more 'pampered' existence and therefore becomes a symbol of it.

As already mentioned, the *situation* in which a communication act is taking place reveals itself in our speech. It is, of course, the decisive factor in determining the relative formality/informality of our language at a particular moment. For example, though we might swear quite loudly at a friend who inadvertently steps on our foot on the terraces at the football match, we would probably change the volume of our speech and the actual words – to say nothing of any accompanying gestures – if the identical act were to occur inside a place of worship. Situation is, then, most obviously concerned with the speech environment (that is, the physical realities surrounding the speech act), but it also includes other factors such as the number of people present, the number of interlocutors (as opposed to noninvolved or nonparticipating bystanders), and whether the event has been planned in advance or is simply spontaneous.

Finally, and of equal importance to all the previously discussed revelatory aspects of our speech, we come to *attitude*. When we speak, unless we are making a special effort to disguise our true feelings, we normally reveal our attitude to the interlocutor(s), to the topic, and to the situation. Through the various linguistic and paralinguistic means at our disposal our speech will reflect whether we feel ill at ease or relaxed, whether we feel nervous or confident, hostile or friendly, and so on.

As an example we may consider two old friends from university days who have made names for themselves as a successful politician and a successful television reporter, respectively. The reporter may interview his friend before the cameras, but we may be sure that, however informal and relaxed the interview might seem to be, the answers given will largely be governed by the attitude of the politician to the reporter in his professional capacity, to the topic as a seriously posed question, and to the situation (that is, a television studio whose cameras will project the interview before millions of potential voters).

The same question put to the politician by his old friend over a pint of beer in a pub might get a very different response. If the politician considers the question to be absurd or irrelevant he will, in all likelihood, say so. His attitude to the reporter in his role as an old friend, his attitude to the topic, which he thinks foolish, and his attitude to the situation, which allows informality and honesty, will permit him to say, for example, 'Oh, come on, Alan! What a daft question! You know perfectly well that . . .' and so on.

14

Fiction and reportage: two accounts compared

David Lodge

From Lodge, David 1977: *The modes of modern writing: metaphor, metonymy, and the typology of modern literature*. London: Edward Arnold, 9–17, 246–51. 'Michael Lake describes what the executioner actually faces' is from *The Guardian* 9 April 1973; 'A Hanging' by George Orwell was first published in the *Adelphi*, August 1931.

George Orwell's 'A Hanging'* is undoubtedly part of 'English Literature', but surely, it may be objected, it is a factual document, and to say that it is literature because we can read it as if it were fiction can only deprive it of its main claim to be valued, namely that it is telling the truth, making us 'face the facts' of capital punishment.

When I first read 'A Hanging' I certainly assumed that it was a true story, an eye-witness account. The more I studied it, the more I suspected that Orwell had added or altered some details for literary effect, but I did not doubt that the piece was essentially factual and historical. I think this is probably the response of most readers of 'A Hanging' – certainly nearly all the published commentary on it assumes that it is, like its companion piece 'Shooting an Elephant', a true story based on Orwell's own experience. The exception is the interesting biography of Orwell's early years, *The Unknown Orwell* (1972) by Peter Stansky and William Abrahams. They have interviewed Orwell's friend Mabel Fierz, who was largely responsible for getting *Down and Out in London and Paris* (1933) published and whom he met in 1930. They report:

> he appears to have told her things he told no-one else – from a literary point of view, the most sensational confidence was that his essay 'A Hanging' which came out in the *Adelphi* the next winter† was not, as it purported to be, an eye-witness account but a work of the imagination, for (she remembers him telling her) he had never been present at a hanging.[1]

Stansky and Abrahams have also talked to Orwell's colleagues in the Burmese police force, who agreed that

> It would have been most unusual, though not impossible . . . for him to have been present at a hanging. As Headquarters ASP [Assistant Superintendent of Police] at Insein his duties would not normally require his presence there.[2]

Writing in *The Road to Wigan Pier* (1937) about his experience of administering the British Empire, Orwell says, 'I watched a man hanged once. It seemed to me worse than a thousand murders'[3] – which appears to be a fairly clear reference to,

---

* See Appendix A. Figures in square brackets refer to the numbered paragraphs of this text.
† Actually August 1931.

and authentication of, 'A Hanging'. But Stansky and Abrahams show that Orwell, like most of us, did not always tell the strict truth, either in conversation or in print. So there is at least an element of doubt about the eye-witness authenticity of 'A Hanging', a possibility that it is a fiction.

To entertain this possibility may be a shock at first, involving a sense of having been deceived. But on reflection we can see, I think, that the factors which made us read the text as an eye-witness account are mainly *external* to the text. First, most of us read it, no doubt, in a volume of Orwell's essays, a context which implies that it is a factual, rather than a fictional account. The volumes of essays in which it appeared, *Shooting an Elephant* (1950) and *Collected Essays* (1961) were, however, posthumous publications: Orwell himself was not responsible for placing 'A Hanging' in this non-fiction context. In his lifetime the piece was published only twice – in the *Adelphi* for August 1931 and in the *New Savoy* in 1946. Secondly, we read 'A Hanging' knowing that George Orwell was a police officer in Burma, a job which he grew to detest and repudiate, but one that would plausibly enough involve him in witnessing an execution. We may, indeed, read 'A Hanging' with that reference in *The Road to Wigan Pier* at the back of our minds.

The original readers of 'A Hanging' in the *Adelphi* had no such knowledge of its author. 'Eric A. Blair', as the piece was signed (he did not adopt the name George Orwell until 1933) was known to them only as the author of a few book reviews in the same periodical and of a first-person sketch of a weekend spent in an English workhouse – 'The Spike' – published in April 1931, and later incorporated into *Down and Out in Paris and London*. The text of 'A Hanging' itself gives no information about the 'I' figure who narrates: no explanation of why he is present at the hanging, or what his function is supposed to be. This absence would have been more striking to the original readers than it is to us, who read back into the text all the biographical information we have acquired about George Orwell/Eric Blair, much of which he himself supplied in his books from 1936 onwards. Stansky and Abrahams observe the same ambiguity about the 'I' figure in 'The Spike' and in *Down and Out*, which Orwell was writing at about the same time. They argue that the invention of this narrator, originally in 'The Spike', was the crucial technical breakthrough in Eric Blair's early struggles to find a style for himself that was not hopelessly derivative and conventionally 'literary'.

> The material he had accumulated until now had to be reinvented if he was to use it truthfully – which meant not a surface honesty but to get under the surface (any honest reporter could take care of the surface) and get down to the essence of it. He began to write in the first person without intervention: simply, I was there.[4]

But since the focus was to be on '*there*', the personal history of '*I*' had to be rigorously curtailed. (Stansky and Abrahams plausibly suggest that Blair adopted the pseudonym 'George Orwell' when *Down and Out* was published not, as he claimed, because he feared the book would be a failure, but to reinforce the anonymity of the narrator. They also show how he rather clumsily attempted to conceal the fact that he had collected much of the material by deliberately posing as a down-and-out).

It is very unlikely, at this date, that we shall ever be able to establish definitely whether Orwell attended a hanging or not, and more or less impossible that we should ever be able to check the particular circumstances of 'A Hanging' against historical fact. It may be completely factual, it may be partly based on experience, or partly on the reported experience of others, or partly fictional, or wholly fictional – though the last possibility seems to me the least likely. The point I wish to make is that it doesn't really matter. As a text, 'A Hanging' is self-sufficient, self-authenticating – autotelic, to use the jargon word. The internal relationships of its component parts are far more significant than their external references. In fact, when we examine the text carefully we see that these external references – to time, place, history – have been kept down to a minimum. There are no proper names except 'Burma' and the Christian name of the head warder. There are no dates. There is no explanation of the prisoner's crime. And it is because the external references of the text are reduced in this way that the internal relationships of its component parts – what has been referred to earlier as systematic foregrounding or patterns of linguistic organization – are correspondingly important, as I shall show.

'A Hanging' is literature, therefore, not because it is self-evidently fictional, but because it does not need to be historically verifiable to 'work'. Although it is possible, and perhaps natural in some circumstances, to read 'A Hanging' as history, the text will, I believe, survive the undermining of that assumption. It is equally satisfying, equally successful read as a true story or as a fiction or as something in between, and nothing we might discover about its relationship to history will affect its status as literature.

It may seem that I am making too simple a distinction here between fiction and history, and taking a naively positivistic view of the latter. But while it is true that historians construct fictions in the sense that they inevitably select and interpret 'the facts' according to conscious or unconscious ideological predilections, no neutral or total reconstruction of the past being possible, nevertheless history is based on the assumption that there is a body of facts to be selected from and interpreted, and that our understanding of an event can be improved or revised or altered by the discovery of new facts or the invalidation of old ones.[5] There is no way in which our understanding of 'A Hanging' could be improved or revised or altered by the discovery of new facts. In this respect it contrasts instructively with an account of a hanging by Michael Lake that appeared in the *Guardian* for 9 April, 1973 under the title 'Michael Lake Describes What the Executioner Actually Faces'.* This text has many features in common with 'A Hanging', and superficially the same narrative design: the procession to the scaffold, the numbed state of the condemned man, the abrupt operation of the gallows, the whisky and the macabre joking of the officials afterwards, the narrator's residual sense of guilt. 'Michael Lake Describes . . .' seems to me a good piece of journalism, and as a polemic against capital punishment perhaps more effective than Orwell's piece. But it *is* journalism, and remains this side of literature. Its effectiveness depends on our trust that it is historically verifiable. If we discovered that there was no such person as Walter James Bolton, or that Michael Lake had never attended a hanging, the text would collapse, because it would be impossible to read it, as one can read 'A Hanging', as an effective piece of fiction. Once its external references were cut, the comparative weakness of its internal structure would become all too evident. We should become aware of clichés, opportunities missed, a lack of variety in tempo and in intensity of feeling. Details like 'Mr Alf Addison, an old friend of mine' would no longer have any function and would

* See Appendix B.

become irritating irrelevancies. And perhaps we should feel we were being bullied into the desired response by crudely sensationalist means.

Correspondingly, 'A Hanging' has certain qualities which 'Michael Lake Describes . . .' hasn't got: a narrative structure, for instance, that is more than a mere sequence. The structure of Michael Lake's report is a chain of items linked in chronological order and suspended between an opening statement of polemical intent and a closing statement of personal feeling. The structure of 'A Hanging' is also chronological, but it is more complex: the inevitable movement towards the death of the condemned man is deliberately but unexpectedly retarded at two points: first by the interruption of the dog and secondly by the prisoner's invocation of his god. These delays heighten the tension, and they allow the moral protest against capital punishment to emerge out of the narrative instead of being merely signalled at the beginning and end. Another structural difference is that Orwell's piece goes on proportionately longer after the actual execution, enforcing the double concern of the writer: not only with what the execution does to the executed but also what it does to the executioners. In a sense, this extended ending is another form of retardation, since it retards the expected termination of the text.

'Retardation' is one of the basic devices that, according to the Russian Formalist Victor Shklovsky, enable narrative art to achieve the effect of 'defamiliarization' which he held to be the end and justification of all art:

> Habitualization devours objects, clothes, furniture, one's wife and the fear of war. 'If all the complex lives of many people go on unconsciously, then such lives are as if they had never been.' Art exists to help us recover the sensation of life; it exists to make us feel things, to make the stone *stony*. The end of art is to give a sensation of the object as seen, not as recognized. The technique of art is to make things 'unfamiliar', to make forms obscure, so as to increase the difficulty and the duration of perception. The act of perception in art is an end in itself and must be prolonged. *In art, it is our experience of the process of construction that counts, not the finished product.*[6]

Although the last statement leads logically to Shklovsky's celebration of *Tristram Shandy* as the supreme example of narrative art,[7] the quotation in the second sentence is from the diary of Tolstoy, from whom Shklovsky draws several of his illustrations. In other words, there is no incompatibility between the theory of 'defamiliarization' and realistic writing of the kind Orwell practised – indeed 'A Hanging' illustrates the theory very well, for what Orwell is doing is defamiliarizing the idea of capital punishment – the idea, not the experience of it, since only the first is 'familiar'.

Michael Lake is trying to do the same thing, but by the comparatively crude method of filling out the familiar idea with unfamiliar details. He selects and describes aspects of the event he witnessed which will make us recoil from it: the possibility of Bolton's head being torn off by his own weight, the hypocrisy and/or irrelevance of the chaplain's prayers, the macabre fancy-dress of the executioner's get-up, Bolton's inarticulateness, and so on. But these details belong to quite disparate emotive categories – some are nauseating, some ironic, some pathetic – and Lake makes no attempt to relate them to each other. He fires the details at us on the principle of the shotgun: if a few miss the target, enough will hit it to make the desired effect. It would be difficult to say, on the evidence of the text, exactly what aspect of the proceedings was to him the most significant or indeed what it is, precisely, that makes capital punishment inhuman in his view.

There is no such difficulty in the Orwell text. The central paragraph [10] makes clear what the narrator feels to be wrong about capital punishment (though it is an 'unspeakable wrongness' he in fact proceeds to speak it). Interestingly, it is not the most gruesome or solemn part of the proceedings that provokes this realization, but a gesture so small and ordinary that most people, perhaps including Mr Lake, would never have noticed it (always supposing, of course, that it actually happened): the prisoner side-stepping the puddle. Why is this gesture so pregnant with meaning for the narrator? Because in the context of imminent death, it makes him understand what it is to be alive. Orwell has thus defamiliarized the idea of capital punishment by defamiliarizing something in fact much more familiar, much more veiled by habit: simply being alive. Implicitly the incident reveals that there is all the difference in the world between knowing *that* we shall die and knowing *when* we shall die. Human life exists in an open-ended continuum. We know that we shall die, but if we are healthy our minds and bodies function on the assumption that we shall go on living, and indeed they cannot function in any other way. The man instinctively avoids the trivial discomfort of stepping in the puddle on his way to the scaffold. His nails continue growing even as he falls through the air with a tenth of a second to live. So he is in the intolerable position of having to behave as if he is going to go on living, but knowing that he isn't going to. And the spectator is correspondingly impressed by the grim irony that all present are inhabiting the same continuum of experience, but that for one person it is not open-ended: 'he and we were a party of men walking together, seeing, hearing, feeling, understanding the same world' – the present participles emphasize the notions of continuity and community – 'and in two minutes, with a sudden snap, one of us would be gone – one mind less, one world less.'

There is then, in this central paragraph, an emphasis on the idea of time in relation to life and death. 'Time is life, and life is time,' runs the lyric of a modern song.[8] 'Death,' said Wittgenstein, 'is not an event *in* life. We do not live to experience death.'[9] At the level of maximum abstraction that is what 'A Hanging' is about: the paradoxical relationships between the concepts death, life and time, in the context of capital punishment. For capital punishment in a sense seeks to subvert the logic of Wittgenstein's assertion, to force the experience of death into life. That is why it is, or may be held to be, inhuman and obscene. Michael Lake is dimly aware of these paradoxes – at least I think that is why he is shocked and incredulous that the chaplain is reading aloud the Burial Service over the living man. But he hasn't quite worked out what is shocking about it, and without Orwell's piece for comparison we might not have worked it out either.

Throughout 'A Hanging' there are repeated references to the theme of life/death/time which prepare for and sustain the explicit statement of it by the narrator in paragraph 10. In the first paragraph there is the reference to the other 'condemned men due to be hanged in the next week or two'. In paragraph 3, eight o'clock strikes, and the superintendent urges the warders to hurry up: 'The man ought to have been dead by this time. . . . ' In paragraph 5 there is the remark that the prisoners can't get their breakfast until the execution is completed – a reference to the continuum of life/time that will go on without the condemned man.

Then comes the intervention of the dog. This of course is the vehicle for several kinds of ironic commentary on the action, but let us just note for the moment that it is a delay, an interruption of the proceedings and duly recorded as such by the narrator: 'It was several minutes before someone managed to catch the dog. Then we put my handkerchief through its collar and moved off once more . . . '[8]. The association of the narrator with the dog through 'my' handkerchief is interesting, perhaps a way of preparing for the narrator's moral recoil from the execution in the next paragraph, in which the personal pronoun 'I' is used for the first time, 'I' becoming distinguished from 'we'. This paragraph ends with the side-stepping of the puddle, which leads to the explicit reflection upon life/-death/time in paragraph 10.

In paragraph 12 begins the second interruption or delay: the prisoner's prayer to his god. We are now in a position to appreciate the underlying function of these two delaying or 'retarding' incidents, which as we noted above constitute the main structural feature of the narrative. If the genre were romance, or at least a narrative more overtly fictional and 'literary', these delays might be welcomed by the narrator, and vicariously by the reader, as affording some time in which a reprieve might arrive, or some rescue be effected (one thinks of *The Heart of Midlothian* or *Adam Bede*). But of course no such possibility is hinted at in 'A Hanging'. Although the narrator, in paragraph 10, recognizes the 'unspeakable wrongness' of the execution, he has no intention of trying to stop it, and neither have any of the other people present. Therefore, although for the prisoner every cry is 'another second of life', this only draws out the agony. Since he must die, the quicker the better for everyone's comfort: 'the same thought was in all our minds: oh, kill him quickly, get it over, stop that abominable noise.'[13] To the narrator, the repetition of the god's name is not 'like a prayer or cry for help' – not, that is, like human speech – but 'steady, rhythmical, almost like the tolling of a bell' – in other words, a regular notation of passing time. 'Minutes seemed to pass.' The narrator wonders if the superintendent is allowing the man a fixed number of cries, 'fifty, or perhaps a hundred'.[13]

After the execution is carried out and the body of the man has been inspected, the Superintendent glances at his watch: 'Eight minutes past eight.'[16] In paragraph 17 the procession reverses itself, minus one. There is a reference to the other condemned men waiting to die, a reference to the other prisoners receiving their breakfast – recapitulations of details in the opening paragraphs. Now the unbearable contradictions of life/death/time have been temporarily resolved and an almost hysterical wave of relief and callous good-humour flows over the witnesses, temporarily melting away conventional barriers of caste, status and race. Dialogue – direct speech – suddenly begins to dominate narrative. 'I' is absorbed back into 'we', and the ironies of time are replaced by ironies of space: 'We all had a drink together, native and European alike, quite amicably. The dead man was a hundred yards away.'[24]

One might say that Orwell has achieved the 'defamiliarization' of capital punishment by 'foregrounding' the semantic component of time in his text. There is indeed a close connection between these two concepts – defamiliarization being opposed to habitualization in Russian Formalism as fore-grounding is opposed to automatization in the poetics of the Prague school. It is to be noted, however, that the language in which the time motif is reiterated is not itself foregrounded in any obvious way either against the 'norm of the standard' or against the internal norms of the text itself (the nearest equivalent in 'A Hanging' to the foregrounded shift of tense in the last stanza of 'Sweeney Among The Nightingales'* is the shift from 'we' to 'I' in paragraph 9).

* A poem discussed earlier.

To sum up the argument so far: 'Michael Lake Describes . . .' is not axiomatically a literary text and could only become one by responding satisfactorily to a 'literary' reading. This, I suggest, it could not do. Whether or not Orwell's 'A Hanging' is axiomatically a literary text is much more problematical and the answer probably depends upon the context in which it is read, and the expectations of the individual reader. It is not foregrounded as literature in any obvious way – indeed it could be said to disguise itself as nonliterature, to merge like a chameleon into the background of writing like 'Michael Lake Describes . . .', though there are certain significant absences in the text which perhaps operate as signs of literariness at an almost subliminal level, and covertly invite a 'literary' reading. That it responds satisfactorily to a literary reading there is no doubt, and I have tried to connect this with certain features of its internal structure.

Appendix A

'A Hanging' By George Orwell

1 It was in Burma, a sodden morning of the rains. A sickly light, like yellow tinfoil, was slanting over the high walls into the jail yard. We were waiting outside the condemned cells, a row of sheds fronted with double bars, like small animal cages. Each cell measured about ten feet by ten and was quite bare within except for a plank bed and a pot of drinking water. In some of them brown silent men were squatting at the inner bars, with their blankets draped round them. These were the condemned men, due to be hanged within the next week or two.

2 One prisoner had been brought out of his cell. He was a Hindu, a puny wisp of a man, with a shaven head and vague liquid eyes. He had a thick, sprouting moustache, absurdly too big for his body, rather like the moustache of a comic man on the films. Six tall Indian warders were guarding him and getting him ready for the gallows. Two of them stood by with rifles and fixed bayonets, while the others handcuffed him, passed a chain through his handcuffs and fixed it to their belts, and lashed his arms tight to his sides. They crowded very close about him, with their hands always on him in a careful, caressing grip, as though all the while feeling him to make sure he was there. It was like men handling a fish which is still alive and may jump back into the water. But he stood quite unresisting, yielding his arms limply to the ropes, as though he hardly noticed what was happening.

3 Eight o'clock struck and a bugle call, desolately thin in the wet air, floated from the distant barracks. The superintendent of the jail, who was standing apart from the rest of us, moodily prodding the gravel with his stick, raised his head at the sound. He was an army doctor, with a grey toothbrush moustache and a gruff voice. 'For God's sake hurry up, Francis,' he said irritably. 'The man ought to have been dead by this time. Aren't you ready yet?'

4 Francis, the head jailer, a fat Dravidian in a white drill suit and gold spectacles, waved his black hand. 'Yes sir, yes sir,' he bubbled. 'All iss satisfactorily prepared. The hangman iss waiting. We shall proceed.'

5 'Well, quick march, then. The prisoners can't get their breakfast till this job's over.'

6 We set out for the gallows. Two warders marched on either side of the prisoner, with their rifles at the slope; two others marched close against him, gripping him by arm and shoulder, as though at once pushing and supporting him. The rest of us, magistrates and the like, followed behind. Suddenly, when we had gone ten yards, the procession stopped short without any order or warning. A dreadful thing had happened – a dog, come goodness knows whence, had appeared in the yard. It came bounding among us with a loud volley of barks, and leapt round us wagging its whole body, wild with glee at

finding so many human beings together. It was a large woolly dog, half Airedale, half pariah. For a moment it pranced round us, and then, before anyone could stop it, it had made a dash for the prisoner, and jumping up tried to lick his face. Everyone stood aghast, too taken aback even to grab at the dog.

7 'Who let that bloody brute in here?' said the superintendent angrily. 'Catch it, someone!'

8 A warder, detached from the escort, charged clumsily after the dog, but it danced and gambolled just out of his reach, taking everything as part of the game. A young Eurasian jailer picked up a handful of gravel and tried to stone the dog away, but it dodged the stones and came after us again. Its yaps echoed from the jail walls. The prisoner, in the grasp of the two warders, looked on incuriously, as though this was another formality of the hanging. It was several minutes before someone managed to catch the dog. Then we put my handkerchief through its collar and moved off once more, with the dog still straining and whimpering.

9 It was about forty yards to the gallows. I watched the bare brown back of the prisoner marching in front of me. He walked clumsily with his bound arms, but quite steadily, with that bobbing gait of the Indian who never straightens his knees. At each step his muscles slid neatly into place, the lock of hair on his scalp danced up and down, his feet printed themselves on the wet gravel. And once, in spite of the men who gripped him by each shoulder, he stepped slightly aside to avoid a puddle on the path.

10 It is curious, but till that moment I had never realized what it means to destroy a healthy, conscious man. When I saw the prisoner step aside to avoid the puddle, I saw the mystery, the unspeakable wrongness, of cutting a life short when it is in full tide. This man was not dying, he was alive just as we were alive. All the organs of his body were working – bowels digesting food, skin renewing itself, nails growing, tissues forming – all toiling away in solemn foolery. His nails would still be growing when he stood on the drop, when he was falling through the air with a tenth of a second to live. His eyes saw the yellow gravel and the grey walls, and his brain still remembered, foresaw, reasoned – reasoned even about puddles. He and we were a party of men walking together, seeing, hearing, feeling, understanding the same world; and in two minutes, with a sudden snap, one of us would be gone – one mind less, one world less.

11 The gallows stood in a small yard, separate from the main grounds of the prison, and overgrown with tall prickly weeds. It was a brick erection like three sides of a shed, with planking on top, and above that two beams and a crossbar with the rope dangling. The hangman, a grey-haired convict in the white uniform of the prison, was waiting beside his machine. He greeted us with a servile crouch as we entered. At a word from Francis the two warders, gripping the prisoner more closely than ever, half led, half pushed him to the gallows and helped him clumsily up the ladder. Then the hangman climbed up and fixed the rope round the prisoner's neck.

12 We stood waiting, five yards away. The warders had formed in a rough circle round the gallows. And then, when the noose was fixed, the prisoner began crying out on his god. It was a high, reiterated cry of 'Ram! Ram! Ram! Ram!, not urgent and fearful like a prayer or a cry for help, but steady, rhythmical, almost like the tolling of a bell. The dog answered the sound with a whine. The hangman, still standing on the gallows, pro-duced a small cotton bag like a flour bag and drew it down over the prisoner's face. But the sound, muffled by the cloth, still persisted, over and over again: 'Ram! Ram! Ram! Ram! Ram!'

13 The hangman climbed down and stood ready, holding the lever. Minutes seemed to pass. The steady, muffled crying from the prisoner went on and on, 'Ram! Ram! Ram!' never faltering for an instant. The superintendent, his head on his chest, was slowly poking the ground with his stick; perhaps he was counting the cries, allowing the prisoner a fixed number – fifty, perhaps, or a hundred. Everyone had changed colour. The Indians had gone grey like bad coffee, and one or two of the bayonets were wavering. We looked at the lashed, hooded man on the drop, and listened to his

cries – each cry another second of life; the same thought was in all our minds: oh, kill him quickly, get it over, stop that abominable noise!

14 Suddenly the superintendent made up his mind. Throwing up his head he made a swift motion with his stick. 'Chalo!' he shouted almost fiercely.

15 There was a clanking noise, and then dead silence. The prisoner had vanished, and the rope was twisting on itself. I let go of the dog, and it galloped immediately to the back of the gallows; but when it got there it stopped short, barked, and then retreated into a corner of the yard, where it stood among the weeds, looking timorously out at us. We went round the gallows to inspect the prisoner's body. He was dangling with his toes pointed straight downwards, very slowly revolving, as dead as a stone.

16 The superintendent reached out with his stick and poked the bare body; it oscillated, slight, 'He's all right,' said the superintendent. He backed out from under the gallows, and blew out a deep breath. The moody look had gone out of his face quite suddenly. He glanced at his wrist-watch. 'Eight minutes past eight. Well, that's all for this morning, thank God.'

17 The warders unfixed bayonets and marched away. The dog, sobered and conscious of having misbehaved itself, slipped after them. We walked out of the gallows yard, past the condemned cells with their waiting prisoners, into the big central yard of the prison. The convicts, under the command of warders armed with lathis, were already receiving their breakfast. They squatted in long rows, each man holding a tin pannikin, while two warders with buckets marched round ladling out rice; it seemed quite a homely, jolly scene, after the hanging. An enormous relief had come upon us now that the job was done. One felt an impulse to sing, to break into a run, to snigger. All at once everyone began chattering gaily.

18 The Eurasian boy walking beside me nodded towards the way we had come, with a knowing smile: 'Do you know, sir, our friend (he meant the dead man), when he heard his appeal had been dismissed, he pissed on the floor of his cell. From fright. – Kindly take one of my cigarettes, sir. Do you not admire my new silver case, sir? From the boxwallah, two rupees eight annas. Classy European style.'

19 Several people laughed – at what, nobody seemed certain.

20 Francis was walking by the superintendent, talking garrulously: 'Well, sir, all hass passed off with the utmost satisfactoriness. It wass all finished – flick! like that. It iss not always so – oah, no! I have known cases where the doctor wass obliged to go beneath the gallows and pull the prisoner's legs to ensure decease. Most disagreeable!'

21 'Wriggling about, eh? That's bad,' said the superintendent.

22 'Ach, sir, it iss worse when they become refractory! One man, I recall, clung to the bars of hiss cage when we went to take him out. You will scarcely credit, sir, that it took six warders to dislodge him, three pulling at each leg. We reasoned with him. "My dear fellow," we said, "think of all the pain and trouble you are causing to us!" But no, he would not listen! Ach, he wass very troublesome!'

23 I found that I was laughing quite loudly. Everyone was laughing. Even the superintendent grinned in a tolerant way. 'You'd better all come out and have a drink,' he said quite genially. 'I've got a bottle of whisky in the car. We could do with it.'

24 We went through the big double gates of the prison, into the road. 'Pulling at his legs!' exclaimed a Burmese magistrate suddenly, and burst into a loud chuckling. We all began laughing again. At that moment Francis's anecdote seemed extraordinarily funny. We all had a drink together, native and European alike, quite amicably. The dead man was a hundred yards away.

Appendix B

'Michael Lake Describes What the Executioner Actually Faces,' Guardian 9 April, 1973

1 It is doubtful if those who seek the reintroduction of capital punishment have ever seen

a hanging. It is a grim business, far removed from the hurly burly of Parliament, from the dusty gloom of the Old Bailey and a million light years away from the murder.

2 In New Zealand hangings were always in the evening. There were never any crowds, but three journalists were always summoned to witness the hanging. Their names were published later that night, along with those of the sheriff, the coroner and others, in the Official Gazette. I watched the last hanging in New Zealand.

3 Walter James Bolton was a farmer from the west coast of the North Island. He had poisoned his wife. He was 62, and the oldest and heaviest man ever hanged in New Zealand. They had to make sure they got the length of rope right so the drop wouldn't tear off his head.

4 I arrived at Mt Eden Gaol, Auckland, at 6 o'clock on a Monday evening. With the other witnesses I was led through the main administrative block, down some steps, and along a wing which it turned out, was a sort of Death Row.

5 We were led to the foot of the scaffold in a yard immediately at the end of the wing. The sky was darkening and a canvas canopy over the yard flapped gently in the breeze.

6 After a long time, there was a murmuring. Into view came a strange procession; the deputy governor of the prison, leading four warders and among them, walked or rather shambled the hulking figure of Bolton. His arms were pinioned by ropes to his trunk.

7 Behind him walked a parson reading aloud. It was with disbelief and shock that I recognised the Burial Service from the Book of Common Prayer.

8 High upon the scaffold, 17 steps away, the executioner stood immobile. He wore a black broad-brimmed hat, a black trench coat, and heavy boots, and he was masked. Only the slit for his eyes and his white hands gleamed in the light.

9 Bolton was helped up the steps by the warders, who bound his ankles together. The sheriff then asked him if he had anything to say before sentence was carried out.

10 Bolton mumbled. After a few seconds mumbling the parson, apparently unaware that the prisoner was talking, interrupted with further readings from the Burial Service.

11 I checked my shorthand notes with the other reporters. One, an elderly man who had witnessed 19 hangings, had heard nothing. The other man's shorthand outlines matched my own. He had said: 'The only thing I want to say is. . . .'

12 The warders did all the work. They bound him and put a white canvas hood over his head as he stood there, swaying in their grasp. Then they dropped the loop over his head, with the traditional hangman's knot, tidied it up, and stepped back.

13 The sheriff lifted his hand and lowered it. The executioner moved for the first and only time. He pulled a lever, and stepped back. Bolton dropped behind a canvas screen. The rope ran fast through the pulley at the top, and then when the Turk's Head knotted in the end jammed in the pulley, the block clanged loudly up against the beam to which it was fixed. The rope quivered, and that was the end of Walter James Bolton.

14 A doctor repaired behind the screen which hid the body from us. A hanged man usually ejaculates and evacuates his bowels. In New Zealand, at any rate he also hanged for an hour. Bolton hung while we sat back in the deputy governor's office drinking the whisky traditionally provided by the Government for these occasions – 'Who's for a long drop,' asked some macabre wit.

15 The city coroner, Mr Alf Addison, an old friend of mine, called us across to his office where we duly swore we had seen the sentence of the court carried out.

16 I went back to my newspaper office and wrote three paragraphs. No sensations, I told the night editor, the bloke hadn't made a fuss. Then I went home with a sense of loss and corruption I have never quite shed.

Section III

Perception, interactive behaviour, interpretation

'Seeing is believing', we are told from early childhood, and for many people what we see is unproblematically *true* in a way that what we read or are told is not (an assumption that has important implications for the study of the mass media).

We know that people all over the world speak different languages, and the comparison of our own speech with that of our parents or our children provides evidence that languages change over time. Language then, we can easily be led to believe, is a cultural barrier between us and objective reality, that reality which we *see* directly and objectively. 'I saw it with my own eyes' has more force than 'I read it with my own eyes'. We know that translation from one language to another is problematic, but when we see a beautiful sunset, or a photograph of a film star, or a gesturing street salesman, we assume that anyone, from no matter what culture, speaking no matter what language, would see what we see. Our Physics lessons at school taught us that the human optical system can be described in a purely technical manner, and if there is something wrong with our sight the optician does not ask about our cultural background or our political beliefs. We assume, therefore, that we all see the same world, even if we may respond to and explain it in different ways.

Such an assumption may sometimes mislead us. We hope that the previous section will have convinced you that language is as much a window on as a barrier between us and objective reality (and that both of these metaphorical views of language are really too simplistic to be very helpful). This section will concentrate mainly upon visual perception, but much of what is said can be applied to perception by means of our other senses. So far as our physical perceptions of the world are concerned there is clearly a certain truth in the assertion that we all see the same world, if what is meant by that is that (ignoring defects in our optical system) much the same messages are sent from the eyes to the brains of two people looking at the same object. But what is of interest is what happens to these messages once they reach these two different brains. (It is also relevant to ask what went on in the two different brains to lead the two people to look at the object in the first place). We believe that most readers new to the study of perception will be very surprised to find out from the first two extracts in this section how much even our simple perceptions of physical objects involve highly complex and structured processes, processes which human beings have to a certain extent to learn. And if this is true of our perception of physical objects, our perceptions of other people in person-to-person contact or in photographed or artistically portrayed form are even more complicated than may be suggested by common sense.

The editors of this Reader do not subscribe to that position of radical philosophical scepticism which holds that every individual actually creates the world that he or she perceives. But the rejection of such an extreme scepticism does not prevent our acknowledging that two different people looking at the same physical object or human being can carry away different information from their scrutiny, and may construct from that information different versions of the thing or person seen. Moreover, many aspects of the reality in which we live are not directly equatable with physical objects. Social norms, standards of beauty, interpersonal gestures – our perception of such things cannot build unproblematically upon our perception of the physical world.

Our extract from **A.R. Luria**'s *Cognitive development* is an appropriate starting point for this section, as it indicates that even simple optical illusions can be differentially perceived by people with varying cultural and educational backgrounds. Luria's work is based upon investigations carried out in Soviet Uzbekistan and Kirghizia during the late 1920s and 1930s, when enormous developments were taking place in these regions. A largely illiterate, peasant population was being transformed through the collectivization of farming and the introduction of mass education. Other cultural factors were also being radically altered; women were receiving formal education for the first time in the history of the culture, and their whole social role was being scrutinized and opened up to change.

In the previous section we saw some of Luria's findings. In the present section we can look at the evidence for his claim that if perceptual processes are not wholly *determined* by social and cultural factors, they are certainly thoroughly *conditioned* by them. We should note that this ties in with the positions advanced in item 16 in the present section, and by Bernstein in the extract from his work in the previous section. For if the authors of the former piece are correct to assert that perception is at least in part reliant upon categories provided by language, and if Bernstein is right to argue that our use of language is impregnate with social factors, then it follows logically that our perceptions can be structured and formed by social factors. This is not of course to suggest that there can be no innate predispositions involved in human perception, nor that there are no perceptual processes that are universal and supra-cultural. *Some* of the optical illusions Luria used were perceived in an identical manner by all his subjects.

Hastorf, Schneider and **Polefka** move very interestingly from an examination of people's perception of objects to that of their perception of one another. Perhaps the most stimulating aspect of their piece is its stress upon the *active* nature of our perceptions. We are not blank sheets of paper passively receiving impressions, but active agents who, individually and collectively, search out and process our perceptions. We may not make our own reality, but reality makes us work to possess aspects of it, and we interpret this information in the light of our needs and interests. Hastorf *et al.* argue that 'The categories we use are derived from our past history and are dependent on our language and our cultural background.' This is perhaps exemplified in their piece by the labellings of the ambiguous figure taken from the work of Robert W. Leeper (see p. 135 following). Why 'old hag' and 'young woman' rather than 'old woman' and 'young woman'? Changes effected in our own cultural situation and language use, largely as a result of the development of the Women's Movement in the last decade and a half, help us to perceive these figures rather differently.

The extract from **Stuart Sigman**'s book takes some of these issues a stage further. We now move from how we perceive, to how we interact with others. Rather than seeing interpersonal communication as something which *individuals* do within a space called *society*, Sigman suggests an alternative viewpoint. Communication is a *social process* involving individuals: 'Communication in this view is seen not as an individual-level phenomenon, but as a societal-level phenomenon.' Moreover, 'Just as individual persons are moments in society, so interpersonal behaviour is a moment in social communication.'

Although written earlier, **David Efron**'s piece can be said to test out the value of such an approach. For if one transports individuals at various stages of maturation to a new society and culture, what happens to their interpersonal behaviour? Efron's argument is not narrowly academic: he was replying to the theorists of Nazi 'anthropology' such as Hans Günther and Fritz Lenz, who had claimed that the amount and manner of gesticulation used by an individual, along with his or her bodily posture, were determined racially. Like Luria, Efron uses a fascinating real-life laboratory: in this case the United States of America with its population including generations of immigrants at different stages of social and cultural assimilation. In the bulk of his book Efron concentrates upon the gestural behaviour of first-generation and assimilated Jews and Italians, and convincingly demonstrates that culture rather than race is the determining factor so far as the gestures of his subjects are concerned. In the extract which we reprint in this section he gives a brief historical survey of the gestural changes in certain European societies, changes that can certainly not be accounted for in biological or racial terms. Our own contention is that so far as changes in the gestural behaviour of the British are concerned, the importance of colonialism should not be overlooked. The English 'stiff upper lip' can be seen as one element in the behaviour found appropriate to those wishing to convey their authority in front of 'subordinate' peoples. It is also the case that the Industrial Revolution involved a suppression of personal, expressive behaviour in favour of the development of disciplined habits obedient to the demands of highly organized productive processes, but one would need to explain why its effect on gestural behaviour seemingly varies so much from culture to culture.

In their piece Hastorf *et al.* assert that 'Our past learning has a significant influence on perception, but it always operates within a framework of purposive activity.' This purposive element is stressed in the opening lines of **Erving Goffman**'s discussion of 'self-presentation', which we include in this section. If we are guided by particular purposes in our encounters with physical objects, when it comes to interaction with other human beings we are also impelled by the various goals which we wish to achieve. Interacting human beings are not like billiard-balls on a table, whose movements are determined only by the forces transmitted to them and the strictly mechanical effects of other physical forces. We do not interact as isolated and autonomous beings in a mechanical manner, our mutual behaviour regulated only by pre-established, universal and unchangeable rules. We inter*act* with socially directed and culturally conditioned individuals on the basis of shared as well as private perceptions, disputed as well as common goals. And as Goffman reveals so convincingly, we interact in a manner determined by both private and public intentions, with both conscious and unconscious goals in mind.

In the previous section we suggested that after studying how various factors influenced language, a particular example of language use could be interpreted so as to 'read off' these same factors. We can make a similar point in this section. For if various social and cultural factors condition and enable our perceptions and interactions, then these factors may often in turn be read off from our accounts of our perceptions and interactions. **Wolfgang Iser**'s piece views the relationship between a text (in this case a literary one, but his argument can be extended to a range of other texts) and that text's readers as itself a form of interaction. Iser admits that this interaction differs from social interaction because of the text's inability to respond to the differential responses of various readers. Nevertheless, this comparison of our reaction to texts with our interaction with human beings is thought-provoking so far as the crucial question of *interpretation* is concerned. Human beings who look at pictures, read novels, watch films, are just as much influenced by culture and history as are human beings who perceive optical illusions and interact with one another: probably more so. Moreover, they are just as active – again, probably more so. Iser's discussion of the way in which the reader of – say – a Jane Austen novel will 'fill in the gaps' of the text is directly comparable to what Hastorf *et al.* say about the active nature of perception. And just as Efron is able to read off cultural histories from the gestures of his subjects, so too is **John Berger** able to read off social and political history from the painting by Holbein which he discusses in the extract given from his book *Ways of seeing*. As in many of the other studies in this volume, questions of communicative form are seen to relate to questions of class, race and gender, to the structures of social power.

Our final extract involves an interpretation which we might expect to be rather different: **Sigmund Freud**'s interpretation of a patient's account of a dream. And yet here again one is struck by the involvement of social and cultural factors. The role and position of women in Freud's society, the significance of such things as marriage, virginity, and sexuality in this society: the effect of all of these can be traced, if not in the dream itself, certainly in Freud's analysis. Can we imagine a woman from a very different sort of society having this dream, or an analyst from a very different society interpreting it in the same way?

Further reading

Our recommendations favour books which share our own view of the importance of studying perception, interaction and interpretation in the context of socio-cultural influences, at the expense of more purely technical studies and approaches dominated by behaviourist theories.

Bordwell, David, and Thompson, Kristin 1986: *Film art: an introduction*. Second edition. New York: Knopf.
A highly recommended introductory textbook which assumes no previous knowledge of film methods, and works through a full range of topics such as the basic styles of camera work, editing, the use of sound, the organization of

narrative, and the history of film-making. Includes some excellent extended analyses, and contains very helpful and comprehensive recommendations on further reading in the area.

Burton, Graeme and Dimbleby, Richard 1988: *Between ourselves: an introduction to interpersonal communication.* London and Baltimore: Edward Arnold.
A straightforward and very accessible introductory textbook covering intra-personal communication, the perception of others, social interaction and social skills, transactional analysis, communication in groups, and communication theory. The authors' starting point is that of the individual self, and thus their approach is different from that outlined in the extract from Stuart Sigman's book.

Gombrich, E.H. 1972: *The story of art.* Oxford: Phaidon Press.
A superb book that is as far from an aridly technical history of the visual arts as can be imagined. Gombrich explores the interpenetration of historical, cultural and technical matters in a masterly fashion, and shows how artistic representation and interpretation are always bound up both with current knowledge of the world and also with the development of technical expertise.

Morgan, John, and Welton, Peter 1986: *See what I mean: an introduction to visual communication.* London and Baltimore: Edward Arnold.
An excellent introductory textbook, very accessible and fully illustrated. This book covers many of the basic terms and issues with which it is now essential for Communication Studies students to be familiar.

Potter, Jonathan, and Wetherell, Margaret 1987: *Discourse and social psychology: beyond attitudes and behaviour.* London: Sage.
This book concentrates upon language (it was quoted in our introduction to the previous section of this Reader), but its concern with the 'texts' of social interaction ties in with many issues raised in this section. Its stress on the active nature of text-construction and interpretation is particularly useful.

Rock, Irvin 1983: *The logic of perception.* Cambridge, Mass. and London: MIT Press.
Of the many textbooks on perception currently available this is one of the most recommended, although Rock's emphasis is more technical and less socio-cultural than our own.

Webster, F. 1980: *The new photography.* London: John Calder.
This is a broadly conceived and engaging discussion of how photography is used in modern societies. Webster attempts to identify the social functions of photography (particularly those in advertising and in journalism) by using perspectives drawn from cultural anthropology. He is particularly concerned with the complex symbolic processes which photographs variously depend upon for their power and interpretation, in spite of the fact that they frequently offer themselves as direct 'capturings' of the real.

Williamson, Judith 1978: *Decoding advertisements: ideology and meaning in advertising.* London and New York: Marion Boyars.
A tightly-argued case using Marxist, structuralist and semiotic theories to 'decode' visual advertisements which are reproduced in the text. Other good textbooks on advertising have been produced since this one, including ones which have more to say about interpretative variation and the attitudes of target readerships, but the sustained force of Williamson's argument and the detail of her analyses still impress.

15

Cultural factors in human perception

A.R. Luria

From Luria, A.R. 1976: *Cognitive development*. Cambridge, Mass., and London: Harvard University Press, 41–5.

For a long time the notion that optical illusions differ in some cultures and that they might result from causes other than elementary physiological laws remained entirely alien to psychologists of perception. As a consequence, the literature on perception contains little data to confirm the view that optical illusions are historically conditioned.

The first investigator to suggest the cultural origins of optical illusions was W.H.R. Rivers (1901), who pointed out that the Toda people of India were much less subject to visual illusions than Europeans. He claimed that there are different classes of illusions, some more closely dependent on cultural conditions than others.

The cultural and historical conditioning of illusions has received more attention during the past decade. Illusions about geometrical perspective are much more frequent among city-dwellers ... (Allport and Pettigrew, 1957). Psychologists have advanced the hypothesis that many optical illusions appear only under the economic conditions of city culture (the 'carpentered world'), and are encountered much less frequently among forest-dwellers living in circular wattle-and-daub huts. Hence the roots of optical illusions should be sought less in the physiological laws of visual perception than in external social and historical conditions (Segall, Campbell and Herskovits, 1963, 1966; and others).

In our study (in which Mordkovich and Gazaryants also participated), subjects in different groups observed figures that usually give rise to optical illusions, so as to determine whether these illusions appear in all cases.

We presented various types of illusions (Figure 15.1). Some contained differing figure – ground relationships; in others, some distances were 'filled in' or not; and still others involved misevaluations of some common area.

We attempted to determine whether the familiar illusion phenomena were present in all our subjects. If optical illusions were not universal, which ones specifically were retained under which conditions, and which ones were not?

It turned out that optical illusions are not universal. The number of illusions fluctuated strongly, increasing to 75.6 per cent as the educational level of the subjects rose (Table 15.1). It became apparent that even among the teachers' school students illusions did not always occur (only in 70 – 80 per cent of the subjects). The number of cases dropped proportionately in groups whose

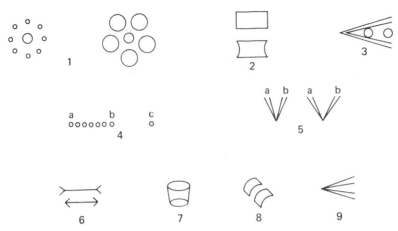

Figure 15.1 Optical illusions presented to subjects in different groups

educational qualifications were lower. Thus the data clearly show that *optical illusions are linked to complex psychological processes that vary in accordance with sociohistorical development.*

As Table 15.1 indicates, the presence of a particular illusion varies from group to group. We can readily distinguish specific geometrical structures that yield a high percentage of illusions among subjects with a higher educational level but that give rise to no such illusions among illiterate subjects.

The Müller–Lyer illusion (see Figure 15.1 item 6) appears among almost all subjects (see Table 15.1), even among ichkari women* (two-thirds of them). Hence, we may assume that the illusion is fairly elementary and independent of cognitive activity. Recent studies (Yarbus, 1967) indicate that eye motion arises from the reflex movement of the eyes over the general area occupied by the figure. This lends a fairly clear explanation to our results.

The illusions perceived primarily by educated subjects include the perspective illusion (3) and others associated with the perception of relationships among geometrical structural elements (5, 7 and 9). There is reason to assume that these illusions result from more complex mental processes and habits acquired through specialized instruction. The perception of perspective, for example, is related to education (Deregowski, 1968a and 1968b).

Our data, however, are preliminary. The mechanisms underlying these illusions might become clearer if we could hit upon a special experiment in which we could vary conditions to produce illusions at will or make them disappear. In our opinion, however, our data clearly show how perceptual processes hitherto regarded as purely physiological (and thus universal) are influenced by sociohistorical development.

We began our analysis of how history shapes consciousness by investigating particular psychological processes, specifically forms of perception usually regarded as fairly elementary and suited only to physiological analysis.

---

* Women living according to Islamic law in separate quarters which they could leave only if veiled, and who enjoyed only a very limited circle of contacts. [Editorial note]

Table 15.1 Number of optical illusions (percentages)

Group	Number of subjects	Illusion number (see Fig. 16.1)									Mean
		1	2	3	4	5	6	7	8	9	
Ichkari women	9	33.3	66.6	0	33.3	11.1	66.6	0	11.1	33.3	29.2
Peasants	25	20.8	36.8	10.5	37.5	25.0	95.8	16.6	29.1	20.8	44.7
Women in preschool courses	25	64.0	60.0	24.0	60.8	36.0	92.0	—	—	—	50.4
Collective-farm activists	40	85.0	72.5	45.0	62.5	77.5	100.0	52.5	47.5	70.0	70.2
Women at teachers' school	38	92.1	68.4	39.4	81.5	71.0	89.9	—	—	—	75.6

The data show that even relatively simple processes involved in perception of colours and geometrical shapes depend to a considerable extent on the subjects' practical experience and their cultural milieu.

The facts thus suggest to us that the conclusions of most current investigations of the perception of colour and shape apply in fact only to individuals shaped by cultural and academic influences, that is, persons with a system of conceptual codes for which such perception is adapted. In other sociohistorical conditions in which life experience is basically determined by practical experience and the shaping influence of school has not yet had effect, the encoding process is different because colour and shape perception fit into a different system of practical experiences, are denoted by a different system of speech terms and are subject to different laws.

16

The perceptual process

Albert H. Hastorf, David J. Schneider and Judith Polefka

From Hastorf, A.H., Schneider, D.J. and Polefka, J. 1970: *Person perception*. Reading, Mass., and London: Addison-Wesley, 3–9.

Both philosophers and psychologists have long been intrigued with the nature of the human perceptual process. One explanation for their interest is that man is naturally curious about his contact with the outside world and wonders how his experiences are caused and to what degree they reflect the world accurately. Beyond general curiosity, the reason for the interest stems from an apparent paradox, the basis of which lies in the difference between the nature of our experiences and our knowledge of how those experiences are caused.

Anyone who takes the trouble to think about and to describe his own experiences usually finds himself overwhelmed with both their immediacy and their structure. One's experience of the world is dominated by objects which stand out in space and which have such attributes as shape, colour, and size. The immediacy of such experiences becomes obvious if one closes his eyes, turns his head in a new direction, and then opens his eyes again. A structured world of objects is immediately present in awareness, without delay and without any consciousness of interpretative or inferential activity. The world appears to be given to us in experience. Yet a causal analysis of these events indicates a very different state of affairs.

You have opened your eyes and you experience a blue vase about six inches high situated on a table. The vase appears to be at a certain distance, and its shape and colour are equally clear. Let us remind ourselves of the causal events that are involved. Light waves of a certain wavelength are reflected off the vase. Some of them impinge on the retina of your eye, and if enough retinal cells are irritated, some visual nerves will fire and a series of electrical impulses will be carried through the sensory apparatus, including the subcortical centres, and will finally arrive at the cortex. This description paints a picture of a very indirect contact with the world: light waves to retinal events to sensory nerve events to subcortical events and finally to cortical events, from which visual experiences result. What is especially important is that this causal description reveals a very different picture than does our naive description of experience. (This causal description led a famous German physiologist to remark that 'we are aware of our nerves, not of objects'.) Thus we have a conflict between our everyday-life experiences of objects together with their properties and an analysis of how these experiences come to exist. How *does* the human being create a coherent perceptual world out of chaotic physical impingements?

Our world of experience has structure

Let us begin with this fact of experience and explore how the structure may be achieved. First of all, we know that our experiences are ultimately dependent on our sensory apparatus, which for visual experiences would include both the retina of the eye and the sensory neurons connecting the retina to the visual areas of the cortex. This apparatus plays, in a manner of speaking, the role of translator. Light waves impinge on the eyes and we experience colour. Sound waves impinge on the ear and we experience pitch. Without the sensory apparatus we would have no contact with the external world. There remains, however, the question of the nature of this translation.

A number of philosophers and psychologists have conceived of the translation process as an essentially passive one, completely determined by the physical properties of the stimulus and by the structure of the receptors and sensory nervous system. They conceive of our sensory apparatus as working somewhat like a high-speed translation device. Physical impingements are looked up and the proper experiential attribute is read out. This conception has led to arguments as to how much of this dictionary is present at birth and how much is the product of our learning history. One reason for the popularity of the passive recording view of perception is the immediacy and 'givenness' of our experience. Our experiences are immediate and they feel direct. These feelings led to the belief that the translation process must be automatic and built in.

The primary argument against that position stems from the fact that our experience of the world is highly selective. If we passively translated and recorded stimuli, our world would be a jumble of experiences; while you were reading a book, you would also be aware of the pressure of your clothes on your body and of all the sounds around you. Actually, from a myriad of impinging stimuli, we are aware of only certain objects and certain attributes of the objects. Anyone who has asked two different persons to describe the same scene has been struck by the fact that they often describe it very differently; each selects different events and different attributes of the events. Given this phenomenon, we must be more than passive translators. In fact, we must be active processors of information. The world is not merely revealed to us; rather, we play an active role in the creation of our experiences.

Let us take an example from the research of Robert W. Leeper to illustrate our point (Leeper, 1935). The stimulus he used was an ambiguous picture which can be seen as either an old hag or an attractive young women (Figure 17.1a). Continued inspection of the picture usually permits an observer to see first one and then the other. Leeper had the original picture redrawn so that one version emphasized the young woman (b) and another emphasized the old hag (c). Subjects who had been exposed to one or the other of these redrawings found themselves 'locked in' on that view when the original ambiguous picture was presented. One hundred per cent of the subjects who had had prior experience with the version emphasizing the young woman saw only the young woman when first looking at the same ambiguous picture. The subjects had been given a set to process the input stimuli in a certain way, and they created a structure consistent with that set. Although our experiences are both immediate and structured, extremely complex participation by the organism, including the active selection and processing of stimulus impingements, is involved in their creation.

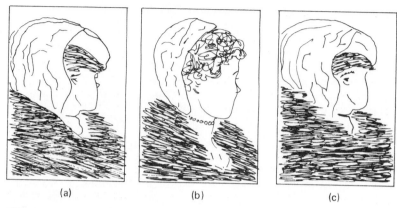

(a)   (b)   (c)

Figure 16.1

One of the most salient features of the person's participation in structuring his experiential world can be described as a categorizing process. He extracts stimuli from the world and forces them into a set of categories. We have here a powerful example of the effects of linguistic coding on the structuring of experience. The subjects in Leeper's experiment did not see a complex pattern of light and dark nor even 'a person' (a possible category); they saw an old hag or a young woman. The categories we use are derived from our past history and are dependent on our language and our cultural background. Some of these categories are markedly ubiquitous and well agreed on by perceivers. Classification of objects according to the attributes of size and shape seems obvious, but some persons may employ different sets of categories. For example, they may perceive in terms of colour and softness. Moreover, there are occasions when all of us change categories in perceiving objects. Instead of size and colour, we may see things in terms of function: the large blue pen and the small green pencil are suddenly similar when we want only to jot down a telephone number. Whatever the nature of the categories we use, they play an important role in the processing of information.

We have begun with the experiential fact that our perceptions are both structured and organized. This structure is immediate and appears to be given by the world of objects. We have argued that a causal analysis of the situation clearly indicates that structured perceptions are the outcome of the organism's engaging in active processing of information, which includes the translation of physical impingements to nerve impulses and the active selection and categorizing of the inputs.

Our world of experience has stability

When we open our eyes and look at a scene, we are not overwhelmed with constant shifts in the picture as our eyes and our attention wander. There is a certain enduring aspect to our experience. We select certain facets of the situation and stick with them. Check this statement against your own experience with the ambiguous picture in Figure 17.1. If it was like the experience of most people, the first organization of the picture, whether it was the old hag or the young woman, continued to demand your attention. It was hard to 'find' the other one. You made various attempts to shift the focus of attention by blinking your eyes or by concentrating on a certain part of the picture, but those strategems did not always work. Although stability in a case of this kind may frustrate us to such an extent that it deserves to be given a different and more pejorative label – rigidity – the example demonstrates that we do *not* experience a world of chaotic instability.

The most obvious example of the maintenance of stability in our experience has been termed *the constancies* in perception. Constancy phenomena have been most carefully described in regard to the perception of size, colour, shape, and brightness. Let us consider an example. You are sitting in a chair in your living room. Another person walks into the room, moves over to a table by the window, picks up a magazine, and then goes across the room to sit down and read it. What are the successive visual-stimulus events impinging on your retina and your successive experiences? Every time the person moves closer to you, the impingement, or *proximal stimulus*, gets larger; in fact, if he moves from 20 feet away to 10 feet away, the height of the image on your eye doubles in size. The opposite occurs as he moves away from you because the size of the retinal image is inversely proportional to a distance of the object from you. Furthermore, when the person moves near the window, more light is available and more light is reflected to the retina. Yet your perception does not fit this description of the stimulus events. While the person is moving about the room, you experience him as remaining relatively constant in size and brightness. In spite of dramatic alterations in the proximal stimulus, you experience a stable world. Given this discrepancy between proximal-stimulus events and experience, the organism must actively process information to produce the stability in his world of experience.

Psychologists are not in total agreement as to how this information-processing takes place, but certain general characteristics of the organism's contribution are apparent. The organism seems to seek *invariance*; that is, he perceives as constant those aspects of the physical world which are most enduring, e.g. size and shape, even though the information he has about them may change radically. The perceived invariance seems to depend on the ability of the organism to combine information from different sources, and to result from the application of equations which define proximal stimulation as a joint function of the distal stimulus (the object) and environmental mediating factors, such as distance and incident illumination. For example, our person moving about the room is always the same height, say six feet. The height of the retinal image, on the other hand, varies, but it is always a constant direct function of his height and an inverse function of his distance from the observer. An invariant function exists:

$$\text{Proximal size} = K \times \frac{\text{Distal size}}{\text{Distance}}$$

Figure 17.2 illustrates the relationships. Note that K is the distance from the lens to the retina, which is assumed to be constant. The invariant relationship allows the formula to be 'solved' by the perceiver; e.g., knowing retinal size and estimating distance, one can arrive at an estimate of the size of the object. By applying this invariant relationship to a particular case, the perceiver can account for variation in proximal size and perceive the object as of a constant size, as he knows from other experiences it must be. Finding invariance by applying relationships such as the above requires the processing of considerable amounts of

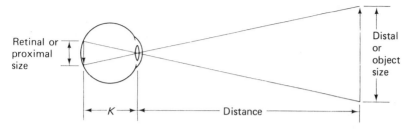

Figure 16.2

information, including the physical size of the object, distance, and illumination; and the information-processing involved in this kind of perceptual act must be quite complicated.

Let us think of the perceptual act as a complex form of problem-solving, the goal of which is to create a stability in which our perceptions bear some relationship to external events. We can then draw an analogy between perceptual problem-solving and scientific problem-solving. Just as the scientist attempts to reduce a complex jumble of events to a small set of variables which serve as a set of determining conditions for a particular event, so we search out the invariant aspects of a situation to produce stable perceptions. The scientist searches for invariance in order to understand and to predict the world; we as perceivers also seek to understand and to predict the world in order that we may behave in it to our advantage. In other words, the perceptual act can be said to generate a prediction that we can use as a basis for action. The goal in both cases is predictability of the environment, and the means to the goal is the specification of causal relationships.

Our world of experience is meaningful

The connotation of 'meaningful' here is that structured and stable events are not isolated from one another but appear to be related in some orderly fashion over time. Both structure and stability are probably necessary for meaning to exist. It is so common for the world of experience to make sense to us that the most powerful way to point out the importance of the phenomenon is to suggest trying to conceive of a world that does not make sense. Events would follow each other with no apparent causal relationships. Almost every event would entail surprise. Nothing would seem familiar. The general experience would be one of chaos. Such a state of affairs is so alien to our everyday-life experience that it is extremely difficult to imagine. Our experiences usually *are* meaningful in that they are structured and they are stable; they are related in the sense that they seem familiar, but particularly in the sense that events have implications for one another.

We must look at the organism as an active processor of input stimuli who categorizes stimulus events and relates them to both past and present events. One property of the organism as an information processor is that he possesses a linguistic coding system which possesses a set of implicative relationships. The impinging stimuli provide the raw material; the organism, with the aid of language, produces the meaning. The organism exists in time: he has a past and he anticipates the future. Past experience, language, and present motivational state or goals for the future influence our perceptions of the present. Our past learning has a significant influence on perception, but it operates within a framework of purposive activity. The experience-derived rules we apply are selected by the purposes we are trying to accomplish. The perceptual process is an achievement by the organism, and perception would not exist without active problem-solving on the part of the perceiver. Our perceptions do have meaning, they do make sense; and meaning and sense derive from both our own past experiences and our present purposes. Without the presence of meaning and sense as active, organizing agents, perception, as we know it, would not exist.

17

Social communication

Stuart Sigman

From Sigman, Stuart 1987: *A perspective on social communication*. New York: Lexington Books, 4–13.

Golding and Murdock (1978) suggest that no theory of communication can be forthcoming without a commensurate theory of society and of the place of communication processes in society. Birdwhistell similarly writes, 'Research on human communication as a systematic and structured organization could not be initiated until we had some idea about the organization of society itself' (1970, 72). The organic approach to communication takes as its starting point society as an 'objective facticity' (Berger, 1963), as an analytic abstraction as real as any other utilized by science (Lundberg, 1939; Mandelbaum, 1973). In Durkheim's (1938) words, society is an entity sui generis, and the behavioural performances of society members are conditioned by regularities that exist at the social level (O'Neill [1973] provides essays on the converse position, methodological individualism). This social level is supraindividual and multi-generational, comprising a history and pattern of behaviour transcending any individual's biography, yet organizing and integrating the behaviour of society members (cf. Kroeber, 1963).

Social communication theory, which is the particular variant of the organic model to be developed in this book (for an alternative, see Watzlawick, Beavin, and Jackson, 1967), is based in part on considerations of society as both a structural entity and a supraindividual behavioural process. Communication in this view is seen not as an individual-level phenomenon, but as a societal-level one. More specifically, communication is conceived of as a process that functions to integrate and support the diverse components of society (or of selected subgroups), of which separate actors are but one of many. Birdwhistell (1970) defines communication as the dynamic or processual aspect of social structure, and as that behavioural organization which facilitates orderly multisensorial interaction. Scheflen similarly writes, 'Communication can be defined . . . as the integrated system of behaviour that mediates, regulates, sustains and makes possible human relationships. We can, therefore, think of communication as the mechanism of social organization.' (1965b, 26). Communication is considered to be a means by which the biosocial interdependencies of species members are maintained (cf. Lundberg, 1939; LaBarre, 1954), and a means by which their behaviour is predictably ordered.

Social communication theory suggests that communication not be reductively defined as a process through which individual cognitions are exchanged, or as a process of information transmission between isolates (for example, 'senders' and 'receivers'). While it is certainly the case that individuals transmit messages to others about internal states and often do so intentionally, it is suggested that interpersonal (or interindividual) messages do not typify or exhaust the human capacity and the group requirement for communication. Pittenger, Hockett, and Danehy write in this regard:

> It is not really useful to think of individuals as the units out of which groups and societies are constructed; it is more fruitful to think of an individual [or the dyad] as the limiting case of a group when, for the moment, there is no one else around. It is treacherously misleading to think of language and other communication systems as cloaks donned by the ego when it ventures into the interpersonal world: rather, we think of ego (or 'mind') as arising from the internalization of interpersonal communicative processes. (1960, 223)

Just as individual persons are moments in society, so interpersonal behaviour is a moment in social communication.

Communication thus appears as a concomitant of all social life and as an exigency of social survival in general, not primarily as a consequence of either individual motivation or initiative. Indeed, from a social communication perspective, motivation and initiative are socially programmed features of mind, that is, delimited options for the appearance of consciousness, emotional display, and verbal reference to consciousness and conduct (cf. Blum and McHugh, 1971; Hochschild, 1983; Denzin, 1984). For example, Heritage and Watson's (1979) analysis of one structural element of conversation, namely, 'formulations', demonstrates that personality attributions or assessments require an understanding not of the presumed 'internal' workings of people but of *standard and non-standard courses of action* available to society members. 'Humourless', 'unsympathetic', 'hostile', and so forth are evidenced in interactants' adherence and non-adherence to specific sequential relationships between and among behaviour units. Personalities do not 'cause' persons to act in certain ways; certain ways of acting provide materials for the construction of social identities and are subject to social regulation and definition. Goffman's focus on the behaviour of interaction is influential here: 'I assume that the proper study of interaction is not the individual and his psychology, but rather the syntactical relations among the acts of different persons mutually present to one another' (1967, 2). In other words, emphasis is placed on the organizing patterns (rules) of behaviour and not on traits of persons.

It follows from this discussion that communication can be defined as a process of information handling – including activities of production, dissemination, reception, and storage – within a social system (cf. Wilden, 1979). This process provides for members' behavioural predictability and ensures societal (group) continuity. Communication is the means by which social reality is created, lived through, sustained, and/or altered. Rather than a process whereby information about an external, 'real' world is shared *by* individuals, it is the mechanism whereby information is used to construct reality *for* individuals (cf. Berger and Luckmann, 1967; Carey, 1975; Pearce and Cronen, 1980). As implied above, it also serves to constitute group membership, to create the social boundaries of persons. Communication establishes meaningful distinctions between and among persons, objects, and behaviours, and defines the structure and goals of interactional events. In this sense, communication is the active or dynamic aspect of social reality, although this does not mean that all persons having membership in a group share identical vantage points on social reality. Rather, as described in greater detail below, there is a supraindividual patterning to the related yet separate social realities, for example, knowledge states and communication rules, which group members are permitted to access. Thus, the suggestion that communication and social reality are related is not intended to mean that individuals, at particular moments of interaction, *construct* or *create* social reality. Instead, social communication proposes that interactants' behaviour serves to *recreate* and *invoke* the historically prior and continuing social reality (cf. McCall and Simmons, 1978).

Communication involves a dynamic structure that allows or prohibits various orders of information or message flow.[1] Research emphasis within social communication is directed toward the continuities and regularities of this information flow over time, rather than toward discrete transmission moments. Focus is placed on the socially constructed limitations or rules governing message flow, and on the functioning of these limitations for the social group under consideration.[2] In this manner, the traditional disciplinary concern for speaker/hearers' message production and reception abilities – that is, 'output' and 'input' trait variables – gives way to analyses of the semiotic codes and the social contexts that sustain *continuous* information flow within society. Communication defines and organizes the spatiotemporal features of interactional events; the sensorial contact among persons 'forcing' either focused or unfocused behaviour (Goffman, 1963); the membership and behavioural requirements sustaining each interactional event; and so on.

It is in the sense of communication as a continuous social phenomenon that the two axioms 'one cannot not communicate' (Watzlawick, Beavin and Jackson, 1967) and 'nothing never happens' (Smith and Trager, cited by Pittenger, Hockett, and Danehy, 1960, 234) take on meaning. The social environment is in a constant state of messagefulness, although selected channels and participants may be momentarily 'silent'. Communication as a totality takes place and endures even though certain channels are not actively employed at particular moments. Moreover, one cannot not communicate because one indeed does not communicate; rather, *one partially contributes behaviour to the supraindividual process of communication.*

It should be stressed that by postulating communication as a social process, organic communication theorists do not intend for the word *social* to imply simply individuals in association, in collectivities, in the physical and interactional co-presence of others. Rather, communication processes are considered *societal* phenomena, prerequisites for the continuity, integration and adaptation of a social system. This social system comprises interdependent members and patterns of behaviour that transcend the individual (Durkheim, 1933, 1938; Linton, 1936, 1940; Kroeber, 1963; Radcliffe-Brown, 1965; Sorokin, 1947).

For example, communication serves to articulate and sustain the processual aspects of the social division of labour. This division of labour functions to allocate responsibility for the group's process and to integrate the diverse activities constitutive of the social group. Individual contributions to the division of labour are not necessarily identical or equivalent. Aberle and his colleagues write of the significance of communication for the division of social labour thus:

'Communication is indispensable if socialization and role differentiation are to function effectively' (Aberle *et al.*, 1950, 106). Kemper similarly notes, 'If actors are engaged in coaction to complete a task, there is inevitably communication between them. . . . Thus, the arrangement of actors in the division of labour coincides in an important sense with the pattern of communication between them' (1972, 743). The behaviour displayed in particular interactional episodes draws upon codes, or integrated sets of rules, which enable the participants to signal (1) their places in the social hierarchy; (2) the amount and type of work responsibility they may be expected to contribute to various activities and contexts; and (3) the integration of their behaviour with that found in other episodes and on the part of other group members. Joos describes one set of such signals for recruiting persons on behalf of the division of labour as follows:

> The community's survival depends on cooperation; and adequate cooperation depends on recognizing the more and less responsible types of persons around us. We need to identify the natural burden-bearers of the community so that we can give them the responsibility which is heaviest of all: we make them responsible for cooperation itself. (1967, 14–15)

Individuals contribute unequally and incompletely to the behaviour that is constitutive of particular interactional scenes and events. Reciprocally, there is a differential distribution of rules and resources for conduct across societal members (see Poole and McPhee, 1983).

Communication is not a single, temporally linear process; a number of subsidiary processes, temporal laminates, and behavioural consequences can be discerned. For example, Erickson and Shultz (1982) recognize two aspects of the social organization of time: *kairos*, the appropriate or right time for a particular action; and *chronos*, the duration of an activity that is mechanically measurable via clock time. Both orders of time contribute to the regulation and structuring of communication.

The multilevel organization of communication can also be seen in terms of multiple message functions. Birdwhistell, for example, distinguishes two dynamic features of messages, which he labels 'integrational' and 'new informational' communication:

> 'Integrational' communication involves such interaction as invokes common past experiences and is related to the initiation, maintenance or severance of interaction. 'New informational', while symbolically consistent with and made up of past experience, involves the inclusion of information not held in common by the communicants. (1952, 3–4)

In a more recent formulation, Birdwhistell (1970) extends the notion of integrational communication processes to comprise regulation of interaction, maintenance of systemic operations, and cross-referencing of particular message units to those contexts providing for their comprehensibility (see also Scheflen, 1968). Lasswell suggests the recognition of three functional processes (see also Jakobson 1960 and Halliday 1978):

> Our analysis of communication will deal with the specializations that carry on certain functions, of which the following may be clearly distinguished: (1) the surveillance of the environment; (2) the correlation of the parts of society in responding to the environment; (3) the transmission of the social heritage from one generation to the next. (1971, 85)

Of special note here is the idea that communication serves multiple social and interactional ends and that a given unit of behaviour can be seen to fulfil several such functions. In addition, there is an awareness of, and an emphasis on, messages of system stability, continuity, monitoring and/or adaptation, rather than on those associated solely with person change.

The social communication position calling for studies of messages of continuity and predictability is designed to contrast with the mechanical model's apparent emphasis (or overemphasis) on novel information transmissions (Thomas, 1980). I have elsewhere written that within contemporary discourse and interaction analysis, the mechanical approach fails to account for the many messages (or message units) which seemingly function to signal the development, stability, and continuity of the participants' social relationships and group affiliations (Sigman, 1983a). Moreover, I suggest that the examination of the verbalizations exchanged within a single interactional episode for some 'internal' organizing principle essentially precludes consideration of the *continuities of information across episodes* that form the full pattern of the social information system.

It should be noted that from a social system perspective, a behavioural function is not always, nor necessarily, seen as isomorphic with an actor's intentions for producing a particular unit of behaviour (see Radcliffe-Brown, 1965; Merton, 1968; Scheflen, 1973; Sigman, 1980a; Giddens, 1984). The usefulness of a distinction between group-level and individual-level (psychological) functions when studying face-to-face interaction is summarized in the following:

> We need not explain the regularities observed in social interaction by reverting to the interests or motives of the individual. Instead, the system of interaction can be treated as having a structure of its own, *sui generis*. . . . Moreover, the structure of the interaction that results may bear little relationship to the motives with which persons entered the situation. (Aldrich, 1972, 171)

In contrast, many definitions of communication explicitly concern themselves with intentional message transmission (cf. Fisher, 1978; Scott, 1977) or delimit that part of social behaviour which is communicative on the basis of presumed intentions (cf. Cushman, 1980). Nevertheless, from the social communication perspective outlined above, an actor's ostensible motive for performing a particular behaviour does not exhaust the regularity of that behaviour or the richness of its contribution to an interactional event and to the social system at large. Although intentionality as a component of some communicative activity cannot be denied, communication analysts should not be limited to this aspect of behaviour. Kockelmans writes that there is a legitimate 'distinction between the meaning a phenomenon has for a society and the meaning the same phenomenon may have for a particular individual who finds himself in this or that particular situation' (1975, 76).

That particular groups define communication in terms of actor intentionality, or differentially judge behaviour as either intentionally or unintentionally performed, is not the same issue as suggesting that the communication theorist examine all examples of socially patterned behaviour. A distinction can be drawn in this manner between a general and a culture-specific definition of communication, between a broad social-scientific approach to the study of communication and a narrower native-delimited conception of what does and does not count as communication. Behaviour for which individuals have intentions, that is, for which socially regulated and defined intentions are available and accountable, is not to be accorded different status for research purposes from that behaviour for which no ostensible (verbalizable) intentions are forthcoming. The ranges of acceptable and unacceptable intentions for behaviour are worthy of systematic study (cf. Gergen, 1982; Harré, Clarke and DeCarlo, 1985).

Thus, this position does not deny or overlook social actors' possession and use of knowledge regarding their conduct and its spatiotemporal location (see Giddens, 1984), but it does situate such knowledge as part of the group's larger system of communication. The very notions of motive, intentionality, individual responsibility, and so on must be seen as semiotic tokens in a more encompassing network of actions and meanings. In this regard, non-Western cultural data remind us that not all groups account for persons' acts in terms of internal psychological states. Rosen writes, for example:

> A person's inner state [in Morocco] is largely irrelevant to an account of events in the world: since motive and intent are discernible in words and deeds, there is no felt need to discuss a person's interior state directly. (1984, 169)
>
> Narrative accounts – whether as conversational exposition, oral history or popular storytelling – work on the assumption that no man acts without contexts; therefore to reveal a person in a variety of circumstances is to reveal him as a social person. (1984, 171)

The more encompassing network of meanings, for example, the vocabularies of motives and the conditions under which persons are socially expected to be responsible for their behaviour (see Gerth and Mills, 1953), is the proper domain of social communication investigations.

The above discussion should not be taken to mean that social communication theorists assume a unilateral correlation between a unit of behaviour and its function. Rather, each functional aspect of the communication process is said to represent only a heuristic abstraction from the total stream of behaviour; communication events and the constituent behaviour 'partials' (see below) may serve numerous functions. Social communication analysts observe such multi-functionality of behaviour in at least three interrelated ways. First, communication behaviour appears to be a hierarchically structured process (cf. Pike, 1967).[3] As such, the contribution or function of communication units on one level of structure may not be the same as on other levels. A unit's functioning may be apparent for some (or all) of the levels considered. As Pittenger, Hockett, and Danehy write, 'In theory, the relative importance of a single small event can be assayed by observing how far its effects 'reverberate' up through more and more inclusive larger events of which it is a constituent' (1960, 250). Moreover, social behaviour is so structured as to involve multiples of hierarchies, and hierarchically arranged hierarchies; the same unit of behaviour may thus be part of, and function within, one or more hierarchies.

A second aspect of multifunctionality concerns the idea that, as noted above, the function and meaning of behaviour for individual participants may not be isomorphic with the function of behaviour for the social group (or for particular subcomponents within a society or group). This again is a consideration of level, although it attends to the relationship among social actors, social systems, and their constitutive behaviour, not to the hierarchical patterning of the behaviour itself. A further consideration here is that the same behaviour may have different consequences (and different message values) for individuals, depending upon where in the social group they occupy statuses. For example, I have previously discussed the different group membership requirements that nursing-home staff members and residents may have for an entering patient; the same behaviour exhibited by a newcomer may be interpreted by one group as a sign of 'health' and 'alertness' while seen by others as a sign of 'mental unfitness' and 'disease', depending on their institutional location and perspective (Sigman, 1982; cf. Annandale, 1985).

Finally, multiple codes constrain the form and contextual placement of participants' behaviour; each such code provides for a meaning or function component of the behaviour (cf. Frentz and Farrell, 1976; Halliday, 1978), and possibly more than one. A simple metaphor may be useful in clarifying this point. A behavioural form in its processing may be thought of as passing through a series of filters or generators before it is finally produced (performed) by a social actor; each filter, representing a particular social-behavioural code, shapes the behaviour according to its own specifications and in interaction with other codes. Interactional behaviour may be assumed to be conditioned by *inter alia* phonological, morphological, discursive and interpersonal regulative principles; the behaviour so produced provides information derived from each one of these semiotic constraints (cf. Halliday, 1978). For example, an utterance such as a greeting – more specifically, the particular form a greeting takes at any one time – may be conditioned by rules for sound production (partially embedding a sociolinguistic message regarding the speaker's socioeconomic background, among other things); social politeness (potentially transmitting information about the speaker's attitude toward the recipient); lexical choice (potentially including information on the speaker's level of education); and so on. In this manner, the multiple codes enable a greeting to serve numerous functions in interaction.

The notion of multifunctionality can be related to the notion of behaviour 'partials' (cf. Birdwhistell, 1970; Wilden, 1979). Individuals only partially possess or evidence all the rules constraining the totality of socially patterned behaviour that constitutes the communication system, and not all individuals share the identical or fully overlapping codes for conduct (see Hymes, 1974; Bernstein, 1975).[4] Interactional events are composed of members' rule-governed behaviour, yet the behaviour of any individual interactant is an incomplete contribution to these events (cf. Mead, 1934; Birdwhistell, 1970). Interactional events require multiparticipant coordination in much the same way that, for example, a formal dinner party is comprised of, and emerges from, the non-overlapping rules and behaviour units of the domestic, who knows to 'serve from the left and take from the right', and the guest, who knows only to signal completion of one course and readiness for the next. In accordance with the division of labour theory noted above, group members must have available to them (1) behaviour for signalling their knowledge states and places within the overall social system, and (2) routines for coordinating their behaviour partials with those of their fellows.

Poole, Seibold and McPhee write, 'Structures cannot be reduced to "cognitive maps" in individual actors' heads' (1985, 77). Nwoye's (1985) discussion of courtship among the Igbo of Nigeria presents a good illustration of the relevance of the concept of structural partials to the ethnographic study of continuous social communication. In the African group studied by Nwoye, courtship is a family affair proceeding from the man's having asked for the girl's hand in marriage: 'The young man is joined by his parents, his relatives, and friends who start treating and behaving toward the girl as his "wife" ' (1985, 188–9). As a communication event, courtship in this group is spread across numerous interactions and is constituted by the partial contributions of a number of individuals (see also Rosen, 1984). The construction of an individual's social identity is likewise illuminated by the concept of interaction partials: 'Evidence of this possession [of a self] is thoroughly a product of joint ceremonial labour, the part expressed through the individual's demeanor being no more significant than the part conveyed by others through their deferential treatment toward him' (Goffman, 1967, 85).

The notion of partials leads to the methodological proposition that the analytic boundaries of a unit of behaviour be seen beyond any individual group member's body; a unit of communication behaviour may be constituted by the separate yet related contributions of several members. As Scheflen remarks, 'A unit is not necessarily performed by one individual. A given unit, usually performed by one person, may be performed by several interactants on some occasions: e.g., one speaker may start a statement, another finish it' (1965b, 20). (See Heritage and Watson's [1979] discussion of the collaborations involved in formulations of conversational topics). Similarly, behaviour performed by an individual may serve as a partial contribution to a group-level function; forms by several individuals, which complement each other or are integrated with each other, may in combination serve this particular function more completely. Discourse units separated by space and time, that is, occurring in what the social actors consider to be discrete events, can still be judged to constitute a single, albeit complex, message unit (see Sigman, 1983a). Birdwhistell (1970) suggests that a communication event may last as briefly as a phoneme or as long as a generation or two. Pearce and Cronen similarly write, 'The patterns of human action that exist in a marriage, a formal organization, or a nation may be extremely complex and take years or generations to emerge' (1980, 161). Leach (1976) notes the message relatedness of symbols separated by many years, for example, as in the case of veils of marriage and of widowhood.

In addition, certain of the partials contributed to the constitution of particular interactional events are only indirectly offered by persons then present in the scene. Rapoport's (1982) discussion of the semiotics of the built environment indicates the importance of various architectural and physical elements for the meaningful construction of interactional events. In such cases, it is reductionistic and simplistic to suggest that the individual architect is communicating *to* the actors, or that the environment is merely a surround ('context') for behaviour; rather, the architect and his/her design can be better seen as meaningful, albeit partial, units of the total scene's structure and composition.

Finally, any one interactional moment is a partial of the larger continuous system of information flow; communication systems, as noted above, are continuous, even though the 'active' and partial message displays of particular individuals may not be.

These observations have implications for the appropriate size of analytic units and the 'ethnographic present' (time framework) selected by researchers for their analyses (see Birdwhistell, 1977). Rather than look at the separate behaviours of various interactants in terms of their apparent role as either 'stimulus' or 'response,' social communication theory highlights the larger scene or event that is accomplished and contributed to by the behaviours. The behaviours of individual interactants can be seen as the partial constituents of communication episodes requiring varying degrees of integration and co-ordination in adherence to the event 'programs' (Scheflen, 1968). When studying interactional events as units of communication constituted by the partial contributions of multiple participants – as in the Igbo case just described – there are several patterns to be explored. The social communication investigator considers (1) the complete array of behaviours constitutive of the event; (2) the assignment of persons, for example, through recruitment and/or self-selection, to the different phases and subsidiary behaviour units of the event; (3) signals available to the participants for co-ordinating their contributions and indicating the progression of the event; and (4) differential outcomes and evaluations of repeated communication events, based on the varying assignments of persons to behavioural contributions.

18

Historical changes in gestural behaviour

David Efron

From Efron, D. 1972: *Gesture, race and culture.* Paris and The Hague: Mouton, 44–7, 53–5. (Originally published 1941 as *Gesture and environment.* New York: King's Crown Press.)

The problem of determining the factors that condition the gestural behaviour of a given human group cannot be solved by speculative assumptions nor by vague generalizations. There are only two legitimate ways of approaching it: (a) the experimental, (b) the historical.

Space forbids description of all the historical material on gestural conduct we have been able to assemble. Tempting as it is, such a description would make up a book in itself. All we can do now is to give a few examples.[1]

> Foreigners talk with their arms and hands as auxiliaries to the voice. The custom is considered vulgar by us calm Englishmen. . . . You have no need to act with the hands, but, if you use them at all, it should be very slightly and gracefully, never bringing down a fist upon the table, nor slapping one hand upon another, nor poking your fingers at your interlocutor. Pointing, too, is a habit to be avoided, especially pointing with the thumb over the shoulder, which is an inelegant action. . . . You should not be too lively in your actions. . . .

Thus reads a passage in a treatise on good manners of the Victorian period.[2] Similar passages may be found in many other social codes of that period.

Unlike Mr Günther *et al.*, the English gentleman of 1870 does not seem to have considered gesticulation an innate impropriety, characteristic only of certain non-'Nordic' groups, but merely a 'foreign' vulgar custom, disliked by 'us calm Englishmen'. He seems to have assumed, however, that *all* Englishmen of all times were as calm and parsimonious in their expressive bodily motions as were apparently the habitués of his club. Had he spent some time looking through the window of history, instead of leisurely watching from his club window the sidewalks of an exclusive section of Victorian London, he might have learned that a good many of his ancestors of the Georgian epoch used to gesticulate as warmly as the 'foreigners' of his own lifetime. Again, had he taken the pains of visiting the British Parliament in the seventies, his belief might have been weakened before the large amount and the forcefulness of gestural movement displayed by the leading orators of that house. This may be ascertained from documents like the following. The first is an excerpt from a satirical description by Steele of a tendency apparently prevalent among the habitués of the coffee-houses of his time to manipulate the wearing apparel of the conversational partner, and to bring him over 'by force of arms'. It is taken from *The Guardian*, 13 and 15 June 1713.

There is a silly habit among many of our minor orators, who display their eloquence in the several coffee-houses of this fair city, to the no small annoyance of considerable numbers of her majesty's spruce and loving subjects, and that is a humour they have got of twisting off your buttons. These ingenious gentlemen are not able to advance three words until they have got fast hold of one of your buttons; but as soon as they have procured such an excellent handle for discourse, they will indeed proceed with great elocution. I know not how well some may have escaped, but for my part I have often met with them to my cost; having I believe within these three years last past been argued out of several dozens; insomuch that I have for sometime ordered my taylor to bring me home with every suit a dozen of spare ones, to supply the place of such as from time to time are detached as an help to discourse by the vehement gentlemen before mentioned. This way of holding a man in discourse is much practised in the coffee-houses within the city, and does not indeed so much prevail at the politer end of the town. It is likewise more frequently made use of among the small politicians, than any other body of men; I am therefore something cautious of entering into a controversy with this species of statesmen, especially the younger fry; for if you offer in the least to dissent from any thing that one of these advances, he immediately steps up to you, takes hold of one of your buttons, and indeed will soon convince you of the strength of his argumentations. . . .

Besides the gentlemen before mentioned, there are others who are no less active in their harangues, but with gentle services rather than robberies. These while they are improving your understanding, are at the same time setting off your person; they will new-plait and adjust your neck-cloth.

But though I can bear with this kind of orator, who is so humble as to aim at the good will of his hearer by being his valet de chambre, I must rebel against another sort of them. There are some, sir, that do not stick to take a man by the collar when they have a mind to persuade him. It is your business, I humbly presume, Mr Ironside, to interpose that man is not brought over his opponent by force of arms. It were requisite therefore that you should name a certain interval, which ought to be preserved between the speaker and him to whom he speaks. For sure no man has a right, because I am not of his opinion, to take any of my clothes from me, or dress me according to his own liking. I am of the opinion that no orator or speaker in public or private has any right to meddle with anybody's clothes but his own. I indulge men in the liberty of playing with their own hats, fumbling in their own pockets, settling their own periwigs, tossing or twisting their heads, and all other gesticulations which may contribute to their elocution; but pronounce it an infringement of the English liberty of a man to keep his neighbour's person in custody in order to force a hearing; and further declare, that all assent given by an auditor under such constraint, is void and of no effect.[3]

That the gestural behaviour of many of the habitués of the London coffee-houses of Steele's time was not restricted to button-twisting and to the manipulation of the interlocutor's wearing apparel we learn from several sketches of some of these people, drawn from life by William Hogarth. Several of these will be found in Samuel Ireland's *Graphic Illustrations of Hogarth* (Vol. 1, London 1794).

Amusingly enough – and with reference to the racist theory of gestural behaviour propounded by Messrs. Günther *et al.* – the Jew Disraeli, in contrast to a good many of his 'Nordic' parliamentary colleagues, 'indulged in little gesticulation. . . . He would hook his fingers in his armholes while speaking.'[4] As a matter of fact, it was precisely Lord Beaconsfield (Disraeli) who introduced the

'Victorian' style of public delivery – that of 'matter-of-factness' – which in years to come made of gestural taciturnity an oratorical virtue.

According to some of the proponents of the racist interpretation of gesture, the French people have a natural propensity to accompany their speech with lively bodily motions. This tendency, they claim, is determined by a hereditary emotional overtness, as contrasted with what they consider a congenital affective restraint in the Anglo-Saxons.

It is rather amusing to learn that a diametrically opposite 'natural' theory was held by a prominent French linguist of the sixteenth century. We are referring to Henri Estienne who, in his book on the 'italianization' of the French language, makes the categorical statement that 'Frenchmen are not gesturers by nature and dislike gesticulation'. Estienne was engaged at that time in fustigating the upper circles of French society for having succumbed to the Italian idioms and manners which were imported into France (particularly into the court of Henri II) by the Florentine retinue of Catherine de Medici. The two satirical dialogues which he wrote to that effect deal also with gestural assimilation. The document is especially interesting in that it indicates that the French courtiers, and apparently also the Frenchmen of other social strata, of the preceding period, considered gesticulation an impolite and 'vulgar' form of behaviour. The habit of the upper-class Frenchmen of Catherine's time to use gestural movement in conversation is resentfully ascribed by Estienne to the strong influence exerted in Paris by the forms of social demeanour of the Italian courtiers of the niece of Clement VII. This may be gathered from statements like the following:

> Celtophile – Do you mean that people have changed not only physically but also mentally?
> Philasvone – Yes, some have – principally courtiers. For they haven't only changed their clothing . . . but also their gestures and expressions and even their bearing – all the behaviours one encounters in ordinary conversation. Indeed, they have gone so far as to turn great vices into virtues and to turn virtues into vices. There has been such a revolution in their thinking that they love what previously they hated and hate what once they loved. That's why you shouldn't be surprised if, at court, you see many things welcomed there which were considered very impolite in the past and which are, truly, most uncouth.
> Celtophile – And are the French Italianizing their gestures? . . .
> Philasvone – . . . I remember what I was going to tell you: more people are adopting the Italian manner . . .[5]

(Editors' translation)

Like the Victorian gentleman, the patriotic Frenchman thought that only 'foreigners' talk with their hands. Had he lived long enough to witness the development of the 'honnête homme' and the 'société polie' in France, with their 'bienséances du corps', and their norms of moderate and graceful gestural conduct, he would have probably been greatly shocked by the fact that also in that case the change was due to no small extent to Italian influence, although of an opposite character, namely: the tradition of 'regola e misura' in expressive movement, transplanted into the upper layers of seventeenth-century French society through the translated works on courteous demeanour of Castiglione, Guazzo, Grimaldi, della Casa, etc.[6] His belief in the 'natural' disinclination of the French people to gestural movement would have strongly been shaken, on the other hand, had he been able to foresee the enthusiastic liking for manual rhetorics of his co-nationals of the revolutionary and the post-Napoleonic periods, when no foreign influence was operative in that respect at all.

19

Introduction to the presentation of self in everyday life

Erving Goffman

From Goffman, Erving 1959: *The presentation of self in everyday life*. New York: Doubleday Anchor.
Extract taken from Penguin books edition: Harmondsworth 1969, 14–27.

When an individual enters the presence of others, they commonly seek to acquire information about him or to bring into play information about him already possessed. They will be interested in his general socio-economic status, his conception of self, his attitude towards them, his competence, his trustworthiness, etc. Although some of this information seems to be sought almost as an end in itself, there are usually quite practical reasons for acquiring it. Information about the individual helps to define the situation, enabling others to know in advance what he will expect of them and what they may expect of him. Informed in these ways, the others will know how best to act in order to call forth a desired response from him.

For those present, many sources of information become accessible and many carriers (or 'sign-vehicles') become available for conveying this information. If unacquainted with the individual, observers can glean clues from his conduct and appearance which allow them to apply their previous experience with individuals roughly similar to the one before them or, more important, to apply untested stereotypes to him. They can also assume from past experience that only individuals of a particular kind are likely to be found in a given social setting. They can rely on what the individual says about himself or on documentary evidence he provides as to who and what he is. If they know, or know of, the individual by virtue of experience prior to the interaction, they can rely on assumptions as to the persistence and generality of psychological traits as a means of predicting his present and future behaviour.

However, during the period in which the individual is in the immediate presence of the others, few events may occur which directly provide the others with the conclusive information they will need if they are to direct wisely their own activity. Many crucial facts lie beyond the time and place of interaction or lie concealed within it. For example, the 'true' or 'real' attitudes, beliefs, and emotions of the individual can be ascertained only indirectly, through his avowals or through what appears to be involuntary expressive behaviour. Similarly, if the individual offers the others a product or service, they will often find that during the interaction there will be no time and place immediately available for eating the pudding that the proof can be found in. They will be forced to accept some events as conventional or natural signs of something not directly available to the senses. In Ichheiser's terms,[1] the individual will have to act so that he intentionally or unintentionally *expresses* himself, and the others will in turn have to be *impressed* in some way by him.

The expressiveness of the individual (and therefore his capacity to give impressions) appears to involve two radically different kinds of sign activity: the expression that he *gives*, and the expression that he *gives off*. The first involves verbal symbols or their substitutes which he uses admittedly and solely to convey the information that he and the others are known to attach to these symbols. This is communication in the traditional and narrow sense. The second involves a wide range of action that others can treat as symptomatic of the actor, the expectation being that the action was performed for reasons other than the information conveyed in this way. As we shall have to see, this distinction has an only initial validity. The individual does of course intentionally convey misinformation by means of both of these types of communication, the first involving deceit, the second feigning.

Taking communication in both its narrow and broad sense, one finds that when the individual is in the immediate presence of others, his activity will have a promissory character. The others are likely to find that they must accept the individual on faith, offering him a just return while he is present before them in exchange for something whose true value will not be established until after he has left their presence. (Of course, the others also live by inference in their dealings with the physical world, but it is only in the world of social interaction that the objects about which they make inferences will purposely facilitate and higher this inferential process.) The security that they justifiably feel in making inferences about the individual will vary, of course, depending on such factors as the amount of information they already possess about him, but no amount of such past evidence can entirely obviate the necessity of acting on the basis of inferences. As William I Thomas suggested:

> It is also highly important for us to realize that we do not as a matter of fact lead our lives, make our decisions, and reach our goals in everyday life either statistically or scientifically. We live by inference. I am, let us say, your guest. You do not know, you cannot determine scientifically, that I will not steal your money or your spoons. But inferentially I will not, and inferentially you have me as a guest.[2]

Let us now turn from the others to the point of view of the individual who presents himself before them. He may wish them to think highly of him, or to think that he thinks highly of them, or to perceive how in fact he feels towards them, or to obtain no clear-cut impression; he may wish to ensure sufficient harmony so that the interaction can be sustained, or to defraud, get rid of, confuse, mislead, antagonize, or insult them. Regardless of the particular objective which the individual has in mind and of his motive for having his objective, it will be in his interests to control the conduct of the others, especially their responsive treatment of him.[3] This control is achieved largely by influencing the definition of the situation which the others come to formulate, and he can influence this definition by expressing himself in such a way as to give them the kind of impression that will lead them to act voluntarily in accordance with his own plan. Thus, when an individual appears in the presence of others, there will usually be some reason for him to mobilize his activity so that it will convey an impression to others which it is in his interests to convey. Since a girl's dormitory mates will glean evidence of her popularity from the calls she receives on the phone, we can suspect that some girls will arrange for calls to be made, and Willard Waller's finding can be anticipated:

> It has been reported by many observers that a girl who is called to the telephone in the dormitories will often allow herself to be called several times, in order to give all the other girls ample opportunity to hear her paged.[4]

Of the two kinds of communication – expressions given and expressions given off – this report will be primarily concerned with the latter, with the more theatrical and contextual kind, the non-verbal, presumably unintentional kind, whether this communication be purposely engineered or not. As an example of what we must try to examine, I would like to cite at length a novelistic incident in which Preedy, a vacationing Englishman, makes his first appearance on the beach of his summer hotel in Spain:

> But in any case he took care to avoid catching anyone's eye. First of all, he had to make it clear to these potential companions of his holiday that they were of no concern to him whatsoever. He stared through them, round them, over them – eyes lost in space. The beach might have been empty. If by chance a ball was thrown his way, he looked surprised; then let a smile of amusement lighten his face (Kindly Preedy), looked round dazed to see that there *were* people on the beach, tossed it back with a smile to himself and not a smile *at* the people, and then resumed carelessly his nonchalant survey of space.
>
> But it was time to institute a little parade, the parade of the Ideal Preedy. By devious handlings he gave any who wanted to look a chance to see the title of his book – a Spanish translation of Homer, classic thus, but daring, cosmopolitan too – and then gathered together his beach-wrap and bag into a neat sand-resistant pile (Methodical and Sensible Preedy), rose slowly to stretch at ease his huge frame (Big-Cat Preedy), and tossed aside his sandals (Carefree Preedy, after all).
>
> The marriage of Preedy and the sea! There were alternative rituals. The first involved the stroll that turns into a run and a dive straight into the water, thereafter smoothing into a strong splashless crawl towards the horizon. But of course not really to the horizon. Quite suddenly he would turn on to his back to thrash great white splashes with his legs, somehow thus showing that he could have swum further had he wanted to, and then would stand up a quarter out of the water for all to see who it was.
>
> The alternative course was simpler, it avoided the cold-water shock and it avoided the risk of appearing too high-spirited. The point was to appear to be so used to the sea, the Mediterranean, and this particular beach, that one might as well be in the sea as out of it. It involved a slow stroll down and into the edge of the water – not even noticing his toes were wet, land and water all the same to *him!* – with his eyes up at the sky gravely surveying portents, invisible to others, of the weather (Local Fisherman Preedy).[5]

The novelist means us to see that Preedy is improperly concerned with the extensive impressions he feels his sheer bodily action is giving off to those around him. We can malign Preedy further by assuming that he has acted merely in order to give a particular impression, that this is a false impression, and that the others present receive either no impression at all, or, worse still, the impression that Preedy is affectedly trying to cause them to receive this particular impression. But the important point for us here is that the kind of impression Preedy thinks he is making is in fact the kind of impression that the others correctly and incorrectly glean from someone in their midst.

I have said that when an individual appears before others his actions will influence the definition of the situation which they come to have. Sometimes the individual will act in a thoroughly calculating manner, expressing himself in a given way solely in order to give the kind of impression to others that is likely to evoke from them a specific response he is concerned to obtain. Sometimes the individual will be calculating in his activity but be relatively unaware that this is the case. Sometimes he will intentionally and consciously express himself in a particular way, but chiefly because the tradition of his group or social status require this kind of expression and not because of any particular response (other than vague acceptance or approval) that is likely to be evoked from those impressed by the expression. Sometimes the traditions of an individual's role will lead him to give a well-designed impression of a particular kind and yet he may be neither consciously nor unconsciously disposed to create such an impression. The others, in their turn, may be suitably impressed by the individual's efforts to convey something, or may misunderstand the situation and come to conclusions that are warranted neither by the individual's intent nor by the facts. In any case, in so far as the others act as if the individual had conveyed a particular impression, we may take a functional or pragmatic view and say that the individual has 'effectively' projected a given definition of the situation and 'effectively' fostered the understanding that a given state of affairs obtains.

There is one aspect of the others' response that bears special comment here. Knowing that the individual is likely to present himself in a light that is favourable to him, the others may divide what they witness into two parts: a part that is relatively easy for the individual to manipulate at will, being chiefly his verbal assertions, and a part in regard to which he seems to have little concern or control, being chiefly derived from the expressions he gives off. The others may then use what are considered to be the ungovernable aspects of his expressive behaviour as a check upon the validity of what is conveyed by the governable aspects. In this a fundamental asymmetry is demonstrated in the communication process, the individual presumably being aware of only one stream of his communication, the witnesses of this stream and one other. For example, in Shetland Isle one crofter's wife, in serving native dishes to a visitor from the mainland of Britain, would listen with a polite smile to his polite claims of liking what he was eating; at the same time she would take note of the rapidity with which the visitor lifted his fork or spoon to his mouth, the eagerness with which he passed food into his mouth, and the gusto expressed in chewing the food, using these signs as a check on the stated feelings of the eater. The same woman, in order to discover what one acquaintance (A) 'actually' thought of another acquaintance (B), would wait until B was in the presence of A but engaged in conversation with still another person (C). She would then covertly examine the facial expressions of A as he regarded B in conversation with C. Not being in conversation with B, and not being directly observed by him, A would sometimes relax usual constraints and tactful deceptions, and freely express what he was 'actually' feeling about B. This Shetlander, in short, would observe the unobserved observer.

Now given the fact that others are likely to check up on the more controllable aspects of behaviour by means of the less controllable, one can expect that sometimes the individual will try to exploit this very possibility, guiding the impression he makes through behaviour felt to be reliably informing.[6] For example, in gaining admission to a tight social circle, the participant observer may not only wear an accepting look while listening to an informant, but may also be careful to wear the same look when observing the informant talking to others; observers of the observer will then not as easily discover where he actually stands. A specific illustration may be cited from Shetland Isle. When a neighbour dropped in to have a cup of tea, he would ordinarily wear at least a hint of an expectant warm smile as he passed through the door into the cottage. Since lack of physical obstructions outside the cottage and lack of light within it usually made it possible to observe the visitor unobserved as he approached the house, islanders sometimes took pleasure in watching the visitor drop whatever expression he was manifesting and replace it with a sociable one just before reaching the door. However, some visitors, in appreciating that this examination was occurring, would blindly adopt a social face a long distance from the house, thus ensuring the projection of a constant image.

This kind of control upon the part of the individual reinstates the symmetry of the communication process, and sets the stage for a kind of information game – a potentially infinite cycle of concealment, discovery, false revelation, and rediscovery. It should be added that since the others are likely to be relatively unsuspicious of the presumably unguided aspect of the individual's conduct, he can gain much by controlling it. The others of course may sense that the individual is manipulating the presumably spontaneous aspects of his behaviour, and seek in this very act of manipulation some shading of conduct that the individual has not managed to control. This again provides a check upon the individual's behaviour, this time his presumably uncalculated behaviour, thus re-establishing the asymmetry of the communication process. Here I would like only to add the suggestion that the arts of piercing an individual's effort at calculated unintentionality seem better developed than our capacity to manipulate our own behaviour, so that regardless of how many steps have occurred in the information game, the witness is likely to have the advantage over the actor, and the initial asymmetry of the communication process is likely to be retained.

When we allow that the individual projects a definition of the situation when he appears before others, we must also see that the others, however passive their role may seem to be, will themselves effectively project a definition of the situation by virtue of their response to the individual and by virtue of any lines of action they initiate to him. Ordinarily the definitions of the situation projected by the several different participants are sufficiently attuned to one another, so that open contradiction will not occur. I do not mean that there will be the kind of consensus that arises when each individual present candidly expresses what he really feels and honestly agrees with the expressed feelings of the others present. This kind of harmony is an optimistic ideal and in any case not necessary for the smooth working of society. Rather, each participant is expected to suppress his immediate heartfelt feelings, conveying a view of the situation which he feels the others will be able to find at least temporarily acceptable. The maintenance of this surface of agreement, this veneer of consensus, is facilitated by each participant concealing his own wants behind statements which assert values to which everyone present feels obliged to give lip service. Further, there is usually a kind of division of definitional labour. Each participant is allowed to establish the tentative official rule regarding matters which are vital to him but not immediately important to others, e.g. the rationalizations and justifications by which he accounts for his past activity. In exchange for this courtesy he remains silent or noncommittal on matters important to others but not immediately important to him. We have then a kind of interactional *modus vivendi*. Together the participants contribute to a single overall definition of the situation which involves not so much a real agreement as to what exists but rather a real agreement as to whose claims concerning what issues will be temporarily honoured. Real agreement will also exist concerning the desirability of avoiding an open conflict of definitions of the situation.[7] I will refer to this level of agreement as a 'working consensus'. It is to be understood that the working consensus established in one interaction setting will be quite different in content from the working consensus established in a different type of setting. Thus, between two friends at lunch, a reciprocal show of affection, respect, and concern for the other is maintained. In service occupations, on the other hand, the specialist often maintains an image of disinterested involvement in the problem of the client, while the client responds with a show of respect for the competence and integrity of the specialist. Regardless of such differences in content, however, the general form of these working arrangements is the same.

In noting the tendency for a participant to accept the definitional claims made by the others present, we can appreciate the crucial importance of the information that the individual *initially* possesses or acquires concerning his fellow participants, for it is on the basis of this initial information that the individual starts to define the situation and starts to build up lines of responsive action. The individual's initial projection commits him to what he is proposing to be and requires him to drop all pretences of being other things. As the interaction among the participants progresses, additions and modifications in this initial informational state will of course occur, but it is essential that these later developments be related without contradiction to, and even built up from, the initial positions taken by the several participants. It would seem that an individual can more easily make a choice as to what line of treatment to demand from and extend to the others present at the beginning of an encounter than he can alter the line of treatment that is being pursued once the interaction is under way.

In everyday life, of course, there is a clear understanding that first impressions are important. Thus, the work adjustment of those in service occupations will often hinge upon a capacity to seize and hold the initiative in the service relation, a capacity that will require subtle aggressiveness on the part of the server when he is of lower socio-economic status than his client. W.F. Whyte suggests the waitress as an example.

> The first point that stands out is that the waitress who bears up under pressure does not simply respond to her customers. She acts with some skill to control their behaviour. The first question to ask when we look at the customer relationship is, 'Does the waitress get the jump on the customer, or does the customer get the jump on the waitress?' The skilled waitress realizes the crucial nature of this question. . . .
> The skilled waitress tackles the customer with confidence and without hesitation. For example, she may find that a new customer has seated himself before she could clear off the dirty dishes and change the cloth. He is now leaning on the table studying the menu. She greets him, says, 'May I change the cover, please?' and, without waiting for an answer, takes his menu away from him so that he moves back from the table, and she goes about her work. The relationship is handled politely but firmly, and there is never any question as to who is in charge.[8]

When the interaction that is initiated by 'first impressions' is itself merely the initial interaction in an extended series of interactions involving the same participants, we speak of 'getting off on the right foot' and feel that it is crucial that we do so. Thus, one learns that some teachers take the following view:

> You can't ever let them get the upper hand on you or you're through. So I start out tough. The first day I get a new class in, I let them know who's boss. . . . You've got to start off tough, then you can ease up as you go along. If you start out easy-going, when you try to get tough, they'll just look at you and laugh.[9]

Similarly, attendants in mental institutions may feel that if the new patient is sharply put in his place the first day on the ward and made to see who is boss, much future difficulty will be prevented.[10]

Given the fact that the individual effectively projects a definition of the situation when he enters the presence of others, we can assume that events may occur within the interaction which contradict, discredit, or otherwise throw doubt upon this projection. When these disruptive events occur, the interaction itself may come to a confused and embarrassed halt. Some of the assumptions upon which the responses of the participants had been predicated become untenable, and the participants find themselves lodged in an interaction for which the situation has been wrongly defined and is now no longer defined. At such moments the individual whose presentation has been discredited may feel ashamed while the others present may feel hostile, and all the participants may come to feel ill at ease, nonplussed, out of countenance, embarrassed, experiencing the kind of anomaly that is generated when the minute social system of face-to-face interaction breaks down.

In stressing the fact that the initial definition of the situation projected by an individual tends to provide a plan for the cooperative activity that follows – in stressing this action point of view – we must not overlook the crucial fact that any projected definition of the situation also has a distinctive moral character. It is this moral character of projections that will chiefly concern us in this report. Society is organized on the principle that any individual who possesses certain social characteristics has a moral right to expect that others will value and treat him in an appropriate way. Connected with this principle is a second, namely that an individual who implicitly or explicitly signifies that he has certain social characteristics ought in fact to be what he claims he is. In consequence, when an individual projects a definition of the situation and thereby makes an implicit or explicit claim to be a person of a particular kind, he automatically exerts a moral demand upon the others, obliging them to value and treat him in the manner that persons of this kind have a right to expect. He also implicitly forgoes all claims to be things he does not appear to be [11] and hence forgoes the treatment that would be appropriate for such individuals. The others find, then, that the individual has informed them as to what is and as to what they *ought* to see as the 'is'.

One cannot judge the importance of definitional disruptions by the frequency with which they occur, for apparently they would occur more frequently were not constant precautions taken. We find that preventive practices are constantly employed to avoid these embarrassments and that corrective practices are constantly employed to compensate for discrediting occurrences that have not been successfully avoided. When the individual employs these strategies and tactics to protect his own projections, we may refer to them as 'defensive practices'; when a participant employs them to save the definition of the situation projected by another, we speak of 'protective practices' or 'tact'. Together, defensive and protective practices comprise the techniques employed to safeguard the impression fostered by an individual during his presence before others. It should be added that while we may be ready to see that no fostered impression would survive if defensive practices were not employed, we are less ready perhaps to see that few impressions could survive if those who received the impression did not exert tact in their reception of it.

In addition to the fact that precautions are taken to prevent disruption of projected definitions, we may also note that an intense interest in these disruptions comes to play a significant role in the social life of the group. Practical jokes and social games are played in which embarrassments which are to be taken unseriously are purposely engineered.[12] Fantasies are created in which devastating exposures occur. Anecdotes from the past – real, embroidered, or fictitious – are told and retold, detailed disruptions which occurred, almost occurred, or occurred and were admirably resolved. There seems to be no grouping which does not have a ready supply of these games, reveries, and cautionary tales, to be used as a source of humour, a catharsis for anxieties, and a sanction for inducing individuals to be modest in their claims and reasonable in their projected expectations. The individual may tell himself through dreams of getting into impossible positions. Families tell of the time a guest got his dates mixed and arrived when neither the house nor anyone in it was ready for him. Journalists tell of times when an all-too-meaningful misprint occurred, and the paper's assumption of objectivity or decorum was humorously discredited. Public servants tell of times a client ridiculously misunderstood form instructions, giving answers which implied an unanticipated and bizarre definition of the situation.[13] Seamen, whose home away from home is rigorously he-man, tell stories of coming back home and inadvertently asking mother to 'pass the fucking butter'.[14] Diplomats tell of the time a near-sighted queen asked a republican ambassador about the health of his king.[15]

To summarize, then, I assume that when an individual appears before others he will have many motives for trying to control the impression they receive of the situation. This report is concerned with some of the common techniques that persons employ to sustain such impressions and with some of the common contingencies associated with the employment of these techniques. The specific content of any activity presented by the individual participant, or the role it plays in the interdependent activities of an on-going social system, will not be at issue; I shall be concerned only with the participants' dramaturgical problems of presenting the activity before others. The issues dealt with by stage-craft and stage management are sometimes trivial but they are quite general; they seem to occur everywhere in social life, providing a clear-cut dimension for formal sociological analysis.

It will be convenient to end this introduction with some definitions that are implied in what has gone before and required for what is to follow. For the purpose of this report, interaction (that is, face-to-face interaction) may be roughly defined as the reciprocal influence of individuals upon one another's actions when in one another's immediate physical presence. *An* interaction may be defined as all the interaction which occurs throughout any one occasion when a given set of individuals are in one another's continuous presence; the term 'an encounter' would do as well. A 'performance' may be defined as all the activity of a given participant on a given occasion which serves to influence in any way any of the other participants. Taking a particular participant and his performance as a basic point of reference, we may refer to those who contribute the other performances as the audience, observers, or co-participants. The pre-established pattern of action which is unfolded during a performance and which may be presented or played through on other occasions may be called a 'part' or 'routine'.[16] These situational terms can easily be related to conventional structural ones. When an individual or performer plays the same part to the same audience on different occasions, a social relationship is likely to arise. Defining social role as the enactment of rights and duties attached to a given status, we can say that a social role will involve one or more parts and that each of these different parts may be presented by the performer on a series of occasions to the same kinds of audience or to an audience of the same persons.

20

Interaction between text and reader

Wolfgang Iser

From Iser, Wolfgang 1980: 'Interaction between text and reader' in Suleiman, S. and Crosman, I. (eds.) *The reader in the text*. Princeton, N.J.: Princeton University Press, 106–13.

Central to the reading of every literary work is the interaction between its structure and its recipient. This is why the phenomenological theory of art has
emphatically drawn attention to the fact that the study of a literary work should
concern not only the actual text but also, and in equal measure, the actions
involved in responding to that text. The text itself simply offers 'schematized
aspects'[1] through which the aesthetic object of the work can be produced.

From this we may conclude that the literary work has two poles, which we
might call the artistic and the aesthetic: the artistic pole is the author's text, and
the aesthetic is the realization accomplished by the reader. In view of this
polarity, it is clear that the work itself cannot be identical with the text or with its
actualization but must be situated somewhere between the two. It must inevitably
be virtual in character, as it cannot be reduced to the reality of the text or to the
subjectivity of the reader, and it is from this virtuality that it derives its
dynamism. As the reader passes through the various perspectives offered by the
text, and relates the different views and patterns to one another, he sets the work
in motion, and so sets himself in motion, too.

If the virtual position of the work is between text and reader, its actualization is
clearly the result of an interaction between the two, and so exclusive concentration on either the author's techniques or the reader's psychology will tell us little
about the reading process itself. This is not to deny the vital importance of each of
the two poles – it is simply that if one loses sight of the relationship, one loses
sight of the virtual work. Despite its uses, separate analysis would only be conclusive if the relationship were that of transmitter and receiver, for this would
presuppose a common code, ensuring accurate communication since the message
would only be travelling one way. In literary works, however, the message is
transmitted in two ways, in that the reader 'receives' it by composing it. There is
no common code – at best one could say that a common code may arise in the
course of the process. Starting out from this assumption, we must search for
structures that will enable us to describe basic conditions of interaction, for only
then shall we be able to gain some insight into the potential effects inherent in the
work.

It is difficult to describe this interaction, not least because literary criticism has
very little to go on in the way of guidelines, and, of course, the two partners in the

communication process, namely, the text and the reader, are far easier to analyse than is the event that takes place between them. However, there are discernible conditions that govern interaction generally, and some of these will certainly apply to the special reader-text relationship. The differences and similarities may become clear if we briefly examine types of interaction that have emerged from psychoanalytical research into the structure of communication. The findings of the *Tavistock School* will serve us as a model in order to move the problem into focus.[2]

In assessing interpersonal relationships R. D. Laing writes: 'I may not actually be able to see myself as others see me, but I am constantly supposing them to be seeing me in particular ways, and I am constantly acting in the light of the actual or supposed attitudes, opinions, needs, and so on the other has in respect of me.'[3] Now, the views that others have of me cannot be called 'pure' perception; they are the result of interpretation. And this need for interpretation arises from the structure of interpersonal experience. We have experience of one another insofar as we know one another's conduct; but we have no experience of how others experience us.

In his book, *The politics of experience*, Laing pursues this line of thought by saying: '*your experience of me is invisible to me and my experience of you is invisible to you*. I cannot experience your experience. You cannot experience my experience. We are both invisible men. All men are invisible to one another. Experience is man's invisibility to man.'[4] It is this invisibility, however, that forms the basis of interpersonal relations – a basis which Laing calls 'no-thing.'[5] 'That which is really "between" cannot be named by any things that come between. The between is itself no-thing.'[6] In all our interpersonal relations we build upon this 'no-thing,' for we react as if we knew how our partners experienced us; we continually form views of their views, and then act as if our views of their views are realities. Contact therefore depends upon our continually filling in a central gap in our experience. Thus, dyadic and dynamic interaction comes about only because we are unable to experience how we experience one another, which in turn proves to be a propellant to interaction. Out of this fact arises the basic need for interpretation, which regulates the whole process of interaction. As we cannot perceive without preconception, each percept, in turn, only makes sense to us if it is processed, for pure perception is quite impossible. Hence dyadic interaction is not given by nature but arises out of an interpretative activity, which will contain a view of others and, unavoidably, an image of ourselves.

An obvious and major difference between reading and all forms of social interaction is the fact that with reading there is no *face-to-face situation*.[7] A text cannot adapt itself to each reader it comes into contact with. The partners in dyadic interaction can ask each other questions in order to ascertain how far their images have bridged the gap of the inexperienceability of one another's experiences. The reader, however, can never learn from the text how accurate or inaccurate are his views of it. Furthermore, dyadic interaction serves specific purposes, so that the interaction always has a regulative context, which often serves as a *tertium comparationis*. There is no such frame of reference governing the text-reader relationship; on the contrary, the codes which might regulate this interaction are fragmented in the text, and must first be reassembled or, in most cases, restructured before any frame of reference *can* be established. Here, then, in conditions and intention, we find two basic differences between the text-reader relationship and the dyadic interaction between social partners.

Now, it is the very lack of ascertainability and defined intention that brings about the text-reader interaction, and here there is a vital link with dyadic interaction. Social communication, as we have seen, arises out of the fact that people cannot experience how others experience them, and not out of the common situation or out of the conventions that join both partners together. The situations and conventions regulate the manner in which gaps are filled, but the gaps in turn arise out of the inexperienceability and, consequently, function as a basic inducement to communication. Similarly, it is the gaps, the fundamental asymmetry between text and reader, that give rise to communication in the reading process; the lack of a common situation and a common frame of reference corresponds to the 'no-thing,' which brings about the interaction between persons. Asymmetry and the 'no-thing' are all different forms of an indeterminate, constitutive blank, which underlies all processes of interaction. With dyadic interaction, the imbalance is removed by the establishment of pragmatic connections resulting in an action, which is why the preconditions are always clearly defined in relation to situations and common frames of reference. The imbalance between text and reader, however, is undefined, and it is this very indeterminacy that increases the variety of communication possible.

Now, if communication between text and reader is to be successful, clearly the reader's activity must also be controlled in some way by the text. The control cannot be as specific as in a *face-to-face-situation*, equally it cannot be as determinate as a social code, which regulates social interaction. However, the guiding devices operative in the reading process have to initiate communication and to control it. This control cannot be understood as a tangible entity occurring independently of the process of communication. Although exercised *by* the text, it is not *in* the text. This is well illustrated by a comment Virginia Woolf made on the novels of Jane Austen:

> Jane Austen is thus a mistress of much deeper emotion than appears upon the surface. She stimulates us to supply what is not there. What she offers is, apparently, a trifle, yet is composed of something that expands in the reader's mind and endows with the most enduring form of life scenes which are outwardly trivial. Always the stress is laid upon character. . . . The turns and twists of the dialogue keep us on the tenterhooks of suspense. Our attention is half upon the present moment, half upon the future. . . . Here, indeed, in this unfinished and in the main inferior story, are all the elements of Jane Austen's greatness.[8]

What is missing from the apparently trivial scenes, the gaps arising out of the dialogue – this is what stimulates the reader into filling the blanks with projections. He is drawn into the events and made to supply what is meant from what is not said. What is said only appears to take on significance as a reference to what is not said; it is the implications and not the statements that give shape and weight to the meaning. But as the unsaid comes to life in the reader's imagination, so the said 'expands' to take on greater significance than might have been supposed: even trivial scenes can seem surprisingly profound. The 'enduring form of life' which Virginia Woolf speaks of is not manifested on the printed page; it is a product arising out of the interaction between text and reader.

Communication in literature, then, is a process set in motion and regulated, not by a given code, but by a mutually restrictive and magnifying interaction between the explicit and the implicit, between revelation and concealment. What is concealed spurs the reader into action, but this action is also controlled by what is revealed; the explicit in its turn is transformed when the implicit has been brought to light. Whenever the reader bridges the gaps, communication begins. The gaps function as a kind of pivot on which the whole text – reader relationship revolves. Hence, the structured blanks of the text stimulate the process of ideation to be performed by the reader on terms set by the text. There is, however, another place in the textual system where text and reader converge, and that is marked by the various types of negation which arise in the course of the reading. Blanks and negations both control the process of communication in their own different ways: the blanks leave open the connection between textual perspectives, and so spur the reader into coordinating these perspectives and patterns – in other words, they induce the reader to perform basic operations *within* the text. The various types of negation invoke familiar and determinate elements or knowledge only to cancel them out. What is cancelled, however, remains in view, and thus brings about modifications in the reader's attitude toward what is familiar or determinate – in other words, he is guided to adopt a position *in relation* to the text.

In order to spotlight the communication process we shall confine our consideration to how the blanks trigger off and simultaneously control the reader's activity. Blanks indicate that the different segments and patterns of the text are to be connected even though the text itself does not say so. They are the unseen joints of the text, and as they mark off schemata and textual perspectives from one another, they simultaneously prompt acts of ideation on the reader's part. Consequently when the schemata and perspectives have been linked together, the blanks 'disappear'.

If we are to grasp the unseen structure that regulates but does not formulate the connection or even the meaning, we must bear in mind the various forms in which the textual segments are presented to the reader's viewpoint in the reading process. Their most elementary form is to be seen on the level of the story. The threads of the plot are suddenly broken off, or continued in unexpected directions. One narrative section centres on a particular character and is then continued by the abrupt introduction of new characters. These sudden changes are often denoted by new chapters and so are clearly distinguished; the object of this distinction, however, is not separation so much as a tacit invitation to find the missing link. Furthermore, in each articulated reading moment, only segments of textual perspectives are present to the reader's wandering viewpoint.

In order to become fully aware of the implication, we must bear in mind that a narrative text, for instance, is composed of a variety of perspectives, which outline the author's view and also provide access to what the reader is meant to visualize. As a rule, there are four main perspectives in narration: those of the narrator, the characters, the plot, and the fictitious reader. Although these may differ in order of importance, none of them on its own is identical to the meaning of the text, which is to be brought about by their constant intertwining through the reader in the reading process. An increase in the number of blanks is bound to occur through the frequent subdivisions of each of the textual perspectives; thus the narrator's perspective is often split into that of the implied author's set against that of the author as narrator. The hero's perspective may be set against that of the minor characters. The fictitious reader's perspective may be divided between the explicit position ascribed to him and the implicit attitude he must adopt to that position.

As the reader's wandering viewpoint travels between all these segments, its constant switching during the time flow of reading intertwines them, thus bringing forth a network of perspectives, within which each perspective opens a view not only of others, but also of the intended imaginary object. Hence no single textual perspective can be equated with this imaginary object, of which it forms only one aspect. The object itself is a product of interconnection, the structuring of which is to a great extent regulated and controlled by blanks.

21

Holbein's *The Ambassadors*

John Berger

From Berger, John 1972: *Ways of seeing*. Harmondsworth: Penguin/London: British Broadcasting Corporation, 89–91, 94–7.
Note: In order to focus on the author's discussion of one painting, two sections of comment and one illustration are omitted.

Holbein's painting of *The Ambassadors* (1533) stands at the beginning of the tradition and, as often happens with a work at the opening of a new period, its character is undisguised. The way it is painted shows what it is about. How is it painted?

It is painted with great skill to create the illusion in the spectator that he is

looking at real objects and materials. We pointed out in the first essay that the sense of touch was like a restricted, static sense of sight. Every square inch of the surface of this painting, whilst remaining purely visual, appeals to, importunes, the sense of touch. The eye moves from fur to silk to metal to wood to velvet to marble to paper to felt, and each time what the eye perceives is already translated, within the painting itself, into the language of tactile sensation. The two men have a certain presence and there are many objects which symbolize ideas, but it is the materials, the stuff, by which the men are surrounded and clothed which dominate the painting.

Except for the faces and hands, there is not a surface in this picture which does not make one aware of how it has been elaborately worked over – by weavers, embroiderers, carpet-makers, goldsmiths, leather workers, mosaic-makers, furriers, tailors, jewellers – and of how this working-over and the resulting rich- ness of each surface has been finally worked-over and reproduced by Holbein the painter.

This emphasis and the skill that lay behind it was to remain a constant of the tradition of oil painting.

Works of art in earlier traditions celebrated wealth. But wealth was then a symbol of a fixed social or divine order. Oil painting celebrated a new kind of wealth – which was dynamic and which found its only sanction in the supreme buying power of money. Thus painting itself had to be able to demonstrate the desirability of what money could buy. And the visual desirability of what can be bought lies in its tangibility, in how it will reward the touch, the hand, of the owner.

In the foreground of Holbein's *Ambassadors* there is a mysterious, slanting, oval form. This represents a highly distorted skull: a skull as it might be seen in a distorting mirror. There are several theories about how it was painted and why the ambassadors wanted it put there. But all agree that it was a kind of memento mori: a play on the medieval idea of using a skull as a continual reminder of the presence of death. What is significant for our argument is that the skull is painted in a (literally) quite different optic from everything else in the picture. If the skull had been painted like the rest, its metaphysical implication would have dis- appeared; it would have become an object like everything else, a mere part of a mere skeleton of a man who happened to be dead.

This was a problem which persisted throughout the tradition. When meta- physical symbols are introduced (and later there were painters who, for instance, introduced realistic skulls as symbols of death), their symbolism is usually made unconvincing or unnatural by the unequivocal, static materialism of the painting- method.

[A section of more general comments is omitted here]

Let us now return to the two ambassadors, to their presence as men. This will mean reading the painting differently: not at the level of what it shows within its frame, but at the level of what it refers to outside it.

The two men are confident and formal; as between each other they are relaxed. But how do they look at the painter – or at us? There is in their gaze and their stance a curious lack of expectation of any recognition. It is as though in principle their worth cannot be recognized by others. They look as though they are looking at something of which they are not part. At something which surrounds them but from which they wish to exclude themselves. At the best it may be a crowd honouring them; at the worst, intruders.

What were the relations of such men with the rest of the world?

The painted objects on the shelves between them were intended to supply – to the few who could read the allusions – a certain amount of information about their position in the world. Four centuries later we can interpret this information according to our own perspective.

The scientific instruments on the top shelf were for navigation. This was the time when the ocean trade routes were being opened up for the slave trade and for the traffic which was to siphon the riches from other continents into Europe, and later supply the capital for the take-off of the Industrial Revolution.

In 1519 Magellan had set out, with the backing of Charles V, to sail round the world. He and an astronomer friend, with whom he had planned the voyage, arranged with the Spanish court that they personally were to keep twenty per cent of the profits made, and the right to run the government of any land they conquered.

The globe on the bottom shelf is a new one which charts this recent voyage of Magellan's. Holbein has added to the globe the name of the estate in France which belonged to the ambassador on the left. Beside the globe are a book of arithmetic, a hymn book and a lute. To colonize a land it was necessary to convert its people to Christianity and accounting, and thus to prove to them that European civilization was the most advanced in the world. Its art included.

[A further section of more general comment is here omitted]

How directly or not the two ambassadors were involved in the first colonizing ventures is not particularly important, for what we are concerned with here is a stance towards the world; and this was general to a whole class. The two ambassadors belonged to a class who were convinced that the world was there to furnish their residence in it. In its extreme form this conviction was confirmed by the relations being set up between colonial conqueror and the colonized.

These relations between conqueror and colonized tended to be self-perpetuating. The sight of the other confirmed each in his inhuman estimate of himself. The circularity of the relationship can be seen in the following diagram – as also the

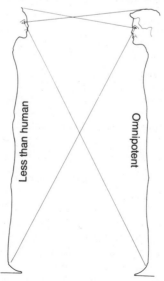

Less than human   Omnipotent

mutual solitude. The way in which each sees the other confirms his own view of himself.

The gaze of the ambassadors is both aloof and wary. They expect no reciprocity. They wish the image of their presence to impress others with their vigilance and their distance. The presence of kings and emperors had once impressed in a similar way, but their images had been comparatively impersonal. What is new and disconcerting here is the *individualized presence* which needs to suggest *distance*. Individualism finally posits equality. Yet equality must be made inconceivable.

22

The flower dream

Sigmund Freud

From Freud, Sigmund 1976: *The interpretation of dreams*. Translated by James Strachey, edited by James Strachey and Alan Tyson, revised by Angela Richards. Harmondsworth: Penguin Books, 493–98.

The naïve dreams of healthy people actually often contain a much simpler, more perspicuous and more characteristic symbolism than those of neurotics; for in the latter, as a result of the more powerful working of the censorship and of the consequently more far-reaching dream-distortion, the symbolism may be obscure and hard to interpret. The dream recorded below will serve to illustrate this fact. It was dreamt by a girl who is not neurotic but is of a somewhat prudish and reserved character. In the course of conversation with her I learnt that she was engaged, but that there were some difficulties in the way of her marriage which were likely to lead to its postponement. Of her own accord she told me the following dream.

' "*I arrange the centre of a table with flowers for a birthday.*"* In reply to a question she told me that in the dream she seemed to be in her own home (where she was not at present living) and had "a feeling of happiness".

' "Popular" symbolism made it possible for me to translate the dream unaided. It was an expression of her bridal wishes: the table with its floral centre-piece symbolized herself and her genitals; she represented her wishes for the future as fulfilled, for her thoughts were already occupied with the birth of a baby; so her marriage lay a long way behind her.

'I pointed out to her that "*the 'centre' of a table*" was an unusual expression (which she admitted), but I could not of course question her further directly on that point. I carefully avoided suggesting the meaning of the symbols to her, and merely asked what came into her head in connection with the separate parts of the dream. In the course of the analysis her reserve gave place to an evident interest in the interpretation and to an openness made possible by the seriousness of the conversation.

'When I asked what flowers they had been, her first reply was: "*expensive flowers; one has to pay for them*", and then that they had been "*lilies of the valley, violets and pinks or carnations*". I assumed that the word "lily" appeared in the dream in its popular sense as a symbol of chastity; she confirmed this assumption, for her association to "lily" was "*purity*". "*Valley*" is a frequent female symbol in

---

* In the present analysis all the material printed in italics occurs in English in the original, exactly as here reproduced.

dreams; so that the chance combination of the two symbols in the English name of the flower was used in the dream-symbolism to stress the preciousness of her virginity – *"expensive flowers, one has to pay for them"* – and to express her expectation that her husband would know how to appreciate its value. The phrase *"expensive flowers, etc."*, as will be seen, had a different meaning in the case of each of the three flower-symbols.

"Violets" was ostensibly quite asexual; but, very boldly, as it seemed to me, I thought I could trace a secret meaning for the word in an unconscious link with the French word *"viol"* ["rape"]. To my surprise the dreamer gave as an association the English word *"violate"*. The dream had made use of the great chance similarity between the words *"violet"* and *"violate"* – the difference in their pronunciation lies merely in the different stress upon their final syllables – in order to express "in the language of flowers" the dreamer's thoughts on the violence of defloration (another term that employs flower symbolism) and possibly also a masochistic trait in her character. A pretty instance of the "verbal bridges"* crossed by the paths leading to the unconscious. The words *"one has to pay for them"* signified having to pay with her life for being a wife and a mother.

'In connection with *"pinks"*, which she went on to call *"carnations"*, I thought of the connection between that word and "carnal". But the dreamer's association to it was *"colour"*. She added that *"carnations"* were the flowers which her *fiancé* gave her frequently and in great numbers. At the end of her remarks she suddenly confessed of her own accord that she had not told the truth: what had occurred to her had not been *"colour"* but *"incarnation"* – the word I had expected. Incidentally *"colour"* itself was not a very remote association, but was determined by the meaning of *"carnation"* (flesh-colour) – was determined, that is, by the same complex. This lack of straightforwardness showed that it was at this point that resistance was greatest, and corresponded to the fact that this was where the symbolism was most clear and that the struggle between libido and its repression was at its most intense in relation to this phallic theme. The dreamer's comment to the effect that her *fiancé* frequently gave her flowers of that kind was an indication not only of the double sense of the word *"carnations"* but also of their phallic meaning in the dream. The gift of flowers, an exciting factor of the dream derived from her current life, was used to express an exchange of sexual gifts: she was making a gift of her virginity and expected a full emotional and sexual life in return for it. At this point, too, the words *"expensive flowers, one has to pay for them"* must have had what was no doubt literally a financial meaning. – Thus the flower symbolism in this dream included virginal femininity, masculinity and an allusion to defloration by violence. It is worth pointing out in this connection that sexual flower symbolism, which, indeed, occurs very commonly in other connections, symbolizes the human organs of sex by blossoms, which are the sexual organs of plants. It may perhaps be true in general that gifts of flowers between lovers have this unconscious meaning.

'The birthday for which she was preparing in the dream meant, no doubt, the

---

* Freud here refers the reader to the following footnote from earlier in the volume: *Footnote added 1909:* See my volume on jokes (1905a) [especially the later part of Chapter VI] and the use of 'verbal bridges' in the solution of neurotic symptoms. [See, e.g., the synthesis of Dora's first dream at the end of Section II of Freud, 1905b (where the term 'switch-words' is also used), and the solution of the 'Rat Man's' rat-obsession in Section I (G) of Freud, 1909.] (Comment in square brackets added by Angela Richards.)

birth of a baby. She was identifying herself with her *fiancé*, and was representing him as "arranging" her for a birth – that is, as copulating with her. The latent thought may have run: "If I were he, I wouldn't wait – I would deflower my *fiancée* without asking her leave – I would use violence." This was indicated by the word *"violate"*, and in this way the sadistic component of the libido found expression.

'In a deeper layer of the dream, the phrase *"I arrange . . ."* must no doubt have an auto-erotic, that is to say, an infantile, significance.

'The dreamer also revealed an awareness, which was only possible to her in a dream, of her physical deficiency: she saw herself like a table, without projections, and on that account laid all the more emphasis on the preciousness of the *"centre"* – on another occasion she used the words, *"a centre-piece of flowers"* – that is to say, on her virginity. The horizontal attribute of a table must also have contributed something to the symbol.

'The concentration of the dream should be observed: there was nothing superfluous in it, every word was a symbol.

'Later on the dreamer produced an addendum to the dream: *'I decorate the flowers with green crinkled paper."* She added that it was *"fancy paper"* of the sort used for covering common flower-pots. She went on: *"to hide untidy things, whatever was to be seen, which was not pretty to the eye; there is a gap, a little space in the flowers. The paper looks like velvet or moss."* – To *"decorate"* she gave the association *"decorum"*, as I had expected. She said the green colour predominated, and her association to it was *"hope"* – another link with pregnancy. – In this part of the dream the chief factor was not identification with a man; ideas of shame and self-relevation came to the fore. She was making herself beautiful for him and was admitting physical defects which she felt ashamed of and was trying to correct. Her associations *"velvet"* and *"moss"* were a clear indication of a reference to pubic hair.

'This dream, then, gave expression to thoughts of which the girl was scarcely aware in her waking life – thoughts concerned with sensual love and its organs. She was being "aranged for a birthday" – that is, she was being copulated with. The fear of being deflowered was finding expression, and perhaps, too, ideas of pleasurable suffering. She admitted her physical deficiencies to herself and over-compensated for them by an over-valuation of her virginity. Her shame put forward as an excuse for the signs of sensuality the fact that its purpose was the production of a baby. Material considerations, too, alien to a lover's mind, found their way to expression. The affect attaching to this simple dream – a feeling of happiness – indicated that powerful emotional complexes had found satisfaction in it.'

Ferenczi (1917)* has justly pointed out that the meaning of symbols and the significance of dreams can be arrived at with particular ease from the dreams of precisely those people who are uninitiated into psycho-analysis.

---

* This paragraph was added in 1919.

Section IV
Media: institutions and meanings

Most programmes of work in Communication Studies include a large amount of material on aspects of mass communications or the media. Although everyone easily understands these two categories to include television, radio and the press, there is a variation in usage such that study of other forms – of cinema, or popular music or of book publishing – may or may not be included.

However, what both terms try to do is to separate out as *different*, and therefore worthy of distinctive kinds of study, those *means and processes* of communication which are *industrialized* and thus able to carry out 'messaging' activities on a large scale (via mass production and mass distribution).

Another of their characteristics which seems to justify special consideration is the heavily 'unbalanced' nature of the processes involved when viewed within the general context of human communicative interaction. For a start, a very few people are senders, whereas quite often millions of them are receivers. Whilst we should be very careful about regarding media reception as essentially passive (it's quite easy to confuse physical with mental activity!), a strong one-way character would appear to be central to the very nature of modern media systems. Yet although the number of receivers is great, the actual business of reception does not, in the main, occur within group situations, but in relatively individualized forms (the private scanning of the newspaper, the watching of TV, perhaps with members of the family or friends). To complicate things further, many of the 'message products' which media systems produce and disseminate are very much the result of intensive group activity rather than of individually exercised intentions and skills.

This rather paradoxical combination of 'mass', 'group' and 'individualized' dimensions is an important feature of media processes and many of the studies in this section attempt to come to terms with it.

There are a number of reasons why academic work on communication should so frequently place study of the media near the centre of its concerns. The varieties of visual and verbal signification used by these systems in exploiting their medium-specific possibilities (e.g. in photography, film editing, page layout and speech styles) and the kinds of adaptive transformations which can be worked upon primary behaviour (as in the interview, the talk-show, the forms of radio and television drama and of documentary) provide a range of discourses whose formal complexity understandably attracts analytical attention. There are thus good technical reasons for academic interest.

But for the primary cause of this interest we must perhaps look at the continuing and widespread *concern* about the linked economic and cultural activities of media systems, and the growing recognition of their importance in not only informing and entertaining, but in actually helping greatly to keep in meaningful existence what in many modern societies is referred to as 'the public'. Clearly, most inquiries informed by this concern are essentially ones into *media power*.

That the media are powerful and do exert an influence over social organization and social change would appear to be the strong if unspecified assumption of most people. At this level of generality, it would be an assumption very difficult to counter too.

If we look, for instance, at the changes which television has brought to British and American political processes, it is clear that the whole business of political leadership, the function of party conferences and the organization and conduct of elections has been modified quite radically. Not only has there been an increased emphasis on *personality* (taking further those conventions of personalization which the popular press's use of photography and informal address had developed) but political campaigning itself has become more and more a *media-based* activity rather than an activity simply 'covered' by the media. The details and, certainly, the implications of this shift are open to analysis and argument, but it would be difficult to deny its basic character and importance. We might well want to consider this as evidence of media power, however generalized the level at which it is perceived. Many comparable instances of shifts and relations of dependence could be drawn from other fields of public life – from the new structures of the entertainment industry, for example, or from the function within the national economy of advertising (revenue from which has played a crucial part in the growth and character both of the press and of broadcasting).

If we want a more specific kind of example of the consequences for *individuals*, rather than for *institutions*, of the various regional and national media systems, we have only to think of the source of many of the images, ideas and sets of associations inside our own heads. What comes into mind when we hear words like 'inflation' for example, or are prompted to consider the problems of 'unemployment', 'race relations' or 'nuclear disarmament'? As like as not, however independently-minded or experienced we consider ourselves to be, some (most?) of the images and terms of classification and evaluation which we draw on and employ in thinking and speaking on such matters will derive from our use of media sources. They will either have been relayed ('mediated') to us through the media or actually devised by media professionals themselves. This certainly doesn't mean that we are programmed into an uncritical dependence on the accounts and judgements of others. But it does mean that any attempt to look at aspects of contemporary *consciousness* – for instance, at how people think and feel about themselves and about their relations with others across differences of gender, race, social class and age – must necessarily take acount of the extended 'symbolic environment' from which such mental activities of the individual subject are now likely to be resourced.

It is worth noting, too, that here we are concerned with more than narrowly journalistic sources. A feature film, or a situation-comedy, may have as much a modifying influence on our thought processes and our personal 'image-bank' as a news item, perhaps even more so given the relative levels of imaginative engagement they encourage. Think, for example, of how much Europeans may feel they know about life in a modern American city, about the 'way things are' there – the kinds of personality and social relationship which are characteristic, with perhaps special reference to the very rich and to criminal behaviour! All this is thanks largely to the success of the American film industry and to the extensive importing of US television series.

But we don't really need to cite the example of knowledge about another culture. What about our sense of our own history (the Second World War?) or of how labelled groupings to which we may not belong ('northerners', 'students', 'housewives', the 'professional middle class') conduct their lives? How far does this rely, in however fragmented and personally reworked a fashion, on the kinds of stories, scenes and characterizations, the kinds of popular narrative, which the institutions of mass communication routinely provide?

Using three quite influential terms in media research, we can sum this up by saying that in addition to performing both a *gate-keeping* function (giving certain images and ideas public prominence whilst ignoring or filtering out others) and a related *agenda-setting* function (establishing a kind of national agenda of issues to be remarked on and talked about), the media also have a *reality-defining* effect. That is to say, they provide us with many of the bits and pieces out of which we fashion our sense of the 'way things are'.

Studying as precisely as possible the institutional conditions, communicational character and consequences of the 'reality-defining' aspect of media operations (*not* a matter of brainwashing despite the frequency with which debates on violence or on politics suggest this) has been the goal of much of that intensive research interest noted above.

Questions of *how* exactly to study media processes and at what *points* or *phases* they are best studied have been the subject of much debate within those arts and social science disciplines from which research has developed. Broadly speaking, there has tended to be a division into three, unfortunately often isolated, fields of work – policy and production studies, content or textual analysis and audience research. Until quite recently, the kinds of concern which are to be found elsewhere in this book, concern with the dynamics of meaning-production and communicational form, were to be found only in research on media texts, where the influence of ideas in Linguistics, Literary Criticism and Film Studies was most strong. Now, however, a recognition of the complex character of the media's linguistic and symbolic functions, of the interplay between public conventions and individual subjectivity in the business of meaning-making, has been shown either side of work on media texts in work on institutions and audiences. Complementing this, there has been a sharper awareness shown by textual researchers of the problems which can result from studying formal properties of media output without consideration of production histories or the circumstances of distribution and of reception among different audiences and readerships.

So, for example, we are beginning to see historians of the media investigating not only matters of policy and organization but questions of developing forms and styles; researchers of output attempting to take into account as fully as possible the activities involved in media production, and inquiries into audience response which are based on a detailed analysis of how the verbal and visual features of print and electronic messages are organized. This latter initiative, towards a more sophisticated kind of reception studies, echoes linguistic pragmatics in working from the observation that meanings do not somehow exist *in* texts (as inherent properties) but are the product of *conventions* being *applied* to those significations out of which texts are made. When these interpretative conventions differ, the text may mean different things to different viewers or readers. To put the matter this way opens up more fully for investigation the range of interpretative resources upon which people draw in 'making sense' out of media items and highlights the different levels of activity involved in sense-making. When added to the 'reality-defining' idea, it also gives a new dimension to inquiry into the mechanisms of media influence and media effects.

Perhaps one of the biggest questions for current research is the relationship between, on the one hand, the various factors of institutional and textual power, and on the other, the variations of audience interpretation and use. It is important not to emphasize one to the exclusion of the other because this merely reproduces the see-saw movement between simplistic 'all powerful' and 'hardly powerful at all' positions. Further development will need to be based on exploration at a number of levels and may well require a radical reformulation of the terms currently used in thinking both about media power and about audiences. A recognition of the fact that the audience's activity, whatever this may be, is itself circumscribed and conditioned by larger socio-cultural structures (a *variant* reading is not necessarily an *optional* one) is also required if a crude perspective, opposing 'viewer freedom' to 'media control', is to be avoided.

In the extracts which follow, we have concentrated on broadcasting, largely because a number of advances in the study of television have been made in the last few years. This, in turn, is probably because television, as a result of its dominance within the national media pattern, has attracted a far greater amount of research attention than either radio or the press. There are some signs that this situation is slowly shifting as a new wave of researchers recognizes the continuing importance of other media, particularly at the regional and local level.

Nevertheless, we think that our focus gives greater cohesion to the items in the section and that this is thematically reinforced by the illuminating concern which nearly all the items have with tracing the relationships between practices and meanings. That is to say, rather than being exclusively either accounts of programme production or critical studies of programmes, the pieces interconnect factors of institution, form and activity so as to pose questions of meaning (and, often, of power) in a richer and more productive way and in a way which connects firmly with material in the earlier section of this Reader.

In our first extract, **John Ellis** looks at television in relation to cinema, a comparison and a contrast which nicely points up some of the distinctive features of television as a *medium*. In particular, Ellis wants to explore the different ways in which television is 'domestic', a notion which he sees as essential to our understanding of its processes and its social power. He has something to say, too, about how the facility of direct address (by which people appear to 'look out from the screen' and speak directly to the viewer) regulates the relationship between programme material and audience. It's perhaps worth testing out his propositions as honestly as you can against your own viewing experience and viewing habits before considering further their pertinence for our understanding of television's political and cultural functions. The argument is nicely designed to establish some basic ideas about the character of the medium as a communicative system, to explore some of the currently-used formats and conventions, and then to move on to more general and speculative arguments about the consequences of the kind of spectatorial experience offered.

A rather tighter perspective is adopted by **Richard Paterson** in his article on Britain's long-running and popular television serial, *Coronation Street*. What assumptions underpin the relationship between this hugely successful programme and its audience? Paterson's piece is notable for its attempt at working across a number of related levels at which he feels the programme should be considered, from its nature as a product within a commercial enterprise having its own history and distinctive cost-structures through to the particular kinds of identification and emotion which the specific uses of image and of narrative seek to elicit. In this latter area, the discussion usefully complements that of Ellis.

As well as providing the student with a lot of information, Paterson succeeds admirably in relating together the various factors of production and signification, offering the reader a clear and suggestive account of that dramatic construction of community upon which the programme's appeal is based.

Programme appeal is the specific topic in **Ien Ang's** study of responses to *Dallas*. Using the idea of the interpretative productivity of the reader (the links here with Iser, Section III item 20, are very close), Ang asks questions about the enjoyment which viewers derive from the programme and about the assessments they make of the characters. Her sample is drawn from letters which she invited by advertising in the (Dutch) press. Thus, rather than coming to the text via production contexts in the manner of Ellis and Paterson, she attempts to a large extent to reconstruct the '*Dallas* experience' from her viewers' accounts. This leads her to query the terms of the 'realist effect' which the programme exerts and to open up for analysis a number of questions both about the pleasure and the ideological power of popular television.

Ang's study is useful, among other things, for its focus on the local detail of interpretative activity and something of this comes through, too, in the study by **Todd Gitlin**. Gitlin's interests are complementary to the Ang approach – working across the relations between production intentions, conventions and final product he gives us a remarkably well-documented account of the ideas and decisions behind the successful and innovatory series, *Hill Street Blues*. How conscious are producers of those social and aesthetic values which come to be associated with their programmes? What kind of strategy lies behind the often intriguingly indirect and yet also highly 'immediate' narratives of modern popular drama? Gitlin draws together a number of factors in the production process, connecting them with over-arching industrial imperatives and therefore with commercial concern about the likely *responses* of viewers too. Students will want to draw parallels with other items in this section where related issues are discussed.

Our final item, by **Ericson, Baranek and Chan,** concerns the use of television as a medium for journalism. Like Gitlin's account, it takes production aims and means as its primary topic, following them through into observations about textual form and particularly about the relations of visuals to speech. Connections with work contained in sections II and III of this volume should be clear as Ericson *et al.* discuss the kinds of viewing relationships which news teams try to establish and the various ways in which these teams seek to 'naturalize' their selective and constructive activity through artful linking, visual continuities and narrative pace. The authors usefully cite the seminal studies of the Glasgow University Media Group in addressing the question of how the principles and practices of television reporting are vulnerable to an ideological shaping. A proper answer might require more evidence of the kind that Ang offers about actual viewing experiences but close examination of news-in-the-making as provided here is invaluable.

We think that all the pieces in this section cross-relate interestingly in respect of the various processes and relationships of production, textual form and reception which constitute 'the media' as an aspect of modern society. They help to draw attention, too, to that crucial interplay, mentioned earlier, between 'top down' theories of how the media structure and influence audiences and 'bottom up' accounts examining the range of variables and differentiations at work, both in the production process and among viewers' own perceptions and understandings. In many parts of the world, this issue will undoubtedly become more central as the new global television environment ushered in by satellite and cable systems changes both patterns of provision and patterns of viewing, both 'institutions' and 'meanings'.

Further reading

In the last few years, the media have attracted a lot of attention from an increasing number of arts and social science specializations. One consequence of this has been a huge growth in the number of publications on media topics. The books listed below should be useful to students wanting to 'get their bearings' and all of them can be used for independent study as well as for course reading.

Armes, R. 1988: *On video*. London: Routledge.
  An excellently concise and lucid discussion of the development of video as a medium. Connects with research in film and television analysis to provide an original account of the relationships between technologies, production methods and meanings. Detailed references and suggestions for further reading.
Collins, R. *et al.* (eds.) 1986: *Media, culture and society: a critical reader*. London: Sage.
  A collection of some of the best work from the journal of the same name. The main emphasis here is on scholarly studies of the political and cultural contexts for broadcasting. The aim of the journal, to develop a general economic, political and cultural analysis of the media rather than to proceed by individual textual studies, informs most of the pieces. Several essays are of great value in providing information on media structures and activities and in giving·a background to current policy debates.
Curran, J. and J. Seaton. 1988: *Power without responsibility* (third edition). London: Routledge.
  Good, substantial accounts of the history of the press and of broadcasting in Britain, together with a discussion of current research issues and an examination of conflicts over national media policy. Some inconsistency in the quality of the writing and an unacceptable degree of 'pottedness' from time to time but still a very helpful guide to British developments which has been improved

by the revisions and additions incorporated in the third edition.

Corner, J. (ed.) 1986: *Documentary and the mass media*. London: Edward Arnold. Articles on aspects of documentary history, production, textual form and reception. One of the few books to bring together different approaches to media research around the study of a genre. Although many pieces are written with a specialist readership in mind, the originality of much of the work and the importance of the kinds of media use to which it refers makes the book a useful text for introductory studies too.

Crisell, A. 1986: *Understanding radio*. London: Methuen. A thorough examination of radio as a means of public communication. Very good in raising questions both about the special appeal of radio formats and about the established conventions of radio practice. Clarity and a generous supply of examples give the book considerable strength as an introductory text, with a relevance for Communication Studies which goes beyond its own immediate concerns.

Hartley, J. 1982: *Understanding news*. London: Methuen. An attractively written introduction to the study of journalism. It covers a range of analytic methods, offers summaries of research findings and is particularly notable for its imaginative and unstinting use of illustrations. Both the press and broadcasting are considered.

Masterman, L. (ed.). 1984: *TV mythologies*. London: Comedia. A collection of short articles on contemporary television form. Most contributors focus on one particular programme or series and develop a pithy and often highly critical account of its workings. The volume is designed to be entertaining as well as informative and, although a few pieces fail and there is a problem with repetition, the scope is broad and the overall effect stimulating.

Morley, D. 1986: *Family television: cultural power and domestic leisure*. London: Comedia. A small-scale but intensive survey of family contexts of television viewing which develops out of the author's earlier, pioneering work on 'decoding'. An ethnographic approach, making extensive use of transcripts of viewers' speech, is combined with a sensitivity to questions of gender and 'family politics' to produce a provocative and influential study.

23

Broadcast TV as sound and image

John Ellis

From Ellis, John 1982: *Visible fictions*. London: Routledge and Kegan Paul, 127–44.

TV offers a radically different image from cinema, and a different relation between sound and image. The TV image is of a lower quality than the cinematic image in terms of its resolution of detail. It is far more apparent that the broadcast TV picture is composed of lines than it is that the cinema image is composed of particles of silver compounds. Not only this, but the TV image is virtually always substantially smaller than the cinema image. Characteristically, the size of TV sets ranges from the 12 inch portable to the 24 inch or sometimes 30 inch model: all these measurements refer to the distance across the screen diagonally. The TV image shows things smaller than they are, unless it is a close-up of a small object, or of a person in head and shoulders only, when they appear more or less their real size. Such simple observations have profound effects on the kind of representations and spectator attitudes that broadcast TV creates for itself.

First, it is a characteristic of broadcast TV that the viewer is larger than the image: the opposite of cinema. It seems to be a convention also that the TV image is looked down on, rather than up to as in cinema. TV sets that are produced with stands are about two feet off the floor, which gives the effect of being almost but not quite level with the eyes of an individual lounging in an easy chair (as indeed we are meant to watch TV according to the advertisements it screens for itself.) TV takes place in domestic surroundings, and is usually viewed in normal light conditions, though direct sunlight reflects off the screen to an unacceptable degree. The regime of viewing TV is thus very different from the cinema: TV does not encourage the same degree of spectator concentration. There is no surrounding darkness, no anonymity of the fellow viewers, no large image, no lack of movement amongst the spectators, no rapt attention. TV is not usually the only thing going on, sometimes it is not even the principal thing. TV is treated casually rather than concentratedly. It is something of a last resort ('What's on TV tonight, then?') rather than a special event. It has a lower degree of sustained concentration from its viewers, but a more extended period of watching and more frequent use than cinema.

This has two major effects on the kind of regime of representation that has developed for TV. First, the role that sound plays in TV is extremely important. Second, it engages the look and the glance rather than the gaze, and thus has a different relation to voyeurism from cinema's. Sound on TV is a strange paradox;

although it is manifestly important, the manufacturers of TV sets provide speakers of dismal quality, even though the broadcast sound signal in many places has a wide tonal range. TV sets come with speakers that are massively geared towards the acceptable reproduction of speech. Music, especially rock music, does not reproduce at all well. This provides an alibi for broadcast TV to provide a minimum of rock music, and to provide the wasteful simultaneous stereo radio and TV transmissions of classical music on occasions.

The role played by sound stems from the fact that it radiates in all directions, whereas view of the TV image is sometimes restricted. Direct eye contact is needed with the TV screen. Sound can be heard where the screen cannot be seen. So sound is used to ensure a certain level of attention, to drag viewers back to looking at the set. Hence the importance of programme announcements and signature tunes and, to some extent, of music in various kinds of series. Sound holds attention more consistently than image, and provides a continuity that holds across momentary lapses of attention. The result is a slightly different balance between sound and image from that which is characteristic of cinema. Cinema is guaranteed a centred viewer by the physical arrangement of cinema seats and customs of film viewing. Sound therefore follows the image or diverges from it. The image is the central reference in cinema. But for TV, sound has a more centrally defining role. Sound carries the fiction or the documentary; the image has a more illustrative function. The TV image tends to be simple and straightforward, stripped of detail and excess of meanings. Sound tends to carry the details (background noises, music). This is a tendency towards a different sound/image balance than in cinema, rather than a marked and consistent difference. Broadcast TV has areas which tend towards the cinematic, especially the areas of serious drama or of various kinds of TV film. But many of TV's characteristic broadcast forms rely upon sound as the major carrier of information and the major means of ensuring continuity of attention. The news broadcast, the documentary with voice-over commentary, the bulk of TV comedy shows, all display a greater reliance on sound than any form that cinema has developed for itself. The image becomes illustration, and only occasionally provides material that is not covered by the sound-track (e.g. comedy sight-gags, news actuality footage). Sound tends to anchor meaning on TV, where the image tends to anchor it with cinema. In both, these are a matter of emphasis rather than any simple reliance one upon another. Sound and image exist in relation to each other in each medium rather than acting as separate entities. However, the difference of emphasis does exist between the two. It gives rise to two critical attitudes that are fundamental to the way in which newspaper critics and practitioners alike tend to conceive of the two media. Any film that contains a large amount of dialogue is open to the criticism that 'it could have been a radio play', as was Bergman's *From the Life of Marionettes* (*Aus dem Leben der Marionetten*, 1980). A similar accusation is never hurled at a TV play, however wordy. Instead, there are unwritten rules that govern the image for TV. Especially in British broadcast TV (possibly the most hide-bound in the world), the image is to be kept literal for almost all the time. There are licensed exceptions (science fiction, rock music programmes) where experimentation with the physical composition of the video image can take place, but the rule is that the image must show whatever is before the camera with the minimum of fuss and conscious technique. The image is to be kept in its place. Both these attitudes refer to occasions in which the subservient partner in the sound/image relationship tends to assert itself too much: for cinema, it is sound; for TV it is the image.

TV's lower level of sustained concentration on the image has had another effect upon its characteristic regime of representation. The image on broadcast TV, being a lower grade image than cinema's, has developed in a particular way. Contrasting with cinema's profusion (and sometimes excess) of detail, broadcast TV's image is stripped-down, lacking in detail. The visual effects of this are immediately apparent: the fussy detail of a film shown on TV compared to the visual bareness of a TV cop series, where cars chase each other through endless urban wastes of bare walls and near-deserted streets. The broadcast TV image has to be certain that its meaning is obvious: the streets are almost empty so that the movement of the car is all the more obvious. The walls are bare so that no writing distracts attention from the segmental event. This is not an effect of parsimony of production investment (rather, it enables it to happen). It is a more fundamental aspect of the broadcast TV image coming to terms with itself. Being small, low definition, subject to attention that will not be sustained, the TV image becomes jealous of its meaning. It is unwilling to waste it on details and inessentials. So background and context tend to be sketched rather than brought forward and subject to a certain fetishism of details that often occurs in cinema, especially art cinema. The narratively important detail is stressed by this lack of other detail. Sometimes, it is also stressed by music, producing an emphasis that seems entirely acceptable on TV, yet would seem ludicrously heavy-handed in cinema. This is particularly so with American crime series, where speed of action and transition from one segment to another dictates the concentration of resources on to single meanings. Where detail and background are used in TV programmes, for example the BBC historical serials, action tends to slow down as a result. The screen displays historical detail in and for itself; characters are inserted around it, carrying on their lengthy conversations as best they can. Segments are drawn out, their meanings unfolding gradually. For historical dramas, especially of the Victorian and Edwardian era, this tends to lend greater authenticity to the fiction: these are assumed to have been the decades of leisure and grace.

The stripped-down image that broadcast TV uses is a central feature of TV production. Its most characteristic result is the TV emphasis on close-ups of people, which are finely graded into types. The dramatic close-up is of face virtually filling the screen; the current affairs close-up is more distant, head-and-shoulders are shown, providing a certain distance, even reticence. Close-ups are regularly used in TV, to a much greater extent than in cinema. They even have their own generic name: talking heads. The effect is very different from the cinema close-up. Whereas the cinema close-up accentuates the difference between screen-figure and any attainable human figure by drastically increasing its size, the broadcast TV close-up produces a face that approximates to normal size. Instead of an effect of distance and unattainability, the TV close-up generates an equality and even intimacy.

The broadcast TV image is gestural rather than detailed; variety and interest are provided by the rapid change of images rather than richness within one image. TV compensates for the simplicity of its single images by the techniques of rapid cutting. Again, the organization of studios is designed for this style of work. The use of several cameras and the possibility of alternation between them produces a style of shooting that is specific to TV: the fragmentation of events that keeps strictly to the continuity of their performance. There is much less condensation of events in TV than in cinema. Events are shown in real time from a multiple of different points of camera view (all, normally, from the same side of the action). Cinema events are shot already fragmented and matched together in editing. Still today, video editing is expensive, and the use of the studio set-up (in which much is already invested: capital and skills alike) provides instantaneous editing as the images are being transferred to tape for later transmission. This enables a rapid alternation of images, a practice which also affects the editing of TV programmes made on film. The standard attitude is that an image should be held on screen only until its information value is exhausted. Since the information value of the TV image is deliberately honed-down, it is quickly exhausted. Variation is provided by changing the image shown rather than by introducing a complexity of elements into a single image. Hence the material nature of the broadcast TV image has two profound effects on the regime of representation and working practices that TV has adopted. It produces an emphasis on sound as the carrier of continuity of attention and therefore of meaning; it produces a lack of detail in the individual image that reduces the image to its information value and produces an aesthetic that emphasizes the close-up and fast cutting with strict time continuity.

However, this is to compare the broadcast TV image with the cinema image. The TV image has further distinct qualities of its own, no doubt the result of a tenacious ideological operation, that mark it decisively as different from the cinema image with its photo effect. The broadcast TV image has the effect of immediacy. It is as though the TV image is a 'live' image, transmitted and received in the same moment that it is produced. For British broadcast TV, with its tight schedules and fear of controversy, this has not been true for a decade. Only news and sport are routinely live transmissions. However, the notion that broadcast TV is live still haunts the medium; even more so does the sense of immediacy of the image. The immediacy of the broadcast TV image does not just lie in the presumption that it is live, it lies more in the relations that the image sets up for itself. Immediacy is the effect of the directness of the TV image, the way in which it constitutes itself and its viewers as held in a relationship of co-present intimacy. Broadcast TV very often uses forms of direct address from individual in close-up to individuals gathered around the set. This is very different from cinema's historic mode of narration, where events do not betray a knowledge that they are being watched. Broadcast TV is forever buttonholing, addressing its viewers as though holding a conversation with them. Announcers and newsreaders speak directly from the screen, simulating the eye-contact of everyday conversation by looking directly out of the screen and occasionally looking down (a learned and constructed technique). Advertisements contain elements of direct address: questions, exhortations, warnings. Sometimes they go further, providing riddles and jokes that assume that their viewers share a common frame of reference with them. Hence advertisements for various staple commodities, beer for example, tend to make oblique and punning references to each other's advertising campaigns. The audience is expected to understand these references. This also is an operation of direct address: an ephemeral and immediate knowledge is assumed in the viewer, who otherwise would have no understanding of the reference or the joke. Hence these advertisements are addressing a viewer as an equal: 'we both know what we are talking about'.

Direct address is recognized as a powerful effect of TV. Its most obvious form, that of an individual speaking directly (saying 'I' and 'you'), is reserved for specific kinds of people. It can be used by those who are designated as politically neutral by TV itself (newsmen and women), or by those who have ultimate political power: heads of state. Otherwise, direct address is denied to individuals who appear on TV. Important personalities are interviewed in three-quarter face. Other strategies of address are open to them, that of recruiting the audience against the interviewer by appealing to a common sense that media persons do not share, for instance. Interviewers in their turn tend to construct themselves as asking questions on behalf of the viewers: 'what the public/the viewers/ordinary people *really* want to know is. . . .' This is also a form of highly motivated direct address. Again, it assumes an audience who is there simultaneously, for whom events are being played out.

Direct address is not the only form of construction of broadcast TV's effect of immediacy. Broadcast TV's own perpetual presence (there every night of the year), and its series formats, breed a sense of the perpetual present. Broadcast TV declares itself as being in the present tense, denying recording as effectively as cinema uses it. TV fictions take place to a very large extent as though they were transmitted directly from the place in which were really happening. The soap opera is the most obvious example of this, where events in a particular milieu are everlastingly updated. Broadcast TV has a very marked sense of presence to its images and sounds which far outweighs any counterbalancing sense of absence, any sense of recording. The technical operation of the medium in its broadcast form strengthens this feeling. The tight scheduling that is favoured by most large broadcast operations means that an audience wanting to see a particular programme has to be present at a very precise time, or they miss it. This increases the sense that broadcast TV is of the specific present moment. In addition, unlike cinema, the signal comes from elsewhere, and can be sent live. The technical origin of the signal is not immediately apparent to the viewer, but all the apparatus of direct address and of contemporaneity of broadcast TV messages is very present. The broadcast signal is always available during almost all normal waking hours. It is ever-present.

The favoured dramatic forms of broadcast TV work within this framework of presence and immediacy. Besides the obvious forms of soap opera, entirely cast in a continuous present, the series format tends towards the creation of immediacy and presence. The open-ended series format of the situation comedy or the dramatic series tends to produce the sense of immediacy by the fact that it presents itself as having no definite end. Unlike the cinema narrative, the end of the episode and the end of the series alike leave events unresolved. They are presented as on-going, part of the texture of life. This sense even extends to the historical reconstruction dramas beloved of the BBC, through the operation of a further mechanism that produces the effect of immediacy.

Immediacy is also produced by the logical extension of the direct address form: by echoing the presumed form of the TV audience within the material of the TV fiction itself. The institution of broadcast TV assumes its audience to be the family; it massively centres its fictional representations around the question of the family. Hence TV produces its effect of immediacy even within dramas of historically remote periods by reproducing the audience's view of itself within its fictions. Hence TV dramas are concerned with romance and the family, both conceived of within certain basic kinds of definition. Broadcast TV's view of the family is one which is at variance with the domestic practices of the majority of domestic units and of individuals in Britain at the moment. Yet broadcast TV's definition has a strength in that it participates in the construction of an idea of the normal family/domestic unit, from which other forms are experienced and remembered as temporary aberrations.

Broadcast TV dramas are constructed around the hetero-sexual romance in its normal and perverse forms, and the perpetual construction of standard families: wage-earning husband, housekeeping wife, two children. Situation comedies play on the discrepancies between this assumed norm and other forms of exist-ence: male and female students sharing a flat (*Man About the House*), the childless, woman-dominated couple (*George and Mildred*), the landlord and his variegated bedsit tenants (*Rising Damp*), the rejuvenated divorced father (*Father Dear Father*). Historical dramas found their sense of the historical on the never-changing patterns of romance and family life: Edward VIII's *amour fou* (*Edward and Mrs Simpson*), the problems of the powerful career woman (*Elizabeth R*), the problems of male lust breaking the confines of the family (*The Six Wives of Henry VIII*), the consequences of one sexual transgression repercussing down the centuries (*The Forsyte Saga, Poldark, etc.*).

The centring of all kinds of broadcast TV drama upon the family (much as direct address assumes a family unit as its audience) produces a sense of intimacy, a bond between the viewers' conception of themselves (or how they ought to be) and the programme's central concerns. So a relationship of humanist sympathy is set up, along the lines of seeing how everyone is normal really, how much they really do desire the norm that our society has created for itself. But the intimacy that broadcast TV sets up is more than just this form of sympathy. It is made qualitatively different by the sense that the TV image carries of being a live event, which is intensified by the habit of shooting events in real time within any one segment, the self-contained nature of each segment, and the use of close-up and sound continuity. All of these factors contribute to an overall impression, that the broadcast TV image is providing an intimacy with events between couples and within families, an intimacy that gives the impression that these events are somehow co-present with the viewer, shared rather than witnessed from outside. The domestic nature of the characteristic use of broadcast TV certainly contri-butes here, but more important is the particular way in which TV has internalized this in its own representations. Broadcast TV has ingested the domestic and bases its dramas upon it. When it does not address its audience directly, it creates a sense of familiarity between its fictions and its audience, a familiarity based on a notion of the familial which is assumed to be shared by all.

Broadcast TV has a particular regime of representation that stresses the imme-diacy and co-presence of the TV representation. Its particular physical and social characteristics have created a very particular mode of representation that includes the image centred upon the significant at the cost of detail, and sound as carrier of continuity. It gives its audience a particular sense of intimacy with the events it portrays. All of these features of broadcast TV create and foster a form of looking by the TV viewer that is different from the kind of voyeurism (with fetishistic undertow) that cinema presents for its spectators.

TV's regime of vision is less intense than cinema's: it is a regime of the glance rather than the gaze. The gaze implies a concentration of the spectator's activity into that of looking, the glance implies that no extraordinary effort is being invested in the activity of looking. The very terms we habitually use to designate the person who watches TV or the cinema screen tend to indicate this difference. The cinema-looker is a spectator: caught by the projection yet separate from its illusion. The TV-looker is a viewer, casting a lazy eye over proceedings, keeping an eye on events, or, as the slightly archaic designation had it, 'looking in'. In psychoanalytic terms, when compared to cinema, TV demonstrates a displacement from the invocatory drive of schopophilia (looking) to the closest related of the invocatory drives, that of hearing. Hence the crucial role of sound in ensuring continuity of attention and producing the utterances of direct address ('I' to 'you').

The different balance between the activities of looking and listening produces a qualitatively different relation to the TV transmission. It is not that the experience is less intense than cinema; rather, it has a distinctive form of its own. In particular, there is far less separation between viewer and image than with cinema. Broadcast TV does not construct an image that is marked by present absence, its regime is one of co-presence of image and viewer. The image is therefore not an impossible one, defined by the separation of the viewer from it, but rather one that is familiar and intimate. The cost of this intimacy is that the voyeuristic mode cannot operate as intensely as in cinema. In particular, the broadcast TV viewer's look is not a controlling look in the same sense as that which operates in cinema. The cinema spectator is secure in the separation from the image that allows events to take place as though they were not watched. The broadcast TV image is quite often directly addressed to the viewer, in a simulation of everyday eye contact. In addition, the sense of cinema's consent to the act of being watched (implied in the event of the projection of a film for spectators) is radically absent from broadcast TV. TV continues whether a particular set is turned on or not. In this sense, it is not for the viewer in the way that the cinema projection is for the spectator. If no one turns up to a film screening, it can be cancelled, but if no one is watching a TV programme, it will be transmitted anyway in blithe ignorance of its lack of reception. The broadcast TV event is just there, it carries no sense with it of being for anyone as the cinema projection is for a definite group. This implies a lack of the consent by the representation to being watched that is vital to the construction of a regime of the voyeuristic gaze in cinema.

Broadcast TV can be left on with no one watching it, playing in the background of other activities in the home. This is perhaps a frequent event; certainly, it also makes impossible the construction of a voyeuristic contract between looker and representation. Instead, broadcast TV uses sound to appeal to its audience, using a large degree of direct address whose function is to attract the look and attention of the viewer, and to hold it. The separation that this practice implies is different from that of cinematic voyeurism. It makes explicit a relationship between viewer and broadcast TV image, designating a TV first person singular or plural ('I', 'we') and a viewing second person ('you', beautifully flexible in its lack of singular/plural difference). Together these first and second person designations can observe and speculate about third persons: 'he', 'she', 'they'. The practice of segmentalizing TV broadcasting means that direct address is present regularly to reaffirm this relationship. It surrounds the segments of dramatic material and comic material so that they become constituted as 'they': the people whom we *and television* both look in upon. But drama's characters are not constituted as a totally separate 'they'. TV drama is constructed around the presumed self-image of the audience: the family. The mobilization of this sense of intimacy, together with TV's effect of co-presence both tend to push even dramatic material into this sense of first and second person togetherness. Characters in drama series on broadcast TV tend to become familiar figures, loved, or excused with a tolerance that is quite remarkable: it is more than is normally extended to members of the family or to neighbours. The construction of a 'real monster' in a TV series is a difficult process: this is perhaps why J.R. Ewing in *Dallas* excited such attention.

The community of address that broadcast TV is able to set up excludes a fully developed regime of voyeurism as found in cinema. This is perhaps why films screened on TV do not quite achieve the same intensity of experience as they would in the cinema, and why broadcast TV's adoption of the cinematic mode has not been more widespread. The community of address sets up a different relation between viewer and representation. The distance between viewer and image is reduced; but a compensatory distance is constructed and separation between the 'I' and 'you' of the community of address and the third person outside that it constructs. The 'they' that is always implied and often stated in direct address forms becomes an other, a grouping outside the consensus that confirms the consensus. Certain characteristic attitudes are taken towards these outsiders: patronization, hate, wilful ignorance, pity, generalized concern, indifference. These are encouraged by the complicity that broadcast TV sets up between itself and its viewers; a series of categories of 'they' has begun to appear, often creating curious dislocations in the operation of TV representations when they are used in news and current affairs. The most obviously dislocating is that of 'housewives'. Housewives suffer from inflation, they worry about their families, they rush out and 'panic buy' when threatened with shortages. 'Housewives' are designated as a 'they' whose actions are scrutinized by the TV institution and its viewers together. This effectively prevents the recognition by women in that audience of themselves as 'housewives'. If they do identify with that term in its use in a news bulletin, they cast themselves outside the consensus of the direct address mode. The effect is that the 'housewife' is presumed to be everywhere, blindly devoted to the maintenance of her little family, but no one recognizes themselves in that designation. Rather, individual women look on at the scene of these strange beings acting in their pitiful ways, rather than recognizing themselves there, even if they would otherwise claim to be ('only') a housewife. The 'they' of a TV direct address news bulletin or announcement is always elsewhere, always outside the consensus between viewer and TV.

Broadcast TV's designation of race has more unilateral consequences in Britain. The 'black community' or 'immigrants' (often and wrongly equated) appear in a news and current affairs context only as problems. The amount of non-current affairs material that appears regularly including coloured people is minimal. There is no continuity of representation of any ethnic minority in British entertainment TV. 'They' are always the exceptions, the cause for concern. A few remarkable (and short-lived) attempts to create such representations have occurred, like BBC 2's *Empire Road*; otherwise, ethnic minorities only appear in their own minority programmes, broadcast at marginal hours of the day like early on Sunday morning. Individuals who are coloured sometimes appear in TV fictions: as a rule, they come weighed down by their colour, supporting a whole invisible culture on their backs. Their colour becomes an obsessive point of dramatic interest, or the butt of jokes in comedy. Perhaps Britain's new Fourth Channel will begin to produce representations that are not so demeaning, but the work has hardly begun on the other three channels. Even the American policy of positive discrimination would be an improvement, producing as it does at least regular appearances of coloured people. On British TV, coloured people are excluded from the world of TV, the world of the familiar and everyday in representations. 'They' appear as a problem or an object of concern only, and are therefore constructed as such for most of the viewing public. Outside the community of TV and viewers, the 'natural' tendency is to conceive of Britain's coloured populations as an 'unnatural' feature of society. Such is the insidious way in which British TV participates in the construction of casual racism. Broadcast TV's particular version of this pervasive attitude is based on its ability to construct a community of address between viewer and TV institution that is capable of excluding any group designated as 'they'.

These examples of casual racism and of the dislocations produced by the designation 'housewife' are both taken from news and current affairs. This is one area in which the construction of the direct address form is most prevalent. Dramatic forms of various kinds occur regularly within TV's direct address context, and are inflected by it to some extent. Dramatic forms are not constructed in broadcast TV for the voyeuristic gaze in the same way as cinematic forms. There is a sense of complicity of the institution of TV in the process of looking at dramatic events which increases their sense of co-presence with the viewer. The effects of immediacy, of segmentation and of the series rather than strong narrative development, and the concentration of TV drama on the family (as presumed reflection of its audience) all intensify this sense of TV drama as part of the consensus between broadcast TV and its audience. Hence drama is crucial in revising and altering the effects of news and current affairs' rather more brutal division of its world into a series of 'theys' beyond the consensus of viewer and TV first persons. The dislocation produced by the designation 'housewife' as beyond the consensus in TV news is made innocuous by the persistent dramatic and advertising use of housewife-figures.

The final effects of TV's low emphasis on the construction of the voyeuristic position lie in the representation of the female body and of female sexuality, and in its characteristic forms of narration of events. Cinematic voyeurism, with its fetishistic counterpart, is centrally concerned with the representation of the female body and of female sexuality as a problem, constructed from the security of a definition of the masculine as positive. TV's concerns are not so heavily centred towards the investigation of the female. This is not only the result of the different mechanisms of self-censorship and imposed censorship that prevail in the two media, nor only of the different sense of the viewing conditions that the two media have of themselves. After all, Hollywood's relentless investigation of the female was carried out under codes of censorship in the 1940s that were every bit as vigilant as those operating in broadcast TV today. TV does not have its equivalents of the *film noir* or of the 'love interest'. Different conditions prevail. Broadcast TV's lack of an intense voyeuristic appeal produces a lack of the strong investigatory drive that is needed alike for tightly organized narration and for intense concern with the 'problem' of the female. Similarly, the regime of broadcast TV does not demonstrate a particular drift towards a fetishistic activity of viewing. Its forms of narration are not particularly repetitive in the fetishistic manner of obsessive replaying of events. The series and the segmental form construct a different pattern of repetition that has much more to do with constructing a pattern of familiarity (as my next chapter demonstrates). The fetishistic regime does operate to some extent, however, as does voyeurism. Its characteristic attention in broadcast TV is not directed towards the whole body, but to the face. The display of the female body on TV, in dance sequences or in a series like *Charlie's Angels*, is gestural rather than fascinating. The techniques of rapid cutting prevent the access of the gaze at the body being displayed. Instead, TV's displays of the female body, frequent and depressing enough as they are, provide material for the glance only. Details and complete bodies are both presented only to the extent that they can be registered as 'a bit of a body/a whole body'. The exception to this is the face, and specifically the female face. In some sense, the female body is hidden, made obscure, by the heavy emphasis that broadcast TV gives to various kinds of close-up. This is particularly so with newsreaders. Newsreaders are on the screen in close-up for long periods of time, but their bodies are never revealed. The face becomes a distraction from the message of the voice for some viewers a lot of the time, and for most viewers some of the time. The fetishistic regime is encouraged by two additional factors: the use of direct address by newsreaders, radically reducing any separation between viewer and image, and the fact that the image of the newsreader is held for a long period (in broadcast TV's terms), with very little alteration. Newsreaders thus can become obsessive objects; when women newsreaders were introduced in Britain in the mid-1970s, they became the targets of a national fetishism. Speculation about their 'private life' was rife in the popular press and in ordinary conversation: a speculation amply rewarded by Anna Ford. The close-up of the face is the one moment where the average TV image is more or less life-sized rather than less than life-size, and the equality of scale between image and viewer contributes to a dramatic reduction of separation between image and viewer that is one aspect of the fetishistic regime. The fetishism is still concentrated upon women, because of the generalized culture of sexual difference under which we suffer . . .

Broadcast TV characteristically offers an image that is stripped down, with no unnecessary details. Cutting produces forms of variation of visual information, and sound has an important role in drawing the viewer's attention back to the screen. The image and sound both tend to create a sense of immediacy, which produces a kind of complicity between the viewer and the TV institution. This can provide a powerful form of consensus, since it tends to define the domestic place of the TV set as a kind of norm, against which the 'outside world' represented on TV can be measured. This regime of image and sound, together with the segment and series forms, has created a distinct form of narration in broadcast TV.

24

The production context of *Coronation Street*

Richard Paterson

From Dyer, R. *et al.* (eds.) 1981: *Coronation Street*, Television monograph 13. London: British Film Institute, 53–66.

Note: Two photographic illustrations which accompanied the original article have had to be omitted from this reprinting.

This essay is concerned with the institutional and organizational context of the production of *Coronation Street* by Granada Television's Manchester studios. Its perspective is that the complex structure of a commercial broadcasting organization, subject to both legislative and IBA pressures, has to be understood when analysing the conditions of existence of its programme production.

The particular features of *Coronation Street* stem from its continuous production, twice weekly since December 1960, which necessitated the setting up of a *Coronation Street* office. Analysis of this office's operation and the routine of production enables us to understand the constraints affecting continuous serials – constraints which are both technical and to do with time. This can be compared with the production of other television drama, such as Thames Television's series *Hazell* and the Euston Films production of *The Sweeney*, to indicate some of the differences between the problems and their resolution within serial drama and series drama. Further, the implications for both the narrative development and significational strategy[1] of series and serial drama derive from different technical problems and from placement in the television schedule. *Coronation Street* has been placed at 7.30 on Monday and Wednesday evenings for most of its existence, and this has ramifications in terms of narrative and audience construction, returning the analysis to the institutional context of British television and the circulation of television as a commodity. This essay seeks to elucidate these factors in the production of *Coronation Street* in order to contextualize the detailed analyses of other essays [in the monograph]. Furthermore, it is the contention of this essay that aesthetic and ideological analyses must take account of these influences on significational strategies.

1. Granada Television

Coronation Street is produced by Granada Television, a subsidiary of the Granada Group Ltd. In addition to the IBA television contract it holds for Lancashire and surrounding areas, the Group lists its principal activities as: television set rental, property investment and development, insurance and life assurance, bingo social clubs and cinemas, motorway services, book publishing and music publishing (*Director's Report* no. 45, p. 1). In 1979 the Group profit was £39 million on a turnover of £277.5 million, with the turnover of the television operation being £65.5 million, contributing 16.3% of the profits. The major profit earner in the Group's 1979 activities was television rental, which contributed 61.9% of the profits.

Comparison with Group activities in 1967 shows a significant change in the proportion of turnover and profit attributable to the television and television rental operations. In 1967 the turnover of the Group totalled £33.1 million (television £20 million), with a Group profit of £4.6 million of which the television operation contributed 87.7% and television rentals only 6.5%. Granada lost the Yorkshire area from its franchise in 1968, which accounts for some loss of revenue from television, but the figures indicate a major diversification of Group activities out of the insecurity of limited tenure television franchise operations and into a wide field of other activities, dominated by television rentals. This diversification – the building up of Granada as a media conglomerate – has been capitalized on the profits accrued in the sixties from the TV franchise.

Granada's original business was luxury cinemas, out of which the initial television operation was a major diversification. Granada commenced transmission in Lancashire on 3 May 1956 and in Yorkshire in November 1956; but, in common with the other early operators, very quickly encountered major financial difficulties:

> In spite of the possibility of limited cost sharing after ATV's Midland station opened in February 1956, Associated Rediffusion and ATV began to wonder how much more money their boards and shareholders would consent to pour into this bottomless well (Black 1972, pp. 96–7).

> Granada . . . lost £176,928 by 30 April 1957, when its financial year ended (Seglow, 1978, p. 93).

In July 1956 Bernstein of Granada and Spencer Wills of Associated Rediffusion signed an agreement whereby Rediffusion provided 85% of Granada's programmes, in consideration of which Granada undertook to pay Associated Rediffusion 'the whole of its net annual advertising revenue, less an agreed proportion' (Black 1972, p. 103). The risks of Granada's television operation were thus taken over by Associated Rediffusion, and up to the termination of the agreement four years later on this resulted in a payment by Granada to Associated Rediffusion of £8,044,238. Thus the initial years of super profits in Independent Television (after 1958) were in large part denied Granada Television, which also had to provide only 15% of its own programmes up to 1960. *Coronation Street* was thus part of a necessary expansion of programme-making by Granada in 1960. Interestingly, this expansion took a radical innovatory form for British television, explainable in part by the nature of the company.

The major shareholder in Granada was, and continues to be, the Bernstein family, which has a tradition of support for the Labour Party. Indeed Sidney Bernstein (until recently chairman of the Granada Group) guaranteed the bank loan of the fledgling Association of Cinematograph Technicians (now the ACTT) in 1935 (Chanan 1976, p. 31).

Granada Television is one of the five network companies within the IBA franchise structure (the others are, currently, Thames, ATV, Yorkshire and London Weekend) charged with providing the programmes for network transmission on Independent Television. IBA franchises are also given to regional companies, whose main function is the provision of programmes for their own areas. Thus within a region programmes come partly from these regional companies and partly from the network companies. Granada's contribution to network programmes is determined by their share of the net advertising revenue, after levy, earned by the entire network (Annan Report 1977, p. 173), and the allocation of responsibility for programmes is worked out by the Programme Controllers Group of the ITCA (consisting of the programme controllers of the five network companies, plus the IBA Director of Television and the Director of the Network Programme Secretariat). One of the major, and continuing, contributions to the network from Granada has been *Coronation Street*, which has aggregated high audience ratings for most of its history. In addition to its profitability (in terms of generating advertising) in Britain, the programme has been sold to many foreign broadcasting stations, while spin-offs have included a series of books (published by Mayflower, a Granada subsidiary) on the early years of the programme: *Coronation Street: Early Days; Trouble at the Rovers;* and *Elsie Tanner Fights Back,* all by H.V. Kershaw. Coverage of the 'stars' of the serial in the popular press is wide and continuing, and the programme makes an important contribution to British popular culture, with a clearly enormous and devoted following.

Granada Television had a reputation for 'radicalism' and innovation in programme production (*World in Action, Sam, Reports Action*) up to the early seventies, and has also established its own regional identity through its network and local output. Its reputation for reflecting its regional base is due in part to the realism of *Coronation Street*. This acts as an important legitimation of the company's claim to remain the contractor for this area, since the IBA has a particular liking for programmes that reflect a regional identity. *Coronation Street* also achieves large audiences in Granada's franchise area and consequent high advertising revenue expectations; it almost invariably tops the ratings in the North West.

The importance of ratings success is evident (cf. Alvarado and Buscombe 1978: *Hazell* p. 28). Bill Podmore's taking over as producer of *Coronation Street* in 1975 from Susi Hush is an illustration of the pressures to which 'popular' programmes are subject. In this case they became public because of Granada's obvious disquiet at the downturn in ratings with the introduction of 'serious' issues. The company's central concern was commercial, and only aesthetic inasmuch as that was seen to determine the ratings.[2] Bill Podmore's reputation as a producer of comedy (e.g. *My Brother's Keeper, Nearest and Dearest*) signalled a change in direction away from 'drama' and a quest for humour and entertainment, and within two years the programme had re-established itself as a ratings success. The rest of the collective authorship (storyline writers, script writers) remained virtually unchanged over this period.

2. The Street

Coronation Street was first broadcast at 7 p.m. on Friday 9 December 1960. This was the first of twelve episodes written by Tony Warren, the programme's creator; and, as Pat Phoenix has written, the programme 'quickly established itself as a firm favourite with viewers in the North . . . From March 1961, it was shown in other parts of the country where it proved equally popular'. The early social realism of the serial, redolent of late fifties British films, and its continuation of a tradition in TV drama documentaries of that period of 'recreating reality' (Scannell 1980, p. 102), has in part been modified by the early standardization of production, the accumulative connotations of the narrative space and the imperatives of the continuous serial form.

In the early days, Friday's episode was transmitted live and was immediately followed by a tele-recording of the Monday episode – that is, the two episodes were recorded in one session. Even after the introduction of VTR, the two programmes were recorded as a continuous performance until 1974. The production of the programme in colour began in 1969. These different technical factors have evident significational importance. Thus continuous performance as opposed to the rehearse-record-edit method used now (see below) caused problems of narrative construction because of the difficulties of time lapse/costume change; while recording in colour has certain ideological implications (cf. E. Buscombe on sound and colour in film, *Jump Cut* no. 17).

A more important determinant of signification in all its aspects is the regularization of production from the *Coronation Street* office. Though this has been modified in minor ways over the years, it has become a continuing, constraining and in part determining feature of significational and narrative possibilities. If the production of *Coronation Street* is compared to that of *Hazell*, both are seen to have an all-powerful producer, a script editor, an original creator, plus a small group of writers and itinerant directors – that is, an office serviced by specialized staff. The early difficulties of a series like *Hazell*, as described by Alvarado and Buscombe – the search for a style, the compromises, the problems of a new production – are of course no longer a part of the production of *Coronation Street*.

The *Coronation Street* office acts with virtual autonomy, although the producer is formally responsible to the Head of Drama. Granada Television's organizational structure has allowed some cross-fertilization between departments through the transference of personnel (cf. Goldie 1977, p. 210, on the importance of this interaction in the genesis of *Tonight*). Many directors have been trained on *Coronation Street*, and indeed the present Granada Programme Controller, Mike Scott, was a director on the early episodes. In addition to the overall producer, the office consists of a programme planner (with responsibility for the logistics of production), two storyline writers, a script editor, a biographical record keeper, and secretarial staff. At any one time three directors, with production assistants, working on various stages of the production of a pair of episodes, will be attached to the office. However, in common with the practice in other companies, cameramen, technicians and other personnel are not allocated permanently to the serial (cf. Alvarado and Buscombe 1978, p. 112).

Every three weeks a story conference is convened to make decisions about the narrative progression of a further six episodes, within the broader framework of a long-term conference held periodically to map out future directions. In attendance at the story conference are the producer, the series planner, the storyline writers and a number of script writers.[3] Plot developments for a three-week period are discussed and proceedings and decisions minuted. The storyline writers then produce the outlines of six episodes based on the decisions of the conference, and these are allocated to suitable writers. Certain writers have established reputations for types of storyline, and this, together with availability, is used as a basis for allocating episodes. Additionally, some writers are used to handle important narrative moments – a small core group whose knowledge and 'understanding' of the programme has been acquired over a long period of association. Each writer is contracted for a set number of scripts over a set period.

The storyline writers' outline indicates which members of the cast are available, who has been written out or is on holiday, and the sets allocated for use in the episode. The plot is broken down into scenes which broadly detail the action, characters involved and set in use. Before the writers start work on the script, a commissioning conference is convened at which the producer, series planner and six writers finalize details of the stories, ensuring that the episodes mesh into a consistent narrative. From the story outline the writer must develop a 26-minute script, utilizing all the narrative points though not necessarily following slavishly the ordering of points or dramatic emphases.

For *Crossroads*, on the other hand, there are 'five or six story lines running at the same time, so that each of [the] writers works on his own story, with his own characters, without concerning himself as to what is happening to the rest of the *Crossroads* folk . . . individual segments which when pieced together make up the whole programme' (Gordon 1975, p. 41). Currently a small team of writers is credited on *Crossroads*, and the practice on *Coronation Street* of using a cohering author (no matter how dubious his or her authorship) is still not employed.

Series formats too are fairly rigid. However, there is a greater leeway allowed to the writer because of the self-contained nature of each episode. There are usually less restrictions in the production timetable and often a greater freedom with production techniques (thus the freedom felt by *The Sweeney* production staff in the use of film rather than video for recording) when compared with the tight limitations of serial production.

Coronation Street's scripts are delivered in sequence over a two to three week period. Each episode is the collective product of conference, storyline writers and script writer – with the script writer credited as author. Coherence with preceding narrative detail, character development, continuity between scripts and maintenance of the 'style' of *Coronation Street* is ensured by the script editor. Thus no out of place characterization is possible, and any biographical details in question are referred to the *Street*'s biographer. As Christine Geraghty points out, [*in another contribution to the collection from which this article was taken*] each episode must attempt to maintain audience interest to ensure repeat viewing, while not progressing too fast so as not to alienate the occasional viewer. A poser – what Geraghty calls the 'cliffhanger device' – is included at the end of each episode, and to a lesser extent before the advertising break in the middle of each episode, in the attempt to ensure repeat viewing.

After passing the script editor, each pair of episodes is allocated to a director, who has responsibility for one week's output. The directors employed tend to be staff members, although it is sometimes necessary to employ freelance workers. Each director is given three weeks to bring the scripts into recorded episode form. The first task is the preparation of a camera script – indicating shot type and camera use, camera deployment in sets etc., for each scene. Set deployment in the studio has to be mapped out. Rehearsal and recording take place in the third week. Monday is used for the recording of any outside scenes – usually on electronic cameras in the Street set near the Manchester studios, although occasionally using film cameras in other parts of Manchester; while Tuesday and Wednesday are taken up with rehearsals. Studio recording of the two episodes is done on Thursday afternoon and all day Friday, moving from set to set rehearsing then recording each scene on electronic cameras. On some occasions several takes are necessary, but the restrictions of time deter unnecessary delay. Technical problems or actor fallibility were more of a hazard when the episode was recorded in one continuous take. The final takes for each scene are edited together in half a day with the director in the week after the recording. The episodes are transmitted two weeks later.

Actor/actress availability for each episode depends mainly on plot requirement. However, an additional constraint is imposed by the fact that their contracts specify appearance in a certain number of episodes over a specified time (the storyline writers keep statistics on appearances), while a character's prolonged absence from the Street, or lack of central plot elements in which characters are involved, may create problems of narrative realism.

Restricted studio space and lack of time for changes during the two days of recording limits the number of sets available for each pair of episodes (generally there are five sets available). However, as will be argued below, this is an important significational factor in continuous serial production, which is further determined by the need to maintain an understandable mythic space.

Coronation Street is, then, an important part of the output from Granada's Manchester studios. The assured use each week of high capital cost equipment and studio facilities (below the line costs) is an important factor in a broadcasting company's resource use. Minimal above the line costs (little expenditure on new sets, location shooting, etc.) enable Granada to provide a very popular production for the ITV network at low cost, with high returns to itself and the other commercial companies from advertising revenue at peak viewing time. This allows for more innovative and expensive programme production, as well as further diversification of the Granada Group. At the same time *Coronation Street*'s success satisfies the IBA's concern for 'regionalism' in production, which is a positive factor when the Authority considers franchise renewals.

3. Series drama and serial drama

Series and serial dramas are central elements of the output of British commercial television. As Goodhardt *et al.* point out, broadcasters believe audiences like repetition, organizationally it is prudent to cope with the enormous demand for programmes by using formulae; and – most important – commercial television requires a fairly stable and predictable audience (Goodhardt *et al.* 1975, p. 6). Scheduling is a fundamental determinant of form and content (Paterson 1980), orientated to the notion (and reinforcement) of a family dynamic: that the domestic environment and patterns of living are related to the television schedule.

The serial and series are different products aimed at different markets using different organizations of the production routine. There are *some* similarities – collective production, the requirement for continuity of characters and places – but these are displaced by production values and by the construction of the programmes into schedules. That is, they are differentiated by the notion of how the aggregated family audience can be maximized at different times and by the suitability of the product for the different slots.

One approach to the difference of two serials – *Coronation Street* and *Cross-roads*, for example – is to examine their position in the schedule and relate this to the IBA time-bands and a professional ideology of broadcasters. If we adopt this method the lack of a total coherence to the *Crossroads* narrative (for the reasons of multiple authorship outlined above) by offering multiple small segments in a serial stripped over three (previously four and five) nights each week at 6.35 or 5.15 p.m. (according to area) can be seen to fit into the professional ideology of a toddlers' truce, as well as the stipulations about time-bands and suitable program-ming made by the IBA. The toddlers' truce (cf. Goldie 1977, p. 209) was based on the idea of no programme transmissions between 6.00 and 7.00 p.m. so that children could be put to bed. Its use is seen to necessitate programmes which consist of multiple short items that a non-static household is able to absorb selectively. That is, the belief that people will put the television on for pro-grammes that do not require constant attention, whereas they would not for a long and involving narrative, was important to the genesis of *Tonight* (and its successor *Nationwide*), and can be seen to fit the *Crossroads* narrative structure. *Crossroads* can also be scheduled at earlier times because it fits the IBA stipulation about the need to cater for a very differentiated audience with a large proportion of children watching alone at either of its transmission times (see above). If this is compared to the audience expected to be watching at 7.30 – a static family audience with the mother present and central in determining channel selection, able to absorb a more coherent narrative, and a need to aggregate a large audience to induce high advertising expenditure – it is clear that the *Coronation Street* narrative fits these requirements. *Hazell* or *The Sweeney*, on the other hand, are both designed for the action series slot after 9.00 p.m. – programmes with greater dramatic licence because the responsibility for what children should watch is believed to lie with parents. Hence stipulations in the IBA *Television Programme Guidelines*: that programmes shown after 9.00 p.m. may be 'progres-sively less suitable (i.e. more adult) material'. After 9.00 p.m. there is an attempt to aggregate a different audience based on the 'adult'.

The placing of programmes in the schedule is an important factor of difference of television forms (and in television drama of the various subgroups: crime thrillers, family sagas, etc.). The series form and the narrative strategies utilized within it have been analysed by Phillip Drummond with reference to *The Sweeney*[4] – a hermeneutic of detection, the necessity for the expulsion of the 'difference' asserted by the villain, within a series motif that includes the mythology of a perpetuity of characters, but with stories not flowing from one episode to the next. The narrative strategies of *Coronation Street* also sometimes rely on the expulsion of any difference (any threat to the integrity of the Street), but the narrative continuity is much more marked without, however, any definite or necessary resolution of the various hermeneutics – continuation does not require resolution. The progression of the narrative is limited by the need not to move on too rapidly. It was discovered in early soap opera production in the United States that too rapid narrative progression annoys an audience and disposes it not to follow. As Stedman says of the radio serial: '. . . on an average a housewife heard between two and three episodes of a given drama each week. . . The pace of the serials at no time bothered her as much as it did researchers and critics . . . Pace bothered the housewife only in one circumstance: when she missed a broadcast and something did happen' (Stedman 1977, p. 275). This is further validated by work on audience behaviour by Goodhardt *et al.* which shows a low repeat-viewing pattern of successive series episodes so that 'for any extended series of episodes . . . almost no one sees all, or even nearly all, the different episodes' (*op. cit.*, p. 126). In fact in April/May 1971 repeat viewing of *Coronation Street* by London housewives in successive weeks was high at 63% (the average for the programmes researched was 54%) (Goodhardt *et al.* 1975, p. 57).

Thus the consumption pattern of the programme is another prime determinant of narrative structure – a narrative slowness is necessitated, together with a pre-signalling of major dramatic events (and here the popular press can be used to ensure both a maximization of audience and a prevention of annoyance at missing the major event – despite 'shocked' reactions of companies to story leaks), and a continuation of the explanation of events in the dialogue of ensuing episodes.

In addition to the importance of schedule placement in the circulation of the *Coronation Street* text, anchorage of the audience into a regular slot as part of the domestic routine, marketing and distribution of associated memorabilia, usually in the form of *TV Times* Souvenir Specials, further contribute to audience involvement. The persistent mythologization of the 'place' in the narrative, and the circulation of myths about Street life, are reinforced. These elements are further elaborated in popular press coverage of key events.

'Publicity', be it events in the lives of the stars, or events in the Street narrative, reported by the press, is a key element in the moving forward of the maze of understanding of the viewer. Furthermore, Granada's publication of three novels based on the early years of the Street was presumably believed to be a potentially profitable enterprise – an assumed demand for archaeological detail.

Independent Television Publications has published four special souvenir publications on *Coronation Street*. The first (in 1967) dealt with the wedding of Elsie Tanner to the American Steve Tanner. Another wedding (that of Len and Rita) was commemorated by a souvenir in 1977. The other two marked the 1,000th episode in 1970 and the 2,000th in 1980. Independent Television Publications sell about half a million of each (including exports to those countries where *Coronation Street* is shown – for example, Australia) and they claim that the main market is with older people. If we examine two souvenir extras – 'There's a Wedding in the Street' and 'Coronation Street 2000' – we can see that they mainly consist of items which reiterate memory points for the Street; they are further elements in the main-tenance of audience interest and commitment. Thus the ritual elements in a wedding are outlined within the ongoing narrative textuality – nodal points in the narrative allow a recapitulation of street history as well as a recasting of character. Hence in the souvenir issue for the wedding of Len and Rita, the biography of Len and Rita situates the history of their relationships with members of the opposite sex and recalls the previous Street weddings; key moments in the story. To engage the further interest of the viewer the wedding is prefigured (and a memory of it provided) by a selection from Rita's wedding album, with comments ascribed to her written alongside. The engagement with the mythic reality of the Street is repeated and circulated to Street 'fans', and the unification of the myths, the spreading out of the memory, all achieved across texts in different media, create repetition and effect reinforcement of the mode of serial consumption – a crucial specificity of continuity and circulation.

4. Signification in the context of production

Central to the understanding of a text is the analysis of its system of representation. However, it can be misleading simply to analyse appearances, or to attempt to transfer concepts employed to analyse one medium (such as a film) to the analysis of another (such as the television serial). As argued above, a central factor in the analysis of a television serial is its mode of reception. Though textual analysis does not itself deal with this area, what it can – and must – engage with is the signifying practices that are determined by the form and its conditions of production, separate from though related to the conditions of existence imposed by the reception mode.

The significational strategy of *Coronation Street* is bounded by significant constraints – place use (limited sets and the restricted narrative possibilities in a 'street'), camera strategy within the spaces used (the conventional shot strategy in the Rovers Return, for instance), a need to maintain the mythic realism of life in a northern street. The title shots and the theme music, opening and closing each episode, map off the street as a separate world; and the televisual construction of space has a central narrative function, which positions the spectator as a unified (and knowing) subject of vision within that world. The sets, and the placing by the camera of the characters in relation to them, constitute spaces that prevalue the foregrounded dialogue – a complex audience-address, interweaving well known spaces and their accumulative value with the dialogue into a constant narrative renewal. These places compensate for the irregular viewing pattern of audience members – nothing is too unexpected, no matter how the dialogue and plot develop.

The centrality of place (and the space within it, realized through camerawork) is a product of the determinations of serialization. In *Coronation Street*, the principal example of the importance of place is the Rovers Return. Here the narrative is made coherent and almost all narrative strands are discussed in this main place of exchange in the Street. At the same time there is a continuous creation of character-text for each character – a biography that has a past and a future within the mythic reality – through a specific televisual signification, meshing performance, kinesis and positioning for camera. For in *Coronation Street* the emphasis is on a group of characters living in a bounded milieu (and in this respect we can compare *Coronation Street* with a series such as *Hazell*, which is focused on one central character moving through a number of constantly changing locations), but this is also contained by the limitations of studio production.

Studio production restricts the size of sets and the number of sets available in any episode. The pre-existing pressure of the serial concept toward an ideology of 'family and community' life in a northern street (no matter how difficult this becomes because of personnel changes) cannot easily be changed to deal, for example, with the central social and economic contradictions of capital and labour in the workplace. It is difficult, if not impossible, to incorporate the industrial situation, with the necessary large sets, into restricted studio space. Narrative progression is orientated to dialogue and action within the home or the place of exchange (the shop, the pub). When industrial problems are introduced they are inevitably trivialized into the spaces available, reinforcing an unsympathetic treatment of the Labour movement. This can account in part for the television serial concentration on the situation of the petit bourgeois family. But of course radio serials of the thirties and forties in the USA also concentrated on the domestic to the exclusion of the industrial, albeit without the problems of televisual signification (cf. Edmondson and Rounds 1973, p. 18).

The style of *Coronation Street* includes a conventionality of camerawork. The particular rhetoric of the shot strategy coheres with the performance of actresses and actors in the realization of the narrative. Normal camera strategy uses two to three cameras on each set, and only a limited vocabulary of shots is utilized. Generally group shots, 2-shots or 3-shots are used (in medium to medium close-up), with emphasis achieved through the medium close-up or close-up of a single character (usually in shot reverse-shot sequence). Sometimes a developing shot is used with the camera panning to follow the action. In an early episode there is a tracking shot, though this is never used in current production. Shots concentrate on characters, and only very seldom are inanimate objects viewed alone, and then for emphasis of some point of the dialogue. The cutting between shots is almost invariably motivated by dialogue. Camera strategy *can* be used, though it is unusual, to provide dramatic emphases, such is the conventionality of the normal shot repertoire.

What has been argued in this section is that camera strategy, set restrictions and conventionalized use of space, together with the limitations of time and technical constraints, impose a certain stylistic rhetoric on the serial. These determinations of the production context are central elements in the construction of the serial-text, and must be taken into account in elaborations of the coded text – i.e. in our understanding of the programme. The technical constraints and conventionalized strategies are as important as those of the schedule or of cultural codes. But there is an overdetermination of the form that is reflected in part in Susi Hush's comment in 1974 that 'it will never get to what I want to see. It's got a reality of its own and you can't pre-empt it.'[5]

25

Dallas between reality and fiction

Ien Ang

From Ang, Ien 1985: *Watching Dallas: soap opera and the melodramatic imagination*. London: Methuen, 24–38, 40–2, 44–5.
Note: In the section before the ones extracted, Ang poses some general questions about *Dallas* as a product of the commercial culture industry and about the 'use-values' and pleasures which its viewers actively take from it. She then moves to a more specific level of commentary, using material from her respondents' letters.

DALLAS as text

In reading the letters we encounter an avalanche of self-given 'reasons' why lovers of *Dallas* like watching the programme. The letter-writers extensively describe their viewing experiences and state what does and does not appeal to them.

> I find *Dallas* a super TV programme. For me it means relaxation twice a week, out of the daily rut. You may wonder why twice a week – well, that's because I watch it on Belgian TV too. You have to switch over, but you quickly pick it up again. I'm interested in the clothes, make-up and hair-dos too. Sometimes it's quite gripping too, for example in Miss Ellie's case. [. . .] And I think Ray Krebbs is wonderful. But I think J.R. is a monster, a hypocrite, etc. (Letter 1)

> The reason I like watching it is that you can easily get really involved in their problems. Yet all the time you know it will all turn out all right again. In fact it's a flight from reality. (Letter 5)

> Why do I watch *Dallas* every Tuesday? Mainly because of Pamela and that wonderful love between her and Bobby. When I see those two I feel warmth radiating from them. I am happily married myself too and perhaps I see myself in Pamela. I find her very beautiful too (which I myself am not). (Letter 8)

> First of all it's entertainment for me, part show, expensive clothes, beautiful horses, something I can just do with by the evening. (Letter 11)

> I think it's marvellous to project myself into *Dallas* and in my mind to give J.R. a good hiding when he's just pulled off yet another dirty trick, or admire Miss Ellie because she always tries to see the best in everyone or to bring it out in them. (Letter 13)

> I find *Dallas* marvellous, though it isn't an absolute 'must' for me. Reasons:
> Everyone is so kind to one another (leaving aside J.R.) and they form a real family, being sociable, having their meals together, for example.
> Witty dialogue.
> Fast, characteristic of an American product. (Letter 17)

> My absorption in *Dallas* has to do with the fact that I follow everything coming from America. I have been there once – last year – and I started watching *Dallas* just to see the American city scene: those beautiful apartment blocks (especially the really beautiful one you see during the titles) and the cars. (Letter 21)

I don't find everything entertaining. The farm doesn't interest me much. Now and then you get a whole episode with nothing but cowboys and cattle. I find that boring, I'm not keen on Westerns. Too macho. Like the episode when the Ewing men went hunting and were chased. Boring. After that it got better again, fortunately. [. . .] I like the pictures of the city too a lot. The office buildings in Dallas. The talks about oil. I really enjoy that. (Letter 23; this letter is from a man)

I find the situations always so well chosen and excellently fitting together and everything runs so well from one thing into another. Then I find the milieu (a rich oil family, etc.) very well chosen. (Letter 40, also from a man)

It is clear that there is not just one 'reason' for the pleasure of *Dallas*, which applies for everyone; each has his or her own more or less unique relationship to the programme. What appeals to us in such a television serial is connected with our individual life histories, with the social situation we are in, with the aesthetic and cultural preferences we have developed, and so on.

But though the ideas of each of the letter-writers are of course personal, they cannot be regarded as a direct expression of their 'motives' or 'reasons' for watching *Dallas*. They can at most be regarded as indications or symptoms of deeper psychological incentives and orientations. Furthermore, although these ideas can *appear* to be strictly personal for the letter-writers themselves, ultimately all these ideas are structured in a specific socio-cultural manner. And so we must take a look behind these ideas; we must subject them to a 'symptomatic reading' to be able to say something about the pleasure of *Dallas* that rises above the merely individual level.

It would be going too far to say that viewers are completely free to handle *Dallas* as they want, as the possibilities of experiencing pleasure in it are not infinite. *Dallas* itself, as an object of pleasure, sets its own limits on those possibilities. From the letter excerpts I have just quoted it emerges that the ideas expressed by these viewers contain many elements referring to what is to be seen in the programme – to its textual characteristics. This fact makes it necessary to go into the specific way in which *Dallas*, as a cultural object, is structured.

Dallas is a weekly television programme. A television programme consists of a series of electronic images and sounds which emerge from a television set. These images and sounds represent something: people talking, walking, drinking, high-rise apartment blocks, moving cars, and so on. From this standpoint a television programme can be looked on as a *text*: as a system of representation consisting of a specific combination of (visual and audible) signs.[1] The problem here, however, is that *Dallas* is a discontinous text: it is a television serial consisting of a large number of episodes, each more or less forming a separate whole. Each episode can then in its turn be called a textual unit. For the sake of clarity I shall view the television serial *Dallas* as a whole as an incomplete, 'infinite' text.[2]

A text functions only if it is 'read'. Only in and through the practice of reading does the text have meaning (or several meanings) for the reader. In the confrontation between *Dallas* and its viewers the reading activity of the latter is therefore the connecting principle. And this reading does not occur just anyhow. As David Morley says: 'The activity of "getting meaning" from [a] message is . . . a problematic practice, however transparent and "natural" it may seem.'[3] A reader has to know specific codes and conventions in order to be able to have any grasp of what a text is about. So it is not by any means a matter of course for viewers to know directly that in *Dallas* they are dealing with a fictional text and not, for example, with a documentary. A great deal of cultural knowledge is necessary to be able to recognize a text as fiction. In *Dallas* – as is the custom in all television serials – certain hints are given for this, such as the titles, presenting the actors one after another, the music, etc.

Any text employs certain rhetorical strategies to arouse the interest of the viewers, and obviously *Dallas* succeeds in attracting the attention of millions of people with very varied social, cultural and psychological backgrounds, and maintaining their involvement in the programme. Very general and widespread structural characteristics of television programmes such as *Dallas* contribute to this.

The function of characters

How do viewers get involved in a television serial like *Dallas*, and what does this involvement consist of? The Belgian media theoretician Jean-Marie Piemme, in his book on the television serial genre,[4] asserts that this involvement occurs because viewers are enabled to participate in the 'world' of the serial. This participation does not come of its own accord, but must be *produced*:

> If, in the serial [. . .] participation can be brought about, this is certainly because this activity has psychological foundations, but it is also because these psychological foundations are confronted by a type of discourse allowing them to be activated. In other words, the structure of the discourse which sustains the serial produces the participation as well as the psychological attitude.[5]

The structure of the text itself therefore plays an essential role in stimulating the involvement of viewers. More importantly still, according to Piemme, it is impossible to watch a television serial without some degree of personal involvement. 'To watch a serial', he states, 'is much more than seeing it: it is also involving oneself in it, letting oneself be held in suspense, sharing the feelings of the characters, discussing their psychological motivations and their conduct, deciding whether they are right or wrong, in other words living "their world".'[6] But what is there so particular about the textual structure of television serials that makes them able to effect such profound involvement?

In commonsense explanations of the attraction of television serials, textual structure and its effects are generally ignored. Often single elements of the story are held responsible for the popularity of a serial. Commentary in the press about *Dallas*, for example, shows a special preference for the striking role of the 'baddie' J.R. One of the letter-writers, however, mentions her preference for another *Dallas* character: 'Sue Ellen is definitely my favourite. She has a psychologically believable character. As she is, I am too to a lesser degree ("knocking one's head against a wall once too often") and I want to be (attractive). Identification, then' (Letter 17). But such identification with one character does not take place in a vacuum. One does not just recognize oneself in the ascribed characteristics of an isolated fictional character. That character occupies a specific position within the context of the narrative as a whole: only in relation to other characters in the narrative is her or his 'personality' brought out. In other words, identification with a character only becomes possible within the framework of the whole structure of the narrative.

Moreover, the involvement of viewers cannot be described exclusively in terms of an imaginary identification with one or more characters. Several other aspects of the text contribute to this, such as the way in which the story is told, or the staging. This does not mean, however, that the characters play a subordinate role in the realization of participation. According to Piemme, in a television serial the characters even function as the pre-eminent narrative element which provides the point of impact for the involvement of viewers. But it is not so much the personalities ascribed to the characters in the story, as their formal narrative status that matters. In a fictional text like the television serial the characters are central. Through the characters the various elements of the text (situations, actions, locations, indications of time and so on) obtain a place and function in the plot. Because the viewer imagines the characters as active subjects, those elements are stripped of their arbitrariness and obtain meaning in the narrative. Furthermore, the 'lifelike' acting style ensures that the distance between actor and character is minimalized, so that the illusion is created that we are dealing with a 'real person'. The character therefore appears for the viewer as a person existing independently of the narrative situations shown in the serial. The character becomes a person appearing to lead an autonomous life outside the fiction of the serial; she or he becomes a person of flesh and blood, one of us. The popular press regularly plays on this illusion: the names of actors and actresses and those of the characters are often used interchangeably or merged – Larry 'J.R.' Hagman.

Being able to imagine the characters as 'real people' thus forms a necessary precondition for the involvement of viewers and is an anchor for the pleasure of *Dallas*. This theoretical assertion is reflected in the letters. When the letter-writers comment on the characters, it is almost always in the same way as we talk about people in daily life: in terms of character traits. The characters are not so much judged for their position in the *Dallas* narrative, as for *how they are*.

That at least is the case for the letter-writers who like *Dallas*. Those who dislike *Dallas* appear to keep a little more distant from the characters. Some of them even criticize their 'unreal' nature.

> One of them (his name escapes me) is always the bastard with his sneaky ideas and tricks, the other son is the goody together with his wife, J.R.'s wife (found the name now) is always 'sloshed' and going off alone to her room. (Letter 32)

> When they can't think up any more problems they send Digger after Miss Ellie and change Sue Ellen around a bit again, while J.R. (over the top) is well away with Sue Ellen's sister. (Letter 36)

> I find the characters appearing in the serial very caricatured [. . .] J.R. with his crazy ideas: always the same teeth-gritting. He is also a very caricatured figure, that is obvious. Oh, how bad he is. It's really laid on thick. I find his wife the most lifelike figure in the serial. I think because she was in such a difficult position the writers had most chances with her. What I really can't stand though is the facial expression she has on. Has on, I can't call it anything else. It looks as though her head is cast in plastic. (Letter 41)

What is striking in these reactions is not only a rejection of the 'personalities' of the *Dallas* people, but also an indignation over their constructedness. Those who like *Dallas*, on the other hand, write much more sympathetically about them. In their descriptions a much greater emotional involvement emerges in the characters as people, even when they find them unsympathetic. As one fan of *Dallas* writes:

Actually they are all a bit stupid. And oversensational. Affected and genuinely American. [. . .] And yet [. . .] the Ewings go through a lot more than I do. They seem to have a richer emotional life. Everyone knows them in Dallas. Sometimes they run into trouble, but they have a beautiful house and anything else they might want. (Letter 21)

The personalities of the characters are for some fans apparently so important that they have spontaneously included a whole list of characterizations and criticisms in their letters. They make clear to us how central the characters are in their viewing experience.

I don't think whether it's what you want but I'll write what I myself think of the characters too.
Miss Ellie: a nice woman.
Jock: mean, doesn't know himself exactly what he wants, I think.
Bobby: someone who has respect everywhere and for everyone (except for J.R. but that's understandable).
J.R.: Just a bastard. I personally can't stand him but I must say he plays his role well.

Pamela: a nice girl (I find her a woman of character; she can be nice, but nasty too).
Sue Ellen: has had bad luck with J.R., but she makes up for it by being a flirt. I don't like her much. And she's too sharp-tongued.
Lucy: she has rather too high an opinion of herself, otherwise she's quite nice (she's made up too old).
I don't know so much about the rest who take part in *Dallas* so I won't write about them. If you need what I've said here about these characters then I hope you can use it. If not tear it up. (Letter 3)

Now I'll describe the main characters a little, perhaps that might be useful for you too. Here we go then.
Jock: a well-meaning duffer, rather surly and hard-headed, a very haughty man.
Miss Ellie: very nice, sensitive, understanding, courageous, in other words a real mother.
J.R.: very egoistic, hard as nails, keen on power, but a man with very little heart.
Sue Ellen: just *fantastic*, tremendous how that woman acts, the movements of her mouth, hands, etc. That woman really enters into her role, looking for love, snobbish, in short a real woman.
Pamela: a Barbie doll with no feelings, comes over as false and unsympathetic (a waxen robot).
Bobby: ditto.
Lucy: likeable, naïve, a real adolescent. (Letter 12)

On the characters: Sue Ellen is definitely my favourite. She has a psychologically believable character. [. . .] (Her friend, Dusty, really loves her and for that reason, although the cowboy business in the serial irritates me and so he does too a bit, I do like him as far as I can judge.)
Miss Ellie is all right too. She looks good, always knows the right thing to do (conciliatory and firm) within the family and her breast cancer gave her some depth.
Lucy has guts, but is a wicked little sod too.
The others don't offer much as characters, I believe. Pamela pouts, and is too sweet. I have absolutely nothing to say about Jock and Bobby; J.R. is really incredible, so mean. (Letter 17)

What is interesting in these extracts is not so much the content of the character descriptions (although the difference in sympathies in itself is worth some attention), but the fact that 'genuineness' forms the basis for evaluation. The more 'genuine' a character appears to be, the more he or she is valued. But what is even more remarkable is that even for the severe critics 'genuineness' is the criterion by which they judge the characters. The only difference is that the severe critics tend to see them as 'unreal', whereas among the fans the opposite is the case. Characters who are 'caricatures' or 'improbable' are not esteemed, characters who are 'lifelike' or 'psychologically believable' are. Also, casually dropped remarks from fans quoted above ('I must say he plays his role well', 'she's made up too old' and 'tremendous how that woman acts, the movements of her mouth, hands, etc.') make clear that these letter-writers are very well aware that they are only dealing with fictional 'real people'. Such remarks indicate that these viewers would like that fictional element eliminated as far as possible. In their eyes actor and character should merge:

> . . . then I find that all the actors and actresses act very well. So well even that, for example, I really find J.R. a bastard, or Sue Ellen a frustrated lady. (Letter 18)

> . . . Because in my opinion they have chosen awfully good actors. I mean suitable for the role they are playing. The whole Ewing family is played so well that they are really human. Sometimes you get a film or a play and you think: God, if I really had to do that, I'd react quite differently. Then it seems so unreal. But usually *Dallas* could really happen, and the actors and actresses make it credible. (Letter 20)

> The people taking part in it act terribly well. (Letter 4)

The effect of 'genuineness' is then the most important thing these viewers expect. Only when they experience the fiction of the serial as 'genuine' can they feel involved in it. They have to be able to believe that the characters constructed in the text are 'real people' whom they can find pleasant or unpleasant, with whom they can feel affinity or otherwise, and so on. It could be said that such involvement is a necessary condition for the pleasure of *Dallas*.

The (un)realistic quality of DALLAS

But genuine-seeming *people* alone are not enough. According to Piemme, the fictional *world* in which the characters live must seem equally real. But how 'real' or 'realistic' is this world? This rather vague concept of 'realism' also seems to play an important part in the letters. 'Realism' seems to be a favourite criterion among viewers for passing judgement on *Dallas*. And here 'realistic' is always associated with 'good' and 'unrealistic' with 'bad'. So it is not surprising that many haters of *Dallas* express their dislike by referring to its – in their opinion – 'unrealistic' content. Here are some letter extracts:

> In *Dallas* no attention at all is paid to any realistic problems in this world. The problems of ordinary people. (Letter 31) . . . in my eyes the characters appearing in it are totally unreal. (Letter 38)

> It is a programme situated pretty far outside reality. The mere fact that a whole family is living in one house comes over as rather unreal. What happens in this serial you would never run into in the street or in your circle of acquaintance: very unreal events. The family relations that are so weirdly involved: this one's married to the sister of the enemy of his brother, etc., etc. (Letter 41)

> 1. It is an improbable story because:
>   1.1 Such a rich family would scarcely live as three families in one house (at least in a Western society), so that privacy for each family is minimal:
>   1.1.1 They breakfast together, etc.

      1.1.2 Other than the common rooms each family only has one bedroom (no separate sitting room or study, etc.).

      1.1.3 The whole family concerns itself with everything.

   1.2 Too much happens in the short time and then it's all dramatic situations, not only for the main characters, but for the minor characters as well. This latter makes things confusing.

   1.3 The actors are rather clichéd types, i.e. they keep up a certain role or attitude. Normal people are more complex.

  2. Thanks to the constant drama there is a certain tension in the story, but this is exaggerated. Even in a more realistic story there can be tension and I actually find that nicer. (Letter 42)

In these extracts a number of things are striking. In the first place these letter-writers find *Dallas* 'unrealistic' because in their opinion the world and the events in the story do not coincide with the world and events outside *Dallas*: reality 'as it is'. A text is called 'realistic' here if the 'reality' standing outside and independent of the text is reflected in an 'adequate' way. But – and this is the second striking point – the letter-writers each invest the notion of 'reality' with a different content. For some the represented reality must coincide with the social reality of 'ordinary people' (i.e. 'real' problems such as unemployment and housing shortages and not the 'mock problems' of the rich); for others that reality must be 'recognizable', i.e. comparable to one's own environment; and for others again the world presented must be 'probable', i.e. cohere, be 'normal'. Finally, a text is also occasionally called 'unrealistic' if people find that it simplifies the 'real' reality (whatever that may be), exaggerates it or reflects it in clichés.

As we can see, the significance of the notion '(un)realistic' can assume different forms. Clearly there is no unambiguous definition of what 'realism' contains. But in the way in which the term is used by the letter-writers quoted, at least an essential community of ideas can be discerned: they all call *Dallas* 'unrealistic' because in their opinion it gives a 'distorted image of reality'. This definition of realism, in which a comparison of the realities 'in' and 'outside' a text is central, we can call 'empiricist realism'.[7] This empiricist concept of realism often fulfils an ideological function in television criticism in so far as its standards are used to furnish arguments for criticizing programmes and to strengthen the concept itself. From this point of view, a text which can be seen as an 'unrealistic' rendering of social reality (however that is defined) is 'bad'. And as we have seen, *Dallas* is often subjected to this judgement.

But having said this, we are immediately confronted by an apparently baffling contradiction. Contrary to the critics and those who dislike *Dallas*, who regard it as particularly 'unrealistic', many fans do find it 'realistic'. Some letter-writers even see the – in their eyes – realistic content of *Dallas* as a reason for the pleasure they experience.

I find *Dallas* super and for this reason: they reflect the daily life of a family (I find). (Letter 3)

It is realistic (for me anyway), other people think I'm mad, things happen in it we might well find happening to us later (or have had). (Letter 12)

How should we interpret this contradiction? Should we ascribe to these letter-writers a 'false consciousness' because their judgement on the 'realistic' content of *Dallas* is totally wrong? Or is there more to it? Reasoning from an empiricist-

206 Dallas *between reality and fiction*

realistic standpoint, we can simply say these letter-writers are misled. In *Dallas*, according to this reasoning, the 'daily life of a family' is certainly not being reflected – for, as one letter-writer suggests: 'I wonder why these people in Heaven's name carry on living in the same house!' (Letter 36). Furthermore, it could be said that the things that happen in it are certainly not things 'we might well find happening to us', for it is clear that in *Dallas* there is an improbable accumulation of sensational events, such as airplane accidents, weird diseases, kidnappings, etc. In short, if *Dallas* is regarded as a mirror of 'the' reality, then we should recognize that it is a big distorting mirror, or more seriously, 'a twisted image of reality'.

But this empiricist conception of realism presents problems for a number of reasons. I shall cite two difficulties here. First, it is wrongly based on the assumption – and this is inherent in empiricism – that a text *can* be a direct, immediate reproduction or reflection of an 'outside world'. This is to ignore the fact that everything that is processed in a text is the result of selection and adaptation: elements of the 'real world' function only as raw material for the production process of texts. The empiricist conception denies the fact that each text is a cultural product realized under specific ideological and social conditions of production. And so there can never be any question of an unproblematic mirror relation between text and social reality: at most it can be said that a text constructs its own version of 'the real'. As Raymond Williams says: 'The most damaging consequence of any theory of art as reflection is that [...] it succeeds in suppressing the actual work on material [...] which is the making of any art work.'[8]

The second difficulty is connected with this. The empiricist conception of realism cannot do justice to the fact that a large number of *Dallas* fans do seem to *experience* it as 'realistic'. Must we regard this experience merely as the result of incorrect reading and must we, consequently, accuse the letter-writers who read 'wrongly' of a lack of knowledge of reality? It is, to say the least, unsatisfactory just to dismiss this very prevalent way of responding to the programme. A more structural explanation must be possible.

DALLAS and the realistic illusion

In the empiricist conception of realism the thematic content of the narrative becomes the guideline for the assessment of the 'realistic' nature of the text. Some literary and film theoreticians on the other hand make the way in which the story is told responsible for what is called the 'realistic illusion': the illusion that a text is a faithful reflection of an actually existing world emerges as a result of the fact that the constructedness of the text is suppressed. Piemme states that it is this suppression which fosters the involvement of viewers in the serial: 'Participation can only function by denying itself as product of discourse. What produces it must suppress the marks of its production in order that the illusion of the natural, the spontaneous, the inevitable, may function.'[9] In other words, the realistic illusion is not something to be blamed on the ignorance or lack of knowledge of the viewers, but is generated by the formal structure of the text itself; the thematic content plays only a subordinate role here.

[The author here offers a brief summary of some of the codes of depiction and of continuity which produce the 'realistic illusion' in film and television fiction – see the items by Ellis and Paterson in this section. She refers to the work of film theorist Colin MacCabe on the self-concealing nature of 'classical realism'.]

According to MacCabe and others[10] it is precisely this constructed illusion of reality which is the basis for pleasure. It is pleasurable to be able to deny the textuality and the fictional nature of the film and forget it: it gives the viewers a comfortable and cosy feeling because they can 'let the narrative flow over them' without any effort. The apparent 'transparency' of the narrative produces a feeling of direct involvement, because it ensures that the viewer can act exactly *as though* the story really happened. In other words, according to this theory pleasure in *Dallas* could be regarded as a pleasure in the obvious, apparently natural meaningfulness of the ups and downs of the Ewing family and the people around them. It is the *form* of the narrative which produces pleasure, not its content.

Yet this explanation of pleasure is not totally satisfactory, precisely because it abstracts from the concrete narrative-content.[11] Transparent narrativity alone is not enough to get pleasure out of a text; not all transparent narrative texts are experienced as equally pleasurable. On the contrary, the thematic differences between such texts are of interest, as one of the letter-writers states: 'For me *Dallas* is comparable to *Dynasty*. Other American series (*Magnum, Hulk, Charlie's Angels, Starsky and Hutch*, in short, violence) I can appreciate less' (Letter 17). Thus the pleasure of *Dallas* is not only to do with the illusion of reality which is produced by its transparent narrativity – although it might be said that this illusion is a general condition of pleasure as it is experienced by a lot of viewers. *What* is told in the narrative must also play a part in the production of pleasure.

DALLAS and 'emotional realism'

Why then do so many fans call *Dallas* 'realistic'? What do they recognize as 'real' in its fictional world?

A text can be read at various levels. The first level is the literal, denotative level. This concerns the literal, manifest content of the *Dallas* narrative: the discussions between the characters, their actions, their reactions to one another, and so on. Is this literal content of the *Dallas* story experienced as realistic by viewers? It does not look like it. Indeed, we can say that the above-quoted letter-writers who dislike *Dallas* are talking on this literal narrative-level when they dismiss the programme as *un*realistic. Let us repeat a letter extract:

> It is a programme situated pretty far outside reality. The mere fact that a whole family is living in one house comes over as rather unreal. What happens in this serial you would never run into in the street or in your circle of acquaintance: very unreal events. The family relationships that are so weirdly involved: this one's married to the sister of the enemy of his brother, etc., etc. (Letter 41)

This indicates that the *Dallas* narrative at the level of denotation is not exactly regarded as realistic; literal resemblances are scarcely seen between the fictional world as it is constructed in *Dallas* and the 'real' world. Again the inadequacy of the empiricist-realistic approach becomes clear here. It is only sensitive to the denotative level of the narrative. Therefore it can only see the fact that so many *Dallas* fans obviously do experience the programme as realistic as a paradox.

A text can, however, also be read at another level, namely at the connotative level.[12] This level relates to the associative meanings which can be attributed to elements of the text. The same letter-writer we have just quoted also wrote the following: 'The nice thing about the serial is that it has a semblance of humanity, it is not so unreal that you can't relate to it any more. There are recognizable things, recognizable people, recognizable relations and situations in it'. (Letter 41)

It is striking; the same things, people, relations and situations which are regarded at the denotative level as unrealistic, and unreal, are at connotative level apparently not seen at all as unreal, but in fact as 'recognizable'. Clearly, in the connotative reading process the denotative level of the text is put in brackets.

[Ang here quotes further from her letters to indicate in what ways viewers find *Dallas* 'recognizable' and 'taken from life' at this level of reading. She notes that it is primarily at this level that the programme is judged to be realistic.]

In naming the 'true to life' elements of *Dallas* the concrete living circumstances in which the characters are depicted (and their wealth in particular springs to mind here) are, it is true, striking but not of significance as regards content; the concrete situations and complications are rather regarded as symbolic representations of more general living experiences: rows, intrigues, problems, happiness and misery. And it is precisely in this sense that these letter-writers find *Dallas* 'realistic'. In other words, at a connotative level they ascribe mainly emotional meanings to *Dallas*. In this sense the realism of *Dallas* can be called an 'emotional realism'.

And now it begins to become clear why the two previous conceptions of realism discussed above, empiricist realism and classical realism, are so unsatisfactory when we want to understand the experience of realism of *Dallas* fans. For however much the two approaches are opposed to one another – for the former realism is a token for a 'good' text, and for the latter for a 'bad' text – in both a cognitive-rationalistic idea dominates: both are based on the assumption that a realistic text offers *knowledge* of the 'objective' social reality. According to the empiricist-realists a text is realistic (and therefore good) if it supplies 'adequate knowledge' of reality, while in the second conception a classic-realistic text is bad because it only creates an illusion of knowledge. But the realism experience of the *Dallas* fans quoted bears no relation to this cognitive level – it is situated at the emotional level: what is recognized as real is not knowledge of the world, but a subjective experience of the world: a 'structure of feeling'.[13]

26

Hill Street Blues

Todd Gitlin

From Gitlin, Todd 1983: *Inside prime time*. New York: Pantheon, 284–96.
Note: This extract is taken from a chapter on the creation of the distinctive 'look' and values of *Hill Street Blues* and is concerned with the development of the initial ideas through the stage of the pilot programme and beyond. Bochco and Kozoll are the co-writers, Stanley is the representative of the Broadcast Standards office (responsible for checking the 'taste and decency' of the material to be transmitted).

Bochco and Kozoll started writing, but old network habits die hard. They were a few days into their script when a program executive called and said, 'When are we going to get together and talk about the story?' Bochco retorted, 'We've already started writing the script.' 'What?' 'We said, "Hey, fellas, come on, you said you were going to leave us alone." ' 'Well, but we want to know what the story is before you go to the screenplay.' 'We'll be more than happy to come in and tell you what we're doing. But we're just going to tell you what we've already started to do.' 'All right, mumble, grumble, mumble, grumble, okay.' 'We went over and we told them certain highlights of our story, and they said, "Well, okay." '

The script Bochco and Kozoll turned in covered a full day of narrative time, from early-morning roll-call to late night. One hundred twenty scenes wedged into each other in the course of fifty-nine pages, introducing thirteen principals and eighteen other speaking parts. Story lines overlapped, interwove, broke off only to resume later. In bare-bones summary, along with many short atmospheric scenes, the plot tracked through everyday crisis upon everyday crisis. The strikingly attractive public defender, Joyce Davenport, stalks into the chaotic, run-down Hill Street Station looking for a client who has disappeared into a bureaucratic pigeonhole. The cocky, handsome detective J.D. LaRue tries to insinuate himself into her good embraces. Davenport tells off the low-key captain, Frank Furillo. Officers Bobby Hill (black, patient, intelligent) and Andy Renko (loud-mouthed, racist urban cowboy) observe two Hispanic teenagers robbing a liquor store and taking hostages. Lt Howard Hunter, the pipe-smoking, tough-talking, self-parodying head of the counterinsurgency squad, counsels an attack with heavy weaponry, while the liberal community-relations officer Henry Goldblume advises careful persuasion. Furillo agrees to let a swaggering Hispanic gang leader enter the negotiations. In the middle of everything, Furillo's ex-wife Fay storms into the station, shrieking because his child-support check has bounced. Meanwhile, Hill and Renko are called to cope with a family feud in a black household. The man of the house has slept with his lover's daughter, and she is threatening to kill him. Hill defuses the skirmish by laying down provisional law: The man has to stay away from the daughter, the daughter has to be less seductive, the woman has to be more available to her man. Leaving the apartment building, Hill and Renko discover that their car has been stolen. Looking for a functioning phone, they amble into an abandoned apartment building, where a group of junkies happen to be shooting up. One of the junkies pulls a gun and fires, leaving Hill and Renko for dead. Back at the liquor store, Furillo coaxes the thieves to give up, just before Hunter's squad blows up the store. Davenport, lured back to the station by LaRue's false claim that her missing client has turned up, charmingly pours coffee all over his pants. Back in her apartment that night, Davenport denounces the police as 'reactionary, fascistic, high-handed, uncaring animals' to her unseen lover – who turns out to be Frank Furillo. They are about to make love when his beeper goes off. The lumbering, baroque Sgt Phil Esterhaus tells him the two men have been found: 'one DOA, one critical.'

Broadcast Standards was not overjoyed. Could Bochco and Kozoll meet with Stanley again? So a second meeting took place, and as Stanley ran through his notes, the writers listened, frowned, and by prior arrangement said nothing. Language . . . sexual innuendo . . . the black family scene . . . the violence of the shooting. Again, each side claims victory. Bochco recalls Stanley backing away from half his notes, in sheer embarrassment. And then, over the next few days, he says, 'We negotiated their remaining notes down to almost nothing. I was amazed. We have done things in our script and put on the screen that I've never seen in a TV show before.' 'Failings that heroes have,' Kozoll chimes in. 'Cops who drink. Cops who smoke controlled substances. We don't show it but we allude to it.'

Stanley thought he had won the important points. First off, he insisted that the show drop specific references to the Bronx and New York; the locale was now made indefinite, universal. Second, Stanley insisted that the show not offend people of colour. Censorship is 'liberal' as well as 'conservative'; in fact, Standards policies in the 70s had the effect of systematically over-representing whites among television's criminals. 'One of the major points of the discussion at the time was, as Steve very astutely pointed out, that the criminal element at this particular precinct was almost 100 per cent black or Chicano. The only whites that live in that kind of neighbourhood are people who are too poor or too old to move away, and consequently they were prisoners in their own environment. Our quarrel with them, if you want to call it that, was that they were simply going to have to fictionalize it to the extent of saying that all criminals weren't black. There are some white Anglo-Saxon Protestant thieves and killers and pimps.' This is one point, he says, that Bochco and Kozoll did not resist. 'What they did to accommodate us – and I don't know that they did it to accommodate us, they may have had it in mind already – was that they put a mixture of various ethnic types in the station, so that you had a counterbalance for the problems that we might be confronted with as broadcasters, [with protesting groups] saying that all the bad guys are Chicanos or blacks. And we were quickly pointing out that a lot of the [cops are] blacks and Chicanos as well, so it's saying that there is good and bad in every group.'

Stanley was also unhappy with what he called the stereotyping of the family feud scene. 'We went round and round on that for a long time,' Stanley says.

'We were not trying to make a specific comment about blacks per se,' Bochco says, 'though there is a very high incidence of abandonment within the black community in ghettoes. There are certain sociological realities there.'

'Ultimately,' says Stanley, 'we conceded that they could do it.' With his faith in Bochco's honourable motives, he struck a custom-made bargain, comparable to the sort of swap that Standards people usually work out with their trigger-list of taboo words, letting the writers swap this 'damn' for that 'hell'. The junkies encountered by Hill and Renko eventually were cast as one black, one white, one apparently Hispanic, and the fourth wholly unrecognizable; the one who pulls the trigger – seen only for a split second – is white. In the end, Bochco and Kozoll were men of liberal conscience. 'We were concerned about that scene, too' Kozoll says. 'We read dozens and dozens of black actors for the parts, and every single one of them we asked if they thought this scene was offensive. We asked other black people who were involved in the show in one way or another if they thought it was offensive. And you might argue that it's really a coercive question, given their situation and our power to hire.' But, Bochco interjected, 'We got some pretty straight answers. Some people were troubled, and they admitted it.' Michael Warren, cast as Hill, was one of them.*

In the end, Stanley was persuaded the black household could have existed, and that was enough. Having a high-level LA police adviser helped. Shows written from the viewpoint of a profession always retain an adviser from that profession. Thus do producers avail themselves of the claim of realism when censors apply their moralism, when protesters write their letters, even when interviewers make nuisances of themselves. Yet this realist stratagem is necessarily selective, if sincere – for the most 'realistic' show is never strictly so. Even in a vérité documentary, filmmakers make choices about where and when to plant cameras and microphones, which scenes will be juxtaposed, what will be edited in and out. And moreover, everyday life in a ghetto precinct is simply too dense, indeed at times too vile and violent, to be exactly 'mirrored'. When *Hill Street* came on the air, along with the many police who lauded it for realism were some who accused it of prettying up the ghetto 'assholes' who Renko and Hunter called 'animals'.

By deploying the claim to realism, producers can beat back some of Broadcast Standards' demands, but only, in effect, by giving some of their autonomy back to authoritative advisers. *Hill Street's* claim to realism makes selectively 'real' police practice the touchstone of creative choices: In a moral universe supervised by censors, fiction establishes its bona fides by borrowing selectively from fact. To protect themselves from censors and potential critics alike, producers make a fetish of fact; they rely not only on official advisers but on fact-checking agencies that specialize in verifying the details intended to guarantee the look of authenticity.

Yet in the end, when official morality is at stake, even the defence of realism may not prevail. Broadcast Standards sometimes intervenes as the strong right arm of ideology pure and simple. Jerry Stanley, for example, was disturbed by what he called the *Hill Street* pilot's 'depiction of the police as being casually indifferent to the law.' In one scene, the script had Officer J.D. LaRue smash open a Laundromat coinbox to find a dime for his call to Joyce. The point could

---

* Stanley didn't register any feminist objection, however. The networks had taken much more heat from angry ethnics than organized feminists. I told Bochco and Kozoll I had heard a feminist object to the scene's suggestion that the family problem was caused by the woman not 'giving' her man enough sex. 'That wasn't what the scene was about,' Kozoll replied. 'The scene was about two police officers using anything at their disposal to cool out a situation, regardless of what impact it really may have. [It was a] con job. We talked with our police technical adviser Jess Brewer about that: "Would you, Jess, have done it that way?" And he said to us he *has* done it that way.' Hill was saying, in other words, 'You cool this off or I'll turn you over to Renko.'

be defended on realist grounds. It does happen that police cut the corners of the law. Besides, by the show's internal logic, LaRue's transgression was a character point. He was a notorious fuck-up who was caught, as we would learn in subsequent episodes, in a downward spiral of alcoholism. But in this case Bochco and Kozoll could not prevail.

'We said absolutely not,' according to Stanley, 'We would not permit that kind of wanton disregard for the law.' After the revision, LaRue got his dime – and his laugh – from a grotesque old woman. It was permissible to show LaRue making a joke at the expense of a *zhlub*, but not to show a cop as a casual criminal.* No police uproar was needed to remind the network to go an extra mile to serve and protect that image. This time censorship was a matter of principle.

A different principle came up in the matter of the shooting of Hill and Renko, where again the claim of realism had to yield – this time to the claim of good taste. Years of organized protest against televised blood and gore had retooled network standards. Stanley was concerned that the shooting of Hill and Renko 'not be exploited. The shooting should be done carefully. We didn't want blood squibs. The point was made that the two guys were shot down, and that's all that was needed.' On this point the writers did not need convincing. What they wanted from that scene was the sting of sudden death, not the horror of smashed corpses . . .

Bochco and Kozoll wanted the show to look singular, and in Greg Hoblit they had an unusually adept and visually sophisticated line producer. Hoblit had gone to Berkeley in the early 60s, gotten involved in the Free Speech Movement and the Vietnam Day Committee, but not managed to balance his dawning politics with his family background (his father was second in charge of the Berkeley FBI office). So he had dropped out, shipped to China in the merchant marine, disabused himself of romantic ideas about the working class, and eventually graduated in film from UCLA. Bochco had seen and admired Hoblit's documentary, *A Difficult Man*, about the Northern California guru Bubba Free John, and later hired him to produce *Paris*, then *Vampire*. Hoblit knew his film lore, and he was quick to learn the nuts and bolts of producing: casting, coping with lost film and compensating for film botched in the lab, massaging the egos of actors, briefing the directors, keeping a sharp eye on the editing, supervising the sound mix. He had opinions but spoke softly, and mostly he worked his ten- to twelve-hour days with a steady humming energy. Entrusted with an unusual degree of authority for a line producer, he got along well with everyone. He was the native Californian in the inner circle. He was Bochco's age, middle thirties, and his hair, like Bochco's, was prematurely gray.

Hoblit was of the film-school generation, Francis Ford Coppola, Martin Scorsese, Paul Shrader, and company, who brought visual stylishness into the Hollywood movies of the 70s. 'I read the script,' Hoblit remembers, 'and immediately a whole visual sense came to me about what it ought to be. Hand-held camera. Let's get the film as dirty as we can. What I said is, "Let's go for the

---

* At least not at the start of the series. In later episodes, when the show was established, and Standards placated, we would see cops screwing up, taking out their frustration in brutality and lies, covering up for buddies, keeping deceptive records in good causes; we would see a bad cop led to bribe-taking and then perjury by way of bigamy. LaRue even got demoted to the motor pool. But it's true that no regular cop was ever again shown as a casual crook.

Serpico look." ' In television even complexity and dirtiness require their own lineage. What was unusual was to find Hoblit's film sensibility erupting in television, the province of the well-trimmed image.

High density, nervous energy, and a look of controlled chaos were alien to commercial television, so who would know how to direct such a show? The industry had cultivated a tame and uniform directorial style. Indeed, instead of style there were techniques. The dialogue would come out mechanical but oh so clear (two-shot, close-up, over-the-shoulder, close-up, cut); actors would be run through their paces with dispatch to meet tight schedules and budgets. The directorial innovations celebrated within the industry were techniques, like the invention of the standard, efficient three-camera method in sitcoms. There were directors who were more or less skilled in working with actors, but with no time to rehearse an episode, and rarely even time for a complete reading by the actors, directors were relatively interchangeable. If movies were a director's medium, television was the producer's.

'People were afraid of the material,' Hoblit says. 'And there were directors who wanted to do two-hour series or miniseries, and they considered one-hour pilots to be less than up to their status at this point.' One of these veterans was Robert Butler, whose experience extended back to the days of live drama on *Playhouse 90*. Butler had directed episodes of *East Side, West Side*, of NYPD, of *The Blue Knight*, and of *Columbo*, Bochco's first show. After 20 years of directing episodes, he had graduated to pilots and a feature film (*Night of the Juggler*). Butler was much in demand for pilots, but had a reputation for being 'unorthodox,' in Greg Hoblit's words, for being a renegade, or delivering what other people would have thought was crappy film.

Butler had once done a project with Grant Tinker. 'They both have eastern prep-school manners, and they do well together,' according to Hoblit. A week before *Hill Street* preproduction began in earnest, Butler happened to call Tinker, who told him he had a new show looking for a director. MTM offered him 'a hell of a lot of money,' Butler says; he loved the script, the dialogue, the story, the 'touches'. Later, when the pilot was complete, Barbara Bosson suggested to her husband Steven Bochco that Butler be hired to shoot the next four episodes. Shooting four shows in a block would give him more than the usual time to achieve some extraordinary effects. Hour-long episodes usually had to be shot in seven days (compared to twelve for a pilot), and such pressures made for sloppiness and corner-cutting. Shooting the episodes together would make for valuable efficiencies. In one day he could shoot all the scenes on a particular location, for example, saving transportation and setup time that could be applied to run-throughs and lighting effects.

In days and weeks of meetings, Bochco, Kozoll, Butler and Hoblit together thrashed out the details of look, sound, costumes, sets, locations. Bochco and Kozoll held final authority, but everyone agreed that Butler deserved much of the credit for the show's tone as he worked to match the show's look and sound to the 'layered, laminated, potentially confusing complication' of its script. No slack time, no flab, momentum was all. The show should look messy because the problems police deal with are messy, solutions are fleeting, the police vulnerable, situations morally ambiguous.

There is much talk in Hollywood about 'production values' – fancy sets and gorgeous costumes and crisp portrayals. But for most shows, the preoccupation is more vivid than the outcome is evident. Craft is hamstrung by the false presumption that only conventional lines of goods will sell. Butler, like the producers, was interested in exploring the boundaries. If this was an ensemble show, dense with principals, filled with short scenes, whose action was 'knitted' from fragments, then the screen should look busy, the editing often abrupt. 'The show is movement,' as Butler put it, and if the characters were to keep moving, then so should the camera in the sort of long takes so splendidly done in movies by Max Ophuls, Orson Welles and Kenzo Mizoguchi. Scenes should flow into each other with minimal editing, as in *Casablanca* or Michael Kozoll's original model, *Grand Hotel*. 'Twelve people standing around looks like the Acropolis. It's the worst,' says Butler.

The camera might open in Furillo's office as he talks to a frantic Hill and Renko about their shooting, but without the usual master shot that shows all three of them together and slows down the action. Esterhaus opens the door, tells Furillo that La Rue has been arrested for taking a bribe, and exits. A phone call tells Furillo that Belker nabbed a rapist. Enter Fay Furillo shrieking about the latest catastrophe in her life. In the background, through the window, we see Goldblume lecturing a gang member. The camera might then follow Furillo out of his office to Goldblume – all this without a cut.

Each strand would be picked up later in the hour, or perhaps in the next episode or several episodes after that, and be taken its own distance, overlapping new ones. Other cops would walk through the background or foreground, filing papers, answering phone calls, typing reports, shuffling suspects in and out of the squad room. With plenty of tight shots, the station would feel cramped. The fragmentation and juxtaposition of shots and conversations would reproduce the fragmentation and simultaneity of society. Characters would brush past each other, reach over each other's shoulders, break into each other's conversations, suggesting that its people depend on each other, crisis is everyday, no man or woman is an island. The heroism of these cops would not be the swagger of loners lording it over society, or over the screen. 'It wasn't new,' Butler said, 'but it had never been done that densely before.'

The camera would avoid the conventional tableau-with-Ping-Pong effect of most television drama, in which each scene begins with the obligatory shot of the whole stiff group on display, followed by close-ups of A, then B, then A again. Butler wanted to break down what he called 'all the heritage of visual cleanliness.' As the script was spare of narrative exposition, so should the film be compact. 'I hate establishing shots,' Butler declares. 'We can go from a close-up of Furillo in his office to a medium shot of Davenport at a restaurant, instead of seeing the cab pull up and the doorman opening the door: all that shoe leather that drives you crazy. If she's tamping a cigarette or having a glass of wine and there are two plates in front of her, you know what's going on. Your establishing shots are a big yawn.' Television had followed Hollywood movies in flashing obvious signals whenever the action moved to a new site: the shot of the name of the building, followed by a pan up the side to the umpty-umpth floor; the shot of the plane landing to suggest a change of locale. Now, at long last, television would follow commercial film's movement into the territory of more economical, more tantalizing kinetic technique. 'Less is more' was Hoblit's slogan for *Hill Street* style. He and Butler were looking for 'lightning in a bottle,' a character's truth in a moment of revelation.

Butler was also tempted by the producers' talk of shooting the whole show with hand-held cameras, in black and white, to heighten the grainy, documentary look. He even proposed shooting in the relatively primitive 16 mm. But 16 mm proved impractical, since the labs were not equipped to handle it on a weekly television schedule; and no one thought the networks were ready for black and white. Accordingly, Butler began shooting the episodes in the normal 35 mm, but with everything hand-held and nervous. This stretched the conventions too far. The producers, Butler recalls, 'got a little spooky with it and asked that I do only certain heightened sequences hand-held,' like the roll-call sequence that opens every show, and certain moments of violence. Influenced by the PBS documentary *The Police Tapes*, he shot roll-call with two cameras running simultaneously. He let the camera operators watch rehearsals with their eyes only, not with their machines. 'I told them, "Don't worry if you have to find focus [in the middle of shooting]." When I saw the dailies they looked pretty raunchy, and I said, Hmm, I wonder, but you mustn't express doubts directorially. But when it strung together, it got smoothed a little bit, and still had the texture and the juice.' Then he told the editors, 'Don't use the stuff once the shot has settled down. Use the bad stuff. It's terrific.'

The edgy look of roll-call was reinforced by sound. While the screen was still black, a background mutter started up. Instantly *Hill Street* looked and sounded ragged. The shaky hand-held frame reinforced the sense of irreverent, antic, raucous, sometimes hung-over cops at seven in the morning, playing against the robust, almost self-mocking orderliness of Sgt Phil Esterhaus as he ticked off his list of items. In the pilot, for example: 'Item fourteen: We've still got a gang of juveniles on 119th Street hitting old people cashing Social Security checks. Now, how about let's give that situation a little extra effort. . . . Item fifteen: At this point in time we've got the same purse-snatcher working Wolf from the projects on South. He is a male black, age approximately thirty, six feet six inches tall, medium build. He is further described as wearing a long blond wig and powder-blue cocktail-style dress, gathered in little tucks at the waist [Snickers from the cops] . . .' And so on through Esterhaus's list to his cautionary trademark, the coda that revealed the precinct's jeopardy in a world it could barely police: 'Let's roll, and hey – let's be careful out there.'

Butler wanted the ragged look of reality in the makeup of individual shots as well. He tried to break camera operators of their training to get clear, neat, balanced shots. 'Make it look messy,' I'm saying to Billy [Cronjager, director of photography]. 'Don't make that pretty stuff we all know how to make. Make it look bad.' They kept coming to me, both on the pilot and on the episodes, saying, 'It's pretty ba-ad.' And I said, 'Make it worse. Make it worse. It makes it more real.' Soft light is unreal. Occasionally there'd be a place where a big shadow would come across somebody, and he wouldn't clean it up, and he'd say, 'It's pretty bad,' and I'd say 'Yeah, I know it is, and it's marvelous. Keep going.' As for the twenty background characters, Butler remembers telling the assistant directors, 'Get the people up, get 'em moving. Have 'em walk right through the scene.' 'Between the lens and the principals?' 'Please.' He wanted background characters 'bumping into principals, reaching across their desks to pick up forms, nobody honouring anybody's privacy.'

Butler dimmed the lighting, too, to make the print look down and dirty. He 'ground the film down' in the lab to get away from 'magazine-cover stuff.' He played tricks with filters, and made sure the cops' wardrobe was irregular, all contributing to an urban tone people generally associate with the East and Midwest. (Actually, the title sequence and a smattering of other exteriors were shot in Chicago; almost all the other exteriors were done on location in the skid row section of Los Angeles.) The multiracial cast also worked against flashy upbeat colour. So did the night-time shooting, the alleys, the litter of dumpsters and dismantled cars dragged into the streets, the graffiti sprayed on walls.

And this messiness extended to sound. In the name of realism, Butler and Hoblit performed the television equivalent of Robert Altman's approach to simultaneous talk in the movies. Less extravagantly than Altman, but more radically than television had seen before, they ushered in overlapping dialogue. Indeed, parts of the script were already written that way, characters talking against each other in the crisis-ridden clutter of precinct life; but Butler pulled out the stops and fought to overcome the normal conventions of TV craft. 'What we're all taught in the business is that one person speaks at a time,' Butler says. 'And you and I know it's nonsense.' To Butler the awkward interference patterns of natural speech were gestures in the name of honesty. This he had to make his editor understand, even while acknowledging the technical fact that dialogue overlaps robbed the editor of some flexibility when it came time to assemble sequences of takes into a continuous dialogue. In the intricate division of labour that stands behind Hollywood performance, craft militates toward conservatism of method. Butler had to push: 'I said to the editor, "Look, let's just not discuss overlaps, because it's too boring. Let's not even get into it. I'm going to do it. I know you can cut. I know you give up freedom; we both give up freedom – let's just do it. It's more real – the hell with it." '

Once the film was assembled, Hoblit laid on a separate background track of ambient sound. He hired an improvisational comedy troupe called Off the Wall to screen selected scenes in a sound studio and improvise everything from squad-room phone murmurs to dispatch calls and crowd noises. When the half dozen comics of Off the Wall recorded their murmurs, they ambled toward and away from their microphones, so the background noise sounded unusually authentic. Off the Wall's buzz set the show's feeling-tone: the sense that foreground action takes place amid the interference of a myriad of events, and that islands of order are, as Robert Frost said about poetry, 'momentary stays against confusion'.

This buzz was the bulk of the show's music. The rest, variations on the muted, downbeat theme by Mike Post, reverberated through odd moments in the show. Post himself was no stranger to blunt, blaring pop styles. He produced records for Dolly Parton, and (with his partner) composed the music for *The White Shadow*, *The Rockford Files*, *Magnum, P.I.*, and other TV shows. But the *Hill Street* producers wanted to avoid the clanging chords by which television melodrama signals strong emotion or imminent disclosure. Sometimes there was so little music on *Hill Street* that Post said to Hoblit, 'I can't charge you for this.' The producers had even toyed with the radical notion of dispensing with music altogether; but that, they concluded, would have been too gross a departure from audience expectations. Post's discreet, wistful theme was a far cry from the peremptory, martial bursts that had once blared forth from *Dragnet*, or the resounding Prokofiev march that had conveyed the strident certitudes of *The FBI*. Whenever *Hill Street* did indulge in musical excess, to plug the holes in a weak script, Hoblit felt abashed.

Butler himself was no theorist of modernist method. He thought he was a realist, period. He said he wanted 'to get the texture and the reality, to bring reality to the people and thereby heighten the trip. I contend that all we're trying to do is transport them anyway. I don't have any philosophical beliefs about the purpose. All I think [TV's] for is to turn it on for an hour because it's been a hard day.' But Butler did enjoy the chance to unfold his craft. For years that craft had crouched in the shadows of convention. How much Bob Butler – or Steven Bochco or Michael Kozoll – had felt, and suppressed, the desire to surpass the limits of paint-by-numbers television is something I couldn't judge; perhaps something they couldn't know either, since the pressure of everyday accommodation renders such desires a demoralizing nuisance. The streamlining of TV production pushes for assembly-line efficiency; too much daydreaming about grand aesthetic designs would prove distracting as well. Anyway, people who are burning to break through the conventional limits are not likely to be making careers in commercial television in the first place. Still, normal pride in craft sometimes flares into an interest in novel methods, and who knows when that interest may slide over into artistry. Enough touches of the relatively novel, in the company of peers who are willing to take a chance, within the right constellation of power relations, can crystallize into a striking piece of work. That is why network executives and admen are disingenuous when they throw up their hands in interviews and say they would love to be patrons of excellence but where is the talent. As *Hill Street* shows, much talent stays hidden right within the confines of television itself, because the system prizes reliability more than native talent. Indeed, a reputation for excessive talent can prove troublesome.

This particular maverick was protected, though, by MTM and – in its own fashion – NBC. The whole amounted to something new, and jarring. It was new to the network and new to the test audience that viewed it for NBC in the spring of 1980. Of all the pilots the network tested during pilot season, *Hill Street Blues* tested among the lowest. Like *All in the Family* and *The Mary Tyler Moore Show* at CBS ten years earlier, this freak defied expectations. 'People didn't get involved with the characters,' Brandon Tartikoff says. Greg Hoblit was told that the test viewers were 'very disconcerted by the speed at which things went. It's an unsettling show. The pilot is very fast, and unresolved, and did not fit any notions that people who go to these tests have about what's a television show. And people were very unhinged by the shooting of Hill and Renko.'

According to one NBC research executive, the test audience thought there were too many characters. They found Furillo a strange hero indeed, an authority who couldn't control his extremist subordinate Hunter, who was publicly embarrassed by his ex-wife, who didn't seem to react emotionally to the shooting of his men. They wanted their heroes to be take-charge men and not plodders, this executive thought. He was convinced the show was going to fail.

Meanwhile, NBC asked a consulting psychologist for a scientific opinion about the number of plots an audience could hold in its mind simultaneously. The general industry assumption was that no more than three sub-plots were manageable within a single episode. The consultant relayed empirical psychology's conclusion that the 'magic number' was seven, plus or minus two; but added the qualification that as the characters became more familiar, their appearance could trigger associated memories and boost the viewers' capacity to handle sub-plots.

27

Visualizing the news

Richard Ericson, Patricia Baranek and Janet Chan

From Ericson, Richard; Baranek, Patricia and Chan, Janet 1987: *Visualizing deviance: a study of news organization*. Milton Keynes: Open University Press, 270–81.

Visuals for television

Television reporters have special requirements in obtaining visuals. These constitute both constraining and enabling features of reporting peculiar to television.

Reporter–Cameraman Relations. The cameraman is a highly valued member of the television newsroom. This was symbolized by the fact that while he was formally under the direction of the reporter, he was paid substantially more than the reporter, sometimes double or more. Moreover, the reporter was very dependent on the cameraman to understand what the story was about so it could be visualized appropriately. 'While the presence on the screen of the television reporter gives the story journalistic credibility in the traditional sense, it is heavily reliant on the news judgment of the cameraman' (Schlesinger, 1978, 160–1).

The basis of the reporter–cameraman relationship was tacit understanding of requirements. The cameraman has to become part of the newsroom culture and learn the vocabulary of precedents of reporters, editors and producers. He must learn the approach of each reporter and the subtle differences in the way each works. Over time a reporter develops a preference to working with a particular cameraman and vice versa. However, since reporter and crew assignments were done on the basis of situational availability rather than keeping a team together, it was not possible to expect a regular matching of those who felt that they worked well together.

Beyond tacit understandings and cues in the field, cameramen often offered specific advice and direct assistance. Advice was given freely on what shots to take, what clips or source quotations to use from shots taken, and what reporter voice-over phrasing might be appropriate for particular visuals. The cameraman also helped to encourage sources to co-operate generally, and to phrase particular notions when they stumbled or seemed unable to articulate in the manner expected.

As would be expected where aesthetic preferences are constantly being worked at rather than already worked out, reporter–cameramen relations were often marked with tension and conflict. Reporters carped about cameramen who took poor shots; packed up too early and therefore missed something of relevance; did not follow directions well; and failed to 'hustle' in the face of time limitations. In turn, cameramen were critical of reporters' judgements about the selection of sources; questioning of sources; overshooting, and otherwise obtaining too much information that risked missing the slot; and making stories where there were none in the opinion of the cameraman. Some of these disputes were taken to the level of supervisors. Underlying the reporter's concern was the fact that he was dependent on the cameraman for a good public face, while the cameraman could remain invisible after completing his visualization work.

On Locations. One picture may not be equivalent to a thousand words, at least not in television news. However, television does have the ability to show as well as to tell. It can show the location of an event and can also picture what the people involved look like, thereby providing for the audience readings of their moral character. It provides a form of tertiary understanding not available to print except through still photographs: during our observations, efforts ranged from committing a crew for hours to obtain a visual of a suspect leaving court with a bag over his head, to hiring a helicopter so a crew could obtain an overview of a fire.

Television actuality shots are quite rare. Visuals rarely capture an actual event in the world, only talk of an event. Hence, most often the choice of a location is a matter of finding some place or someone that will stand for what is being talked about. In terms of physical locations, these were termed 'generic spots'. The release of a government report on domestic violence was represented by a reporter stand-up in front of the legislative building. A politician whose election campaign included disputing a highrise-building development was interviewed near the site of the development to represent this point of the campaign. When a place of a type could provide the sign, then the most convenient one would do: for a story about the contamination of a pharmaceutical product sold in drugstores, the handiest local drugstore was chosen for the visuals; for a story about lawyers' fees for real estate transactions, a street near the newsroom was selected for shots of houses with 'for sale' signs.

If official reports or other documents were being talked about, these were sometimes also shown to exist. These visuals focused on title pages or bold headings, as well as taking key words or phrases to print across the screen with the document shown above or in the background. As in showing events and people, this treatment did not provide documentation of the matter being addressed but only a sign that the document being talked about actually existed and appeared in a particular form.

Most television stories were built around interview clips with a few sources, 'the talking head'. While the key aspect of these clips was the person's words rather than the context in which they were said, as shown in the visuals, the context was often deemed by the reporter to be a relevant component of his visualization of how the source was to be represented. An important consideration for the reporter was how to represent the source's authority, in the context of the matter being reported and the other sources involved. The basic choice was whether talking-head visuals should be 'on the street', or in the physical office which represented the source's official office. One executive producer encouraged 'on the street' accounts from ordinary folk, the vox pop. He circulated memos to reporters to this effect, including one that stressed the need generally of 'going to the street' rather than letting 'institutional mouthpieces get air time with no real people'. However, what was done in this respect depended on the particular story and the contexts in which sources were dealt with.

In stories of the basic point/counterpoint format, involving leading representatives of each of two organizations in dispute, the usual approach was to represent each in the authority of their physical office. An instance of this, in which complications arose, is illustrative. A representative of a citizens' organization trying to establish a halfway house for prisoners was also an executive of a large corporation, but did not want visuals to be taken in his corporate office because the matter did not pertain to that corporation. Similarly, the representative of a citizens' organization in opposition to the establishment of this halfway house did not wish to have his unrelated corporate office used for visuals. The reporter, wishing to represent both as men of significance, found alternative physical space to convey the authority of their offices visually. One person agreed to come to the television station for interview. He was interviewed sitting behind the desk of one of the station's senior executives, appearing as if it was his own. The other interview was done in the lobby of a quality hotel across the street from the source's corporate offices, with permission of the hotel. The lobby furniture was rearranged so that the source could be suitably visualized sitting in a stolid wingback chair, indicating that he too was talking from, and within, an authoritative office.

A reporter was assigned to do a story on the reaction of various ethnic groups to the revelation that RCMP security services had an 'ethnic list' of suspicious persons connected to various ethnic types. The reporter planned to do the story by filming the representatives of different ethnic groups 'on the street' to emphasize the 'voice of the people,' against what was portrayed as a possible sign of totalitarian practice of government. The first representative agreed to a street interview. The reporter then proceeded to interview a doctor who said that in his practice he had many patients who complained of abuse by immigration and RCMP policing authorities. However, upon arriving at this doctor's office it was discovered to be in a poor part of town and the doctor himself did not look the part: he was in his late twenties or early thirties, and casually dressed without tie or jacket. The reporter decided that a street interview with this person would undercut his authority as a family physician speaking sympathetically about aggrieved patients. In spite of crew grumblings about having to set up their lights inside, the reporter insisted on representing the source in the authority of his office to add credence to his story. In contrast, the third source, a representative of a Polish group, was wearing a quality business suit. He refused an interview on the street in spite of the reporter's efforts to convince him. Instead he insisted on being shot behind his desk, flanked by flags of Poland, Canada, and Ontario that were placed there by him for the purpose of the interview. In this instance the source's desire to appear authoritative won out, and the reporter ended up, against her initial wish, with two or three sources 'off the street.'

It was a convention to shoot two sources with opposing views from opposite angles. On one occasion a reporter thought that the cameraman tacitly understood this procedure when he asked him to obtain a clip from each of two opposition-party leaders making statements outside the legislature. When he discovered that the cameraman had taken shots of both from the same angle he was most annoyed, stressing that it was simply 'common sense' to shoot from opposite angles.

When sources were not available to be filmed, or a crew was not available to film them, other means were devised. A common practice was to telephone a source and obtain a voice recording that could be used along with a still photograph of the source and/or a shot of the reporter in the newsroom making the call. This was done in particular when a source was some distance from Toronto and the newsroom did not want to go to the expense of obtaining something that they knew could be captured in essence through a voice clip. In this circumstances something had to be shown with the voice clip, and if a still photograph of the source was lacking, that something was usually the reporter shown to be doing his job. While this representation was useless in terms of its relation to the source's statement, it was at least useful in showing the authority of the reporter's office.

Staging. The imperative of television journalists to represent visually people doing things related to the story often poses difficulties. Crews cannot always be on time at the place where the events are occurring, and even if they are they often face technical difficulties in obtaining shots with proper lighting, sound and focus. When such difficulties arise the solution is to have sources stage their activities, or in the words of the vocabulary of precedents, do a 'fake'. Indeed, the resource limitations and technical requirements of television news are so well known to sources that they usually take elaborate measures to script the event in advance and stage everything so that television crews can obtain their clips expeditiously. In this activity Goffman's dramaturgical model of social life is acted out in considerable detail.

When the requirement is talk about events, and 'talking heads' for television visuals, the news conference is a standard format. Well-prepared and -groomed organizational representatives represent what is organizationally in order. After the basic presentation at a news conference, sources are asked by a television journalist to repeat a part of their performance for the purposes of a television clip. This approach saves film and editing time, since shooting the entire presentation expends a lot of film and requires a lot of sorting out back in the film-editing room.

The two leaders of the Guardian Angels citizen-patrol organization, based in New York City, came to Toronto on several occasions to stage news events that might help them with their cause. They chose significant locations – such as the city-hall square, the main indoor shopping precinct, and a space in a park where a woman had been sexually assaulted – to conduct interviews and give displays of self-defence techniques. On these occasions television journalists cooperated in the staging of each event by helping with locations, props, and suggestions for the enactment of representative action such as self-defence-technique displays.

Similar staging techniques were employed by citizens' groups with other causes. Groups in opposition to nuclear weapons held several marches and demonstrations, engaging in acts guaranteed to result in arrest by police, and equally guaranteed to be visually represented as the dominant frame of television-news items. At one demonstration television reporters from two different outlets discussed the various staging techniques being employed. They were very negative about the sources' representations, but nevertheless felt 'forced' to treat them as a central aspect of how they visualized the deviance. They pointed out that the source organization selected a key location (a plant involved in weapons manufacture); a good day in summer when 'news' was likely to be 'slow' because key source bureaucracies were in recess; and, sent a release, along with promises via telephone calls, that there would be 'violence' of some sort. One television station had three crews on location. The source organization arranged for five people to jump over a fence to throw red paint, signifying blood, on a wall. They were stopped and arrested for trespass or public mischief. Meanwhile two women were able to paint with stencils six green doves on a wall before they were arrested for public mischief. A spokesperson for the organization, wearing a shirt displaying an anti-nuclear statement, was asked by a reporter why these acts were necessary. The source replied that it was a way of educating the public, through the media, about the role of Toronto-based firms in the manufacture of nuclear weapons. The reporter asked what acts of civil disobedience had to do with educating the public and was told that the organization wanted to remind employees of these firms, as well as the general public, that people have strong feelings about disarmament. The source organization had also come equipped with a variety of props – including banners (e.g., 'Ban the Bomb') and a coffin – all of which were focused on by cameramen, along with shots of the paint on the wall and the persons responsible being arrested. The reporters recognized that they were simply following the script of their source, and one remarked while editing that this item was a prime example of creating the news.

Virtually all sources work to create appearances for visuals in some way. Persons are selected who photograph and speak well. Background materials are also attended to, for example, piling papers and documents on the office desk to sustain the dominant cultural impression that good people work hard. If television crews are to be allowed inside private space to visualize what goes on there, it is in the terms of public culture.

Reporters did on occasion object to a source's staging techniques or props and were sometimes able to get rid of them. Ultimately it was for the reporter to decide what was an appropriate sign, and whether it was useful or in good taste. A reporter doing a story on a citizens' group campaigning against anti-Semitism included an interview with a source who had a collection of artifacts that were anti-Jewish, such as bumper-stickers, pamphlets and a Nazi flag. The source offered to hold the Nazi flag as she was being filmed, but the reporter regarded this as out of place and rejected it.

Reporters sometimes moved into the director's seat and used equally elaborate techniques of perfecting the 'fake'. A reporter doing a story on the introduction of a major foot-patrol–beat system for police arranged through the public-relations office of the police to meet two officers on patrol. The location selected was the 'Yonge Street strip,' a segment of a street widely visualized in the city as a centre of vice and disorderliness. One police officer was wired up with a tape recorder, and two were followed down the street by the reporter, cameraman and researcher. Shots were taken of the officers going into stores, talking to people on the street, interviewing people in an automobile accident, and writing a traffic ticket.

Efforts to film events occurring 'naturally' sometimes ran into difficulty so that staging was necessary. Television crews waited in the mayor's office for the arrival of two people who represented an organization wanting to meet the mayor's executive assistant about a social problem. When the two people arrived

and entered the office of the secretary to the executive assistant, they and the
television crews 'broke up' laughing at the effort to appear 'natural' in face of a
pack of reporters and cameramen. After everyone had regained composure, one
television reporter asked the two people to go out of the office and enter again. A
proper representation of the event was made on this 'retake'.

Reporters sometimes set out to recreate what had occurred previously without
always stating to the audience that it was a recreation. The RCMP had sent some
illegal drugs to an incinerator, but part of the shipment was lost. A reporter
decided to visualize the incineration process on film. At the incineration plant,
she had visuals taken of the fire itself, a 'pretend' run of a crane picking up the
garbage and dropping it into the incinerator, the temperature gauge, and a
conveyor belt carrying indestructable materials left behind after the ashes were
washed away. These visuals, visualizing the process, were then used by the
reporter in juxtaposition with a description of what was believed to have taken
place weeks before, when the drugs went missing. The result was a blend
of illusion and accounts of reality, as is evident in the following script of the
story.

Anchorperson roll-up: The RCMP had it . . . but it slipped out of their hands. In the process
of destroying the largest-ever cache of drugs seized in Canada . . . one million dollars'
worth went missing. The mounties had wanted to get rid of the stuff but not in the way
it disappeared. It has been recovered . . . but police are still trying to figure out how it
got lost. [Names reporter] has more.

Reporter: They tried to burn it away . . . faced with the problem of disposing 6 tonnes of
methagaeline . . . a heroin substitute . . . [fire burning in furnace]. RCMP took it to the
Metro Toronto incinerating plant [Sign: Metro Inc. plant]. On that day in June, an
RCMP truck arrived with its precious cargo . . . [truck dumping garbage] it came and
went 4 times with 200 million dollars worth of drugs, packed in Sunlight detergent
boxes . . . [Sunlight detergent box].

While 3 RCMP officers supervised . . . a crane picked up the drugs with the other
garbage and dropped it into the hopper leading to the incinerator. But inside the
incinerator . . . [a Metro works official] explains, the drug made it too hot [crane and
hopper travelling and dropping]. [Metro works official talking head]

Reporter: When the temperature went up to a critical point they shut down the incinerator
. . . One truck load was turned away and the RCMP were informed the drug clogged the
incinerator. Somehow one box was neither burned away nor returned to the RCMP
[temperature gauge, followed by shot of truck coming down ramp].

The RCMP didn't even know 1 million dollars' worth of drugs was missing . . . that
is until Metro Toronto police stopped a car 3 weeks later and found hidden in a
suitcase 35 pounds of meth . . . 3 people were subsequently charged for possession
of drugs and one of them is an employee of the incinerating plant . . . [stand-up]

Inspector [name] and his staff were the ones who announced the huge heist of meth
. . . last October . . . [Super: stock film showing RCMP] it was a dramatic seizure of
drugs at Collingwood airport . . . [still graphic: police firing guns with an airplane in
the background].

Even though the missing box went unnoticed for 3 weeks . . . [the inspector] says
he's sure there isn't any more on the streets . . . [box]

RCMP Inspector: I would be very surprised if there's another box missing . . . [etc.] [talking
head]

Reporter: The RCMP has used this plant three times . . . [Sign: Metro Inc. Plant] workers
don't have special security clearances . . . the RCMP assumes full responsibility [truck
going down ramp]

RCMP Inspector: Our procedure . . . [etc.] completely recalculated to make sure they get into the fire box. [talking head]

Reporter: The remaining drugs will be neutralized by a chemical process [pick up drug in box].

This story used visuals of the incineration process – including 'fakes' – to represent what happens in talking about what happened. The audience was offered the illusion of watching the actual dumping of the drugs, the detergent box used, etc., at the time. There was no mention that this was a reconstruction of what *may* have happened. Similarly, the artist's graphic of the original seizure of drugs ten months before was simply his visualization of what happened at that time. Apart from the talking heads, all the visuals were simply visualizations of how events might have appeared, and of how things might have looked in the improbable event a 'live-eye' television crew had been there at the time. Faced with the impossibility of being 'everywhere,' television news is left to visualize things as if they are.

Stocks. Time and space considerations influenced decisions about whether to use stocks (old visuals) from previous stories to represent something. A reporter faced with a distant event, an event that had already occurred, an event occurring in a physical space he could not penetrate, and/or an encroaching deadline, often turned to the stocks for something to add vision to his story. A considerable amount of 'research' in the television newsroom consisted of searches for appropriate stocks, and special 'researchers' were employed to assist reporters in this regard.

The choice of stocks also involved 'fake' elements. A reporter doing a story on an Ontario government report concerning domestic violence, including police response to it, had difficulty finding appropriate shots of police attending a domestic call. He and an editor searched for and eventually found stock footage from a story done five months earlier, involving the domestic-response team for the city of Detroit, Michigan. This footage visualized police officers talking with a woman, and was used with a voice-over stating. 'The report says wife battering must be treated as a crime . . . that the onus for laying charges in such cases should be with the police.' Of course the reporter's intention was not to lie with these shots of police – not to indicate that Detroit police should be seen to be helping Ontario women – but that the police institution should be doing more of what was represented in these pictures.

The only real concern in using this form of representation was that it not be seen through as an obvious fake. Thus, there was concern that repeated use of the same stock clip, especially to represent aspects of different stories rather than the same continuing story, would look bad. Moreover the stock clips usually had to look as if they appeared to have been taken at the time of the shots actually taken on the day. A reporter was preparing a story about an accused person, released after a preliminary hearing, who had decided to sue various officials for malicious prosecution and negligence. The reporter relied on stocks of the attorney general's office building to use with a voice-over stating this office was named in the suit. This story was in August, but the stock shot of the building showed it to be winter. The reporter had a close-up 'freeze' of the building edited to get rid of the snow in the wider shot. The reporter relied on stocks of police officers on motorbikes to use with a voice-over stating the chief of police and investigating officers were also named in the suit. This stock film had a background of trees with no leaves, indicating that it was not in August, but in this case the reporter did not ask for it to be 'frozen.' The regular memos from the executive producer included critiques about the use of stocks which laid bare the fact that they did not represent the time the story was done. One such memo complained that a particular reporter had all day to shoot new footage, but had relied on stock footage with snow on the ground when it was summer. Even though everyone could see that a particular visual clip was a representation, it was not to appear as a 'fake'.

Visual and Texts. The research literature emphasizes that television journalism is still dominated by the written text, and most of the conventions of print journalism are therefore applied in television journalism. If anything, the visual requirement serves as a limiting factor on television texts, meaning that they have less depth and range of opinion than is available in the quality press. Nevertheless the construction of a coherent text is paramount in most instances. 'The serious business of agenda setting is too important, as far as we can tell, for the visual imperative to be a major consideration' (GUMG, 1980, 248). The early news broadcasts of BBC television included sound only, and even a decade after its establishment in 1957, the BBC television news bulletin was in essence a radio bulletin read to camera, with a few illustrations. Even in the contemporary period television news has been portrayed as 'visual radio' (Gans, 1980) because the spoken word predominates, linking and ultimately binding the visual images (Williams, 1974).

The traditional interpretive role of the print journalist is sustained through the considerable degree to which the journalist himself appears, or voices-over, other visuals, talking about things that happened elsewhere. While clips with sources are termed 'actualities', they too involve the source talking about what has gone on, or is going on, in another time at a different place. The need for talk from sources, and for the reporter to connect their talk in the maintenance of a flow, means the text forecloses on the range of visual options. Visuals only rise to the forefront 'when the material is exclusive, exceptionally dramatic and has unusual immediacy' (GUMG, 1976, 121). A shot of a person leaping from a building that is leaping with flames may speak for itself. However, most visual material consists of people speaking for themselves. In this respect television most often pictures the sources who form part of the text, a capability also available to newspapers through still photographs.

The reporter constantly visualizes what visuals can be obtained in relation to the text he imagines to be appropriate and what can fit with what his sources have said. This relation is dialectical, with amendments to both text and visuals being made at every stage of the reporting process. The extent to which one or the other predominates is related to the nature of the matter being reported on. In a story on a public demonstration several video cameramen were sent to obtain copious material; video was selected because it does not require processing and can be edited with much greater speed. The reporter then returned to the newsroom to screen the videotapes and in that process took notes for an accompanying text. Only after the screening was the text prepared, with the reporter indicating explicitly to the researcher how the script was written in accordance with the visuals obtained. In contrast we witnessed scripts being written in advance and then tinkered with as required by source-interview material obtained and stocks available. When the requirement was simply to update a continuing story, then the updated information – augmented by background information, usually from newspaper clippings – was the core of the matter and written much like a newspaper journalist would write it. However, because something had to be put up on the screen, the journalist scrambled to obtain generic visuals, stocks, graphics, or whatever else would fill the bill.

The importance of visuals was revealed when there were problems in obtaining them. If particular visuals could not be obtained, or if obtained were deemed to be lacking in drama, immediacy, or exclusivity, then the entire story was sometimes dropped. Thus a reporter assigned to a story on Monday regarding a murder on the previous weekend initially screened some film a weekend crew had obtained. The film was of poor quality and there were only two things shown: the apartment building where the incident occurred, showing a third-floor balcony, and two detectives looking around for evidence. With no body and no police-car visuals, the reporter said he did not think he could build a story around it and the item was eventually dropped.

When there were inadequate visuals – often in the face of severe time limitations to search for stocks or to dispatch a crew, or in face of the material limitation of no crew available – one option was to do a script for the anchorperson to read. This script was sometimes accompanied by whatever visuals were available, but usually only included a head-on shot of the anchorperson reading what the reporter had written for him. This situation arose also when physical space was difficult or impossible to penetrate for visuals. For example, reporters doing court stories were prevented from filming in the courtroom or courthouse. They usually relied upon a graphic artist's representation of the key actors during the day in court, supplemented if possible by source interviews outside the courtroom and stocks of the original incident or investigation related to the court hearing. A typical court story we observed entailed the use of five graphics with the reporter's voice-over. We also observed instances in which not even an artist's conception was obtained, and the anchorperson was left to say what the reporter had written.

Visuals were used to make statements beyond the scripted text. A reporter was doing a story on fear among women, in the context of a reported series of incidents of attacks on women. She decided to take shots of a 'secluded' area in a park where a woman had been raped while sunbathing in her swimming suit. On location, there were approximately one hundred men, women, and children in the area. The reporter had the cameraman isolate two women in swimming suits sitting on a bench, with no other people in the background. This clip was later used in the story, suggesting that even after the rape there were women foolhardy enough to be in this 'secluded' area of the park and wearing only scanty clothing.

In the ideological use of visuals there was usually textual material to set the stage and give preferred readings of what the reporter was representing. '[S]uch commentary does not tend iconically to describe the shots, but rather forces the viewer to see shots indexically or even symbolically within a framework of understanding thereby established by the professionals' (GUMG, 1980, 332). A reporter covering a well-policed demonstration by persons opposed to nuclear weapons began his item with a series of shots of police dragging demonstrators off a roadway. Instead of his own words, he used a background audio clip of demonstrators elsewhere on the site singing 'Give Peace a Chance.' A shot of a woman being led by a policeman who had hold of her hair was selected to fit with a textual statement, 'For the most part police used as little violence as possible.' Here the reporter was suggesting visually that this was a possible instance of excessive use of force, even while the text standing by itself was less suggestive of police excesses.

In a story on local residents' opposition to the establishment of a halfway house for prisoners, the reporter wanted to visualize a view that people felt threatened and there was potential for danger. In order to do so she not only obtained a talking-head of a spokesperson for the citizens in opposition, but went to the location of the house proposed for this use to obtain suggestive visuals. On location she had the cameraman picture the house alongside the one next door, which had a for-sale sign on it. This was done in the context of a newspaper story which cited the potential centre's next-door neighbour as being concerned about the safety of her two children. 'Are they sex offenders, drug offenders, or what?' The suggestion to be left was that the house was for sale because the neighbour was concerned about 'criminals' moving into the neighbourhood. Shots were also taken of young children walking through the park across the street from the house, suggestive that with the park so accessible to the house, children might be easy prey. Visualizations of deviance of this type were rendered more easily and subtly with the aid of television visuals. In print, reporters would be quite unlikely to say, 'Since this park is directly across the street from the house, criminals are likely to watch for children playing in the park and calculate whom they can victimize.' They might obtain a quotation from a local resident expressing this fear, but even that is arguably less immediate and dramatic than *showing* the physical possibility with visuals.

Notes and references

I 1: What is communication? (Colin Cherry)

Notes

1 But such reflexes do not form part of true human language; like the cries of animals they cannot be said to be *right* or *wrong* though, as signs, they can be interpreted by our fellows into the emotions they express.
2 John Donne, the Sixteenth Devotion.
3 See Reusch and Kees (1964) for many illustrations and examples of pictures, icons, motifs, gestures, manners, etc.
4 With kind permission of the Clarendon Press, Oxford.
5 With kind permission of the *Journal of the Acoustical Society of America*.
6 Locke used the word 'semeiotic' to denote the 'doctrine of signs'. See Locke (1689). For an appreciation and survey of Peirce's relevant work in digestible form, see Gallie (1952).

References

Gallie, W.B. 1952: *Peirce and pragmatism*. Harmondsworth: Pelican Books. An outline of Peirce's scattered work.
Locke, John 1689: *An essay concerning human understanding*. Numerous editions: e.g. London: Ward, Locke & Bowden.
McDougall, W. 1927: *The group mind*. London: The Cambridge University Press.
Morris, C.W. 1938: Foundations of the theory of signs. In *International encyclopedia of unified science series*, Vol. 1.2. Chicago: University of Chicago Press. A brief introduction.
Morris, C.W. 1946: *Signs, language and behaviour*. New York: Prentice Hall Inc.
Reusch, J. and Kees, W. 1964: *Non-verbal communication*. Berkeley and Los Angeles: University of California Press.
Stevens, S.S. 1950: Introduction: a definition of communication. In Proceedings of the speech communication conference at MIT, *Journal of the Acoustical Society of America* 22, 689–90.

I 2: A generalized graphic model of communication (George Gerbner)

Reference

Halloran, James 1969: The communicator in mass communication research. In Halmos, P. (ed.), *The Sociological Review Monograph* 13. University of Keele, January 1969.

I 3: The analysis of communicative events (Saville-Troike)

References

Bateson, G. 1955: A theory of play and phantasy. *Psychiatric Research Reports 2*, 39–51. American Psychiatric Association.
Birdwhistell, R. 1952: *Introduction to kinesics: an annotation system for analysis of body motion and gesture*. Louisville, KY: University of Louisville Press.
Ekman, P. 1972: Universal and cultural differences in facial expressions of emotion. In J. Cole (ed.), *Nebraska symposium on motivation (1971)*, 207–83. Lincoln: University of Nebraska Press.
Ekman, P., W. Friesen and S. Tomkins 1971: Facial affect scoring technique: a first validity study. *Semiotica 3*: 37–58.
Erikson, F. and J. Shultz 1979: When is a context?: some issues and methods in the analysis of social competence. Unpublished manuscript.
Ervin-Tripp, S. 1969: Sociolinguistics. In L. Berkowitz (ed.), *Advances in experimental social psychology* 91–165. New York: Academic Press.
1972. On sociolinguistic rules: alternation and co-occurrence. In J. Gumperz and D. Hymes (eds.), *Directions in sociolinguistics: the ethnography of communication*, 213–50. New York: Holt, Rinehart & Winston.
Friedrich, P. 1972: Social context and semantic feature: the Russian pronominal usage. In J. Gumperz and D. Hymes (eds.) *op. cit.* 270–300.
Goffman, E. 1971: *Relations in public: microstudies of the public order*. New York: Harper & Row.
Gumperz, J. 1977: Sociocultural knowledge in conversational inference. In M. Saville-Troike (ed.), *Linguistics and anthropology*, 191–212. Washington, DC: Georgetown University Press.
Hall, E. 1963: A system for the notation of proxemic behaviour. *American Anthropologist 65*, 1003–26.
Hymes, D. 1967: Models of interaction of language and social setting. *Journal of Social Issues 33(2)*, 8–28.
1972. Models of the interaction of language and social life. In J. Gumperz and D. Hymes (eds.) *op. cit.*, 35–71.
Philips, S. 1976: Some sources of cultural variability in the regulation of talk. *Language in society 5(1)*, 81–95.
Shimanoff, S. 1980: *Communication rules: theory and research*. Beverly Hills: Sage.
Tannen, D. 1979a: Processes and consequences of conversational style. Dissertation, University of California at Berkeley.
Tsuda, A. 1980: An ethnographic study of sales events and salesman's talk in the American and Japanese speech communities. Dissertation, Georgetown University.

I 4: Defining language (Jean Aitchison)

References

Evans, W.E. and Bastian, J. 1969: Marine mammal communication: social and ecological factors. In H.T. Anderson (ed.), *The biology of marine mammals*. New York: Academic Press.

Hockett, C.F. 1963: The problem of universals in language. In J.H. Greenberg (ed.), *Universals of language*. Cambridge, Mass.: MIT Press.

McNeill, D. 1966: Developmental psycholinguistics. In Smith, F. and Miller, G.A. 1966: *The genesis of language*. Cambridge, Mass: MIT Press.

Marshall, J.C. 1970: The biology of communication in man and animals. In Lyons, J. (ed.), 1970: *New horizons in linguistics*. Harmondsworth: Penguin.

Morton, J. 1971: What could possibly be innate? In Morton, J. (ed.), *Biological and social factors in psycholinguistics*. London: Logos Press.

Robins, L. 1971: *General linguistics: an introductory survey*. Second edition, London: Longman.

Struhsaker, T.T. 1967: Auditory communication among vervet monkeys (*Cercopithecus aethiops*). In Altman, S.A. (ed.), *Social communication among primates*. Chicago: Chicago University Press.

Thorpe, W.H. 1961: *Bird song: the biology of vocal communication and expression in birds*. Cambridge: Cambridge University Press.

Thorpe, W.H. 1963: *Learning and instinct in animals*. Second edition. London: Methuen.

Von Frisch, K. 1950: *Bees: their vision, chemical sense and language*. Ithaca: Cornell University Press.

Von Frisch, K. 1954: *The dancing bees*. London: Methuen.

Von Frisch, K. 1967: *The dance and orientation of bees*. Translated by L.E. Chadwick, Cambridge, Mass.: Harvard University Press.

I 5: Verbal and non-verbal communication (Michael Argyle)

References

Abercrombie, K. 1968: Paralanguage: *British Journal of Disorders in Communication* 3, 55–9.

Argyle, M. 1972: Non-verbal communication in human social interaction. In R. Hinde (ed.), *Non-verbal communication*. London: Royal Society and Cambridge University Press.

Argyle, M., Salter, V., Nicholson, H., Williams, M. and Burgess, P. 1970: The communication of inferior and superior attitudes by verbal and non-verbal signals. *British Journal of Social and Clinical Psychology* 9, 221–31.

Brown, R. 1965: *Social psychology*. New York: Collier-Macmillan.

Burns, T. 1964: Non-verbal communication. *Discovery* 25(10), 30–7.

Chapple, E.D. 1956: *The interaction chronograph manual*. Moroton, Connecticut: E.D. Chapple Inc.

Cook, M. 1969: Anxiety, speech disturbances, and speech rate. *British Journal of Social and Clinical Psychology* 8, 13–21.

Crystal, D. 1969: *Prosodic systems and intonation in English*. London: Cambridge University Press.

Davitz, J.R. 1964: *The communication of emotional meaning*. New York: McGraw-Hill.

Ekman, P. and Friesan, W.V. 1969: The repertoire of non-verbal behaviour: categories, origin, usage, and coding. *Semiotica* 1, 49–98.

Hall, E.T. 1963: A system for the notation of proxemic behavior. *American Anthropologist* 65, 1003–26.

Jourard, S.M. 1966: An exploratory study of body-accessibility. *British Journal of Social and Clinical Psychology* 5, 221–31.

Kendon, A. 1972: Some relationships between body motion and speech: an analysis of an example. In A. Siegman and B. Pope (eds.), *Studies in dyadic communication*. Elmsford, New York: Pergamon.

Lott, R.E., Clark, W. and Altman, I. 1969: *A propositional inventory of research on interpersonal space*. Washington: Naval Medical Research Institute.

Melly, G. 1965: Gesture goes classless. *New Society*, 17 June, 26–7.

Sarbin, T.R. and Hardyk, C.D. 1953: Contributions to role-taking theory: role-perception on the basis of postural cues. Unpublished, cited by T.R. Sarbin 1954: Role theory. In G. Lindzey (ed.) *Handbook of social psychology*. Cambridge, Mass.: Addison-Wesley.

Scheflen, A.E. 1965: *Stream and structure of communication behavior*. Eastern Pennsylvania Psychiatric Institute.

Schlosberg, A. 1952: The description of facial expressions in terms of two dimensions. *Journal of Experimental Psychology* 44, 229–37.

Sommer, R. 1965: Further studies of small group ecology. *Sociometry* 28, 337–48.

I 6:   The analysis of representational images (Bill Nichols)

Notes

1   Excerpts from the transcript of Godard-Gorin's *Letter to Jane, Women and Film* 1 3/4 (1973), 48.

II: The socio-cultural relations of language

Notes

1   Levinson, Stephen C. 1983: *Pragmatics*. Cambridge: CUP, 35, 38.

2   Vološinov, V.N. 1973: *Marxism and the philosophy of language*. Trans. Matejka, Ladislav and I.R. Titunik. New York and London: Seminar Press, 94.

3   Potter, Jonathan, & Wetherall, Margaret 1987: *Discourse and social psychology: beyond attitudes and behaviour*. London: Sage, 6.

II 8:   Social class, language and socialization (Basil Bernstein)

References

Bernstein, B. 1962: Family role systems, socialization and communication. Manuscript, Sociological Research Unit, University of London Institute of Education. Also in: A socio-linguistic approach to socialization. In J.J. Gumpertz and D. Hymes (eds.), *Directions in sociolinguistics*. New York: Holt, Rinehart & Winston.

Bernstein, B. 1970: Education cannot compensate for society. *New Society* 387, February.

Bernstein, B. and Cook, J. 1965: Coding grid for maternal control. Available from Department of Sociology, University of London Institute of Education.

Bernstein, B. and Henderson, D. 1969: Social class differences in the relevance of language to socialization. *Sociology* 3(1).

Bright, N. (ed.) 1966: *Sociolinguistics*. The Hague and Paris: Mouton.

Carroll, J.B. (ed.) 1956: *Language, thought and reality: selected writings of Benjamin Lee Whorf*. New York: Wiley.

Cazden, C.B. 1969: Sub-cultural differences in child language: an inter-disciplinary review. *Merrill-Palmer Quarterly* 12.

Chomsky, N. 1965: *Aspects of linguistic theory*. Cambridge, Mass.: MIT Press.

Cook, J. 1971: An enquiry into patterns of communication and control between mothers and their children in different social classes. PhD thesis, University of London.

Coulthard, M. 1969: A discussion of restricted and elaborated codes. *Educational Review* 22(1).

Douglas, M. 1970: *Natural symbols*. London: Barrie & Rockliff, The Cresset Press.

Fishman, J.A. 1960: A systematization of the Whorfian hypothesis. *Behavioral Science* 5.

Gumpertz, J.J. and Hymes, D. (eds.) 1971: *Directions in sociolingustics*. New York: Holt, Rinehart & Winston. [Volume published 1972.]

Halliday, M.A.K. 1969: Relevant models of language. *Educational Review* 22(1).

Hawkins, P.R. 1969: Social class, the nominal group and reference. *Language and Speech* 12(2).

Henderson, D. 1970: Contextual specificity, discretion and cognitive social-ization: with special reference to language. *Sociology* 4(3).

Hoijer, H. (ed.) 1954: Language in culture. *American Anthropological Association Memoir* 79. Also published by University of Chicago Press.

Hymes, D. 1966: On communicative competence. Research Planning Conference on Language Development among Disadvantaged Children. Ferkauf Graduate School: Yeshiva University.

Hymes, D. 1967: Models of the interaction of language and social setting. *Journal of Social Issues* 23.

Labov, W. 1965: Stages in the acquisition of standard English. In W. Shuy (ed.), *Social dialects and language learning*. Champaign, Illinois: National Council of Teachers of English.

Labov, W. 1966: The social stratification of English in New York City. Washington DC Centre for Applied Linguistics.

Mandelbaum, D. (ed.) 1949: *Selected writings of Edward Sapir*. Berkeley and London: University of California Press.

Parsons, T. and Shils, E.A. (eds.) 1962: *Toward a general theory of action*. New York: Harper Torchbooks. [Chapter 1 especially.]

Schatzman, L. and Strauss, A.L. 1955: Social class and modes of communication. *American Journal of Sociology* 60.

Turner, G. and Pickvance, R.E. 1971: Social class differences in the expression of

234 Notes and references

uncertainty in five-year-old children. *Language and Speech* 14(4).
Williams, F. and Naremore, R.C. 1969: On the functional analysis of social class differences in modes of speech. *Speech Monographs* 36(2).

II 9: Impossible discourse (Trevor Pateman)

Notes

1 This passage was published in 1956. But in his seminar of 1971–2, Barthes was still speaking of the 'social contract' of language.
2 If 'flower' and 'rose' are not hierarchically ordered, then there is no contradiction for the speaker in such statements as 'It's a rose, not a flower' or 'If it's not a flower, is it a rose?' Note that the speaker is not contradicting himself; there is no contradiction for him, only for the hearer.
3 Not all trees are alike. Whorf (Carroll, 1956, 136; see also the whole of the essay *The relation of habitual thought and behaviour to language*, 134–59) suggests that the word 'stone' logico-linguistically implies 'non-combustibility'. However, this implication seems to exist only as the result of belief in a particular theory, namely that stone is non-combustible, and even to this theory there are exceptions (e.g. brimstone). The link between 'monarchy' and 'government' is different in nature. Here, the link is logico-linguistic. One could say that it is a synthetic truth (or falsehood) that 'stone' and 'non-combustibility' have the link they do or are supposed to have, whereas it is an analytic truth that 'government' and 'monarchy' have the relationship which they do. Whorf fails to come to terms with the fact that different theories can be developed within the same language (by speakers of the same language) and this I presume, because of his identification of thought and language.
4 If I am correct in thinking that the conceptual understanding of a word requires reference to a superordinate term, then the most abstract words – those at the tops of trees – with no superordinate words of their own, would be doomed to remain the words for complexes; they could not be concepts. This seems to me paradoxical, for it is my conventional view that the most abstract words ought to be the most rigorously conceptually definable.
5 To a larger degree, this was recognized by the students of schizophrenic thought being criticized. Thus, for instance, Kasanin writes that abstract or categorical thinking (the absence of which was regarded as a trait of schizophrenia) 'is a property of the educated adult person' (1944, 42). And Hanfmann and Kasanin write that 'the difference in [test] scores of this [group, largely composed of attendants at a state mental hospital] and of the college-educated group is sufficiently striking to warrant the conclusion that the highest performance level in the concept formation test is the prerogative of subjects who have had the benefit of college education' (1942, 59–60).
6 The question then arises, What are the specific features of schizophrenia? Some have concluded that there are none, that schizophrenia as a disease-entity does not exist.
7 Many of Wason and Johnson Laird's undergraduate samples do appallingly on reasoning tests. This cannot just be put down to the nature of the tests, for

some do well on them. It could be put down to differential reactions to the test situation. Hudson has explored this (1970).

8 The opposition abstract/concrete helped me a great deal when I started in 1970 on the lines of thought developed here, though it has fallen into a secondary place in this chapter. I would still recommend the books which originally helped me, namely Cassirer (1944) and Goldstein (1963).

9 Compare from a different context the following criticism of Cameron: 'In our opinion all explanations [of failure on the Vygotsky blocks test] in terms of evasion or projection of blame on the task etc., misrepresent the situation of those patients who perform to the best of their ability but are unable even to conceive of the performance required from them' (1944, 96).

10 Based on a discussion in an evening class I once taught.

11 Vygotsky's child has an adequate understanding of both 'cow' and 'dog', otherwise he would not be able to make the particular mistake that he does.

12 This point was brought home to me by Chris Arthur.

13 Some people seek to solve political problems by spatial displacement that is, by *emigration*. It would be interesting to study the political ideology of emigration, perhaps making use of Gabel's theories about spatialization (1969).

14 In contrast, Reich construes apathy as a defence mechanism against recognition of one's class position and interests (1970, 201).

15 'The masses' class consciousness does not consist of knowing the historical and economic laws which rule the existence of man, but: (1) knowing one's own needs in all spheres; (2) knowing the means and possibilities of satisfying them; (3) knowing the hindrances which the social order deriving from private enterprise puts in their way: (4) knowing which inhibitions and fears stand in the way of clearly recognizing one's vital needs and the factors preventing their fulfilment . . .; (5) knowing that the masses' strength would be invincible in relation to the power of the oppressors if only it were coordinated.' (Reich, 1971, 68–9.)

16 'If one wants to lead the mass of the population into the field against capitalism, develop their class consciousness and bring them to revolt, one recognizes the principle of renunciation as harmful, stupid and reactionary. Socialism, on the other hand, asserts that the productive forces of society are sufficiently well developed to assure the broadest masses of all lands a life corresponding to the cultural level attained by society.' (Reich, 1971, 23–4.)

17 Reich, in contrast, has a manipulative concept of song, dance and theatre: 'we must secure the emotional attachment of the masses. Emotional attachment signifies trust, such as the child has in its mother's protection and guidance, and confidence in being understood in its innermost worries and desires including the most secret ones, those relating to sex'. (1971, 58–9.) Apart from the last nine words, this reads more like Stalin than Reich.

18 The Maoist criticism of Stalin, that he made mistakes, is no criticism at all. For it does not challenge his right to have held the kind of power which *permitted him* to make such mistakes.

References

Bachelard, G. 1970: *La formation de l'esprit scientifique*. Paris: Bibliothèque des Textes Philosophiques.

Barthes, R. 1967: *Elements of semiology*. London: Cape.

Barthes, R. 1972: *Mythologies*. London: Cape.

Bernstein, B. 1971: *Class, codes and control: volume one: theoretical studies towards a sociology of language*. London: Routledge.

Carroll, J.B. (ed.) 1956: *Language, thought and reality: selected writings of Benjamin Lee Whorf*. Cambridge, Mass.: MIT Press.

Cassirer, E. 1944: *An essay on man*. New Haven, Conn.: Yale University Press.

Gabel, J. 1969: *La fausse conscience, essai sur la réification*. Third edition, Paris: Editions de Minuit.

Goldstein, K. 1963: *Human nature in the light of psychopathology*. New York: Schocken Books.

Halliday, M.A.K. 1969: Relevant models of language. *Educational Review* 22.

Hanfmann, E. and Kasanin, J. 1942: *Conceptual thinking in schizophrenia*. Nervous and Mental Diseases Monograph Series number 67.

Hudson, L. 1970: *Frames of mind*. Harmondsworth: Penguin.

Kasanin, J. (ed.) 1944: *Language and thought in schizophrenia*. Stanford, Calif.: University of California Press.

Laing, R.D. and Esterson, A. 1970: *Sanity, madness and the family*. Harmondsworth: Penguin.

Lyons, J. 1968: *An introduction to theoretical linguistics*. Cambridge: Cambridge University Press.

McKenzie, R. and Silver, A. 1969: *Angels in marble*. London: Heinemann.

Marcuse, H. 1964: *One-dimensional man*. London: Routledge.

Pateman, T. 1973a: Review of R. Barthes, *Mythologies*. *Human Context* 5.

Pateman, T. 1973b: The experience of politics. *Philosophy and Phenomenological Research* (USA) 33.

Reich, W. 1970: *The mass psychology of fascism*. Trans. V.R. Carfagno. New York: Farrar, Straus & Giroux.

Reich, W. 1971: *What is class consciousness?* London: Socialist Reproduction.

Saussure, F. de 1966: *Course in general linguistics*. Trans. W. Baskin. New York: McGraw-Hill.

Vygotsky, L. 1962: *Thought and language*. Cambridge, Mass.: MIT Press.

Wason, P. and Laird, P. Johnson 1972: *Psychology of reasoning: structure and content*. London: Harvard University Press.

Wertheimer, M. 1961: *Productive thinking*. London: Tavistock.

Wittgenstein, L. 1958: *Philosophical investigations*. Second edition, Oxford: Blackwell.

Wood, J. (ed.) 1970: *Powell and the 1970 election*. Surrey: Elliot Right Way Books.

II 10: The co-operative principle and the rules for conversation (Mary Louise Pratt)

Notes

1   Grice's lectures have not yet been published in their entirety, though a substantial excerpt has appeared in Cole and Morgan (1975). My own discussion of Grice is based on the unpublished manuscript of the lectures. In this and following page references I have used a roman numeral to indicate the number of the lecture, followed by an Arabic numeral indicating the page number within the lecture text.

2 The term 'illocutionary act' was coined by the philosopher J.L. Austin to denote speech acts such as asserting, warning, apologizing, promising, and so on. Austin claimed that there were over a thousand such illocutionary acts in English. [Editors' note].

References

Cole, Peter & Morgan, Jerry L., eds. 1975: *Syntax and semantics*, vol. III, *Speech acts*. New York: Academic Press.

II 11: The structures of speech and writing (Gunther Kress)

References

Brazil, D.C. 1975: *Discourse intonation*. Discourse analysis monographs no. 1. Birmingham: English Language Research.
Hymes, Dell 1972: On communicative competence. In Pride, J.B., and Holmes, J. (eds.) 1972: *Sociolinguistics*. Harmondsworth: Penguin.

II 12 Beyond alienation: an integrational approach to women and language (Deborah Cameron)

Notes

1 Simone de Beauvoir, *Memoirs of a Dutiful Daughter*, Trans. Kirkup (Penguin 1963) p. 17.
2 Camilla Gugenheim, 'Man Made Language?' *Amazon*, no. 4, 1981.
3 Audre Lorde, *The Cancer Journals*, (Spinsters Ink, 1980) p. 19.
4 Genesis, 11: 6–9.
5 For Ferdinand de Saussure see the editors' introduction to this section. Benjamin Lee Whorf is representative of a 'strong' version of linguistic determinism. Basing his views on a study of the language of the North American Hopi Indians, he claimed that because their language structured reality differently from, say, English, the Hopi perceived the world differently from native English speakers. [Editors' note].
6 Trevor Pateman, *Language, Truth and Politics*, 2nd edn (Jean Stroud, 1980) p. 129.
7 Cora Kaplan, 'Language and Gender', *Papers on Patriarchy* (WPC/PDC, 1976).
8 *Ibid.*, p. 21.
9. J. Gumperz, *Discourse Strategies* (CUP, 1982) and J. Gumperz (ed.), *Language and Social Identity* (CUP, 1982).
10 Gumperz, *op. cit.*, pp. 4–5.
11 D. Maltz and R. Borker, 'A Cultural Perspective on Male/Female Miscommunication', in Gumperz, *op. cit.*
12 Colin MacCabe, 'The Discursive and the Ideological in Film', *Screen*, 19/4.
13 M. Black and R. Coward, 'Linguistic, Social and Sexual Relations', *Screen Education*, 39, p. 78.
14 Dalston Study Group, 'Was the patriarchy conference "patriarchal"?', in *Papers on Patriarchy*, p. 76.

15 M. Jenkins and C. Kramarae 'A Thief in the House', in *Men's Studies Modified*, ed. Spender (Pergamon, 1981).

16 Kaplan, op. cit., p. 21.

17 Shirley Ardener, *Perceiving Women* (John Wiley, 1975); Philip Smith, 'Sex Markers in Speech', in *Social Markers in Speech*, ed. K. Scherer and H. Giles (CUP, 1979).

18 Marielouise Janssen-Jurreit, *Sexism* (Pluto Press, 1982) p. 284.

19 O. Jespersen, *Language: Its Nature, Development and Origin* (Allen & Unwin, 1922), p. 246.

20 Elino Keenan, 'Norm Markers, Norm Breakers' in *Explorations in the Ethnography of Speaking*, ed. R. Bauman and J. Sherzer, (CUP, 1974).

21 E. Marks and I. de Courtivron (eds), *New French Feminisms*, p. 5.

22 J.J. Rousseau, *Emile*, quoted in J. O'Faolain and L. Martines, *Not in God's Image*, (Fontana, 1974) p. 259.

23 Dale Spender, *Man Made Language* (Routledge & Kegan Paul, 1980) p. 107.

24 Cf. Jenkins and Kramarae, *op.cit.*, pp. 16–17.

25 See M. Jenkins and C. Kramer, 'Small group process: learning from women', *WSIQ*, 3, 1980', D. Jones, 'Gossip: notes on women's oral culture', *WSIQ*, 3, 1980.

26 Basil Bernstein, *Class, Codes and Control*, vol. 1, (Routledge & Kegan Paul, 1970).

27 W. Labov, *The Logic of Non-Standard English*, repr. in Giglioli, P. P. (ed.), *Language and Social Context* (Penguin, 1972).

28 Jespersen, *Language*, ch. 24.

29 Dalston Study Group, 'Was the patriarchy conference "patriarchal"?', *Papers on Patriarchy*, p. 77.

II 14 Fiction & reportage: two accounts compared (David Lodge)

Notes

1 Peter Stansky and William Abrahams, *The Unknown Orwell (1972)* p. 224.

2 *Ibid.* pp. 163–4.

3 George Orwell, *The Road To Wigan Pier* (Harmondsworth, 1962) p. 128.

4 Stansky and Abrahams, *op. cit.* p. 205.

5 For a perceptive discussion of this point, see 'The Language Field of Nazism', *Times Literary Supplement*, 5 April 1974, pp. 353–4.

6 Victor Shklovsky, 'Art as "Technique"', quoted by Robert Scholes, *Structuralism in Literature* (1974) pp. 83–4. Scholes follows the translation of Lee T. Lemon and Marion J. Reis, *Russian Formalist Criticism* (Lincoln, Nebraska, 1965), but emends the final sentences (italicized) for reasons explained in a note.

7 Victor Shklovsky, 'Tristram Shandy: Stylistic Commentary', Lemon and Reis, *op. cit.* p. 57.

8 'Coming Apart' by James Griffin & Robb Royes of 'Bread'.

9 Ludwig Wittgenstein, *Tractatus Logico-Philosophicus (1922)* 6.4311.

III 15: Cultural factors in human perception (A.R. Luria)

References

Allport, G.W. and Pettigrew, T.F. 1957: Cultural influence on the perception of movement: the trapezoidal illusion among Zulus. *Journal of Abnormal and Social Psychology* 55, 104–13.
Deregowski, J.B. 1968a: Difficulties in pictorial depth perception in Africa. *British Journal of Psychology* 59, 195–204.
Deregowski, J.B. 1968b: On perception of depicted orientation. *International Journal of Psychology* 3, 149–56.
Rivers, W.H.R. 1901: Primitive color vision. *Popular Science Monthly* 59, 44–58.
Segall, M.H., Campbell, D.T. and Herskovits, M.J. 1966: *The influence of culture on visual perception*. Indianapolis: Bobbs-Merrill.
Yarbus, A.L. 1967: *Eye movements and vision*. New York: Plenum.

III 16: The perceptual process (Albert H. Hastorf, David J. Schneider and Judith Polefka)

References

Leeper, R. 1935: The role of motivation in learning: a study of the phenomenon of differential motivational control of the utilization of habits. *Journal of Genetic Psychology* 46, 3–40.

III 17: Social communication (Stuart Sigman)

Notes

1 The careful reader will have noted that I alternate between describing communication as a 'process' and as a 'structure.' Communication is an *organized activity*, and can thus be studied from the two interrelated vantage points.
2 'Rule' is used in a most general sense to refer to statements about socially patterned procedures for behaving and interpreting (see Sigman [1980a]; Shimanoff [1980] for various uses of the term). Rules are analytic devices to account for behaviour units; relations among behaviour units; contextuality; and normative force (Sigman, 1985a). The degree of constraint that rules place on persons, and the definitions of the relevant interacting body or bodies, for example, persons, groups, and so on, to which rules apply are cross-culturally variable and are subject to empirical observation. Thus, social communication theory leaves open the possibility that normative and interpretive views of the social order and communication rules will be appropriate to varying degrees to different cultures (cf. Donohue, Cushman, and Nofsinger, 1980).
3 This is an axiom that guides certain structuralist methodologies (see Birdwhistell, 1970; Scheflen, 1973). For a limited criticism of this approach, see Condon (1980), who presents some data that question the total hierarchical

organization of behaviour. Note also that the guiding principle of hierarchy does not directly address the issue of whether a top-down or bottom-up view is most appropriate (cf. Scheflen, 1973; Kendon, 1982), that is, whether the hierarchy is seen as an organization of frame levels that constrain the appearance of behaviour units on lower levels or as a structure built up from lower units. See chapter 2.*

4 The mechanical model often seems to assume a nonequivalence of the interactants as well, at least in terms of their information states. However, this model usually sees communication as bringing the participants' information states more in line with each other, as in the case of the sender sending information to an unknowledgeable receiver. See chapters 4 and 5* for an elaboration on the social communication suggestion that communication need not involve isomorphic rules guiding participants' behaviour or isomorphic information states resulting from interaction.

References

Aberle, D.F., Cohen, A.K., Davis, A.K., Levy, M.J. Jr., and Sutton, F.X. 1950: The functional prerequisites of a society, *Ethics* 6, 100–11.

Aldrich, H. 1972: Sociability in Mensa: characteristics of interaction among strangers. *Urban Life and Culture* 1, 167–86.

Annandale, E. 1985: Work roles and definitions of patient helath. *Qualitative Sociology* 8, 124–48.

Berger, P.L. 1963: *Invitation to sociology: a humanistic perspective.* Garden City, NY: Doubleday Anchor.

Berger, P.L. and Luckmann, T. 1967: *The social construction of reality.* Garden City, NY: Doubleday Anchor.

Bernstein, B. 1975: *Class, codes and control: theoretical studies towards a sociology of language.* New York: Schocken.

Birdwhistell, R.L. 1977: Some discussions of ethnography, theory, and method. In Brockham, J. (ed.) 1977: *About Bateson.* New York: Dutton, 103–41.

—— 1970: *Kinesics and context.* Philadelphia: U. of Philadelphia Press.

—— 1952: *Introduction to kinesics.* Washington, D.C.: Foreign Service Institute.

Blum, A.F. and McHugh, P. 1971: The social ascription of motives. *American Sociological Review* 36, 98–109.

Carey, J.W. 1975: A cultural approach to communication. *Communication* 2, 1–22.

Condon, W.C. 1980: The relation of interactional synchrony to cognitive and interactional process. In Key, M.R. (ed.) 1980: *The relationship of verbal and nonverbal communication.* The Hague: Mouton, 49–65.

Cushman, D.P. 1980: A functional approach to rules research. Paper presented to the Eastern Communication Association, Ocean City, Maryland.

Denzin, N.K. 1984: *On understanding emotion.* San Francisco: Jossey-Bass.

Donohue, W.A., Cushman, D.P., and Nofsinger, R.E. 1980: Creating and confronting social order: a comparison of rules perspectives. *Western Journal of Speech Communication* 44, 5–19.

* Not included in this extract.

Durkheim, E. 1938: *The rules of the sociological method*. Chicago: U. of Chicago Press.
—— 1933: *The division of labor in society*. New York: Free Press.
Erickson, F. and Shultz, J. 1982: *The counselor as gatekeeper: social interaction in interviews*. New York: Academic Press.
Fisher, B.A. 1978: *Perspectives on human communication*. New York: Macmillan.
Frentz, T.S. and Farrell, T.B. 1976: Language-action: a paradigm for communication. *Quarterly Journal of Speech* 62, 333–49.
Gergen, K.J. 1982: *Toward transformation in social knowledge*. New York: Springer-Verlag.
Gerth, H. and Mills, C.W. 1953: *Character and social structure*. New York: Harcourt, Brace.
Giddens, A. 1984: *The constitution of society*. Berkeley: U. of California Press.
Goffman, E. 1967: *Interaction ritual*. Chicago: Aldine.
—— 1963: *Behavior in public places*. New York: Free Press.
Golding, P. and Murdoch, G. 1978: Theories of communication and theories of society. *Communication Research* 5, 339–56.
Halliday, M.A.K. 1978: *Language as social semiotic: the social interpretation of language and meaning*. London: Edward Arnold.
Harré, R., Clarke, D., and DeCarlo, N. 1985: *Motives and mechanisms: an introduction to the psychology of action*. London: Methuen.
Heritage, J.C. and Watson, D.R. 1979: Formulations as conversational objects. In Psathas, G. (ed.) 1979: *Everyday language: studies in ethnomethodology*. New York: Irvington, 123–62.
Hochschild, A.R. 1983: *The managed heart*. Berkeley: U. of California Press.
Hymes, D. 1974: *Foundations in sociolinguistics*. Philadelphia: U. of Pennsylvania Press.
Jakobson, R. 1960: Closing statement: linguistics and poetics. In Sebeok, T. (ed.) 1960: *Style in language*. Cambridge, Mass.: MIT Press.
Joos, M. 1967: *The five clocks*. New York: Harcourt, Brace and World.
Kemper, T.D. 1972: The division of labor: a post-Durkheimian analytical view. *American sociological review* 37, 739–53.
Kendon, A. 1982: The organization of behavior in face-to-face interaction: observations on the development of a methodology. In Scherer, K.R. and Ekman, P. (eds.) 1982: *Handbook of methods in nonverbal behavior research*. Cambridge: CUP, 440–505.
Kockelmans, J.J. 1975: Toward an interpretative or hermeneutic social science. *Graduate Faculty Philosophy Journal* 5, 73–96.
Kroeber, A.L. 1963: *Anthropology: culture patterns and processes*. New York: Harcourt Brace Jovanovich.
LaBarre, W. 1954: *The human animal*. Chicago: U. of Chicago Press.
Lasswell, H.D. 1971: The structure and function of communication in society. In Schramm, W., and Roberts, D.F.W. (eds.) 1971: *The process and effects of mass communication*. Urbana, I11.: U. of Illinois Press, 84–99.
Leach, E. 1976: *Culture and communication*. Cambridge: Cambridge UP.
Linton, R. 1940: A neglected aspect of social organization. *American Journal of Sociology* 45, 870–86.
—— 1936: *The study of man*. New York: Appleton-Century-Crofts.
Lundberg, G. 1939: *Foundations of sociology*. New York: Macmillan.

Mandelbaum, M. 1973: Societal facts. In O'Neill, J. (ed.) 1973: *Modes of individualism and collectivism*. London: Heinemann, 221–36.

McCall, G.J. and Simmons, J.L. 1978: *Identities and interactions*. Rev. ed. New York: Free Press.

Mead, G.H. 1934: *Mind, self, and society*. Chicago: U. of Chicago Press.

Merton, R.K. 1968: *Social theory and social structure*. Enlarged ed. New York: Free Press.

Nwoye, G. 1985: Eloquent silence among the Igbo of Nigeria. In Tannen, D. and Saville-Troike, M. (eds.) 1985: *Perspectives on silence*. Norwood, N.J.: Ablex, 185–91.

O'Neill, J. (ed.) 1973: *Modes of individualism and collectivism*. London: Heinemann.

Pearce, W.B. and Cronen, V.E. 1980: *Communication, action, and meaning: the creation of social realities*. New York: Praeger.

Pike, K.L. 1967: *Language in relation to a unified theory of the structure of human behavior*. The Hague: Mounton.

Pittenger, R.E., Hockett, C.F., and Danehy, J.J. 1960: *The first five minutes: a sample of microscopic interview analysis*. Ithaca, NY: Paul Martineau.

Poole, M.S. and McPhee, R.D. 1983: A structurational analysis of organizational climate. In Putnam, L.L., and Pacanowsky, M.E. (eds.) 1983: *Communication and organizations: an interpretive approach*. Beverly Hills: Sage, 195–219.

Poole, M.S., Siebold, D.R., and McPhee, R.D. 1985: Group decision-making as a structurational process. *Quarterly Journal of Speech* 71, 74–102.

Radcliffe-Brown, A.R. 1965: *Structure and function in primitive society*. New York: Free Press.

Rapoport, A. 1982: *The meaning of the built environment*. Beverly Hills: Sage.

Rosen, L. 1984: *Bargaining for reality: the construction of social relations in a Muslim community*. Chicago: U. of Chicago Press.

Scheflen, A.E. 1973: *Communicational structure: analysis of a psychotherapy transaction*. Bloomington, Ind.: Indiana UP.

—— 1968: Human communication: behavioral programs and their integration in interaction. *Behavioral Science* 13, 44–55.

—— 1965b: Systems in human communication. Paper presented to the Society for General Systems Research, Berkeley, California.

Scott, R.L. 1977: Communication as an intentional social system. *Human Communication Research* 3, 258–68.

Shimanoff, S. 1980: *Communication rules*. Beverly Hills: Sage.

Sigman, S.J. 1985a: Some common mistakes students make when learning discourse analysis. *Communication Education* 34, 119–27.

—— 1983a: Some multiple constraints placed on conversational topics. In Craig, R.T. and Tracy, K. (eds.) 1983: *Conversational coherence*. Beverly Hills: Sage, 174–95.

—— 1982: Some communicational aspects of patient placement and careers in two nursing homes. Unpublished PhD. dissertation, University of Pennsylvania.

—— 1980a: On communication rules from a social perspective. *Human Communication Research* 7, 37–51.

Sorokin, P.A. 1947: *Society, culture, and personality*. New York: Harper and Brothers.

Thomas, S. 1980: Some problems of the paradigm in communication theory. *Philosophy of Social Sciences* 10, 427–44.

Watzlawick, P., Beavin, J.H., and Jackson D.D. 1967: *Pragmatics of human communication*. New York: Norton.

Wilden, A. 1979: Changing frames of order: cybernetics and the *Machina Mundi*. In Krippendorff, K. (ed.) 1979: *Communication and control in society*. New York: Gordon and Breach Science Publishers, 9–29.

III 18: Historical changes in gestural behaviour (David Efron)

Notes

1 For a fuller description, see our book, *Race and gesture*.

2 The Man in the Club Window, 1870: *The habits of good society: a handbook for ladies and gentlemen*. London: Low & Company, 284–5.

3 The following anecdote by Charles Lamb suggests that the habit of button-holding in gesticulation was also practised by Anglo-Saxons of a subsequent period.

> I was going from my house at Enfield to the India-house one morning, and was hurrying, for I was rather late, when I met Coleridge, on his way to pay me a visit; he was brimful of some new idea, and in spite of my assuring him that time was precious, he drew me within the door of an unoccupied garden by the roadside, and there, sheltered from observation by a hedge of evergreen, he took me by the button of my coat, and closing his eyes commenced an eloquent discourse, waving his right hand gently, as the musical words flowed in an unbroken stream from his lips. I listened entranced; but the striking of a church recalled me to a sense of duty. I saw it was of no use to attempt to break away, so taking advantage of his absorption in his subject I, with my penknife, quietly severed the button from my coat and decamped. (Richard W. Armour and Raymond F. Howes, *Coleridge the talker* [Cornell University Press, 1940] p. 279.)

With very slight alterations, Steele's description of the tactile gestures of the English coffee-house orators of the beginnings of the eighteenth century fits perfectly the gestural behaviour of a good many of the habitués of any café in the East Side Jewish ghetto of New York City today.

Button's was one of the rendezvous places of the upper and middle classes, and was kept by no less a lady than the Countess of Warwick. Cf., e.g., Addison: *The Spectator*, No 556: 'I was a Tory at Button's and a Whig at Child's'. Also Johnson's *Lives of the most eminent English poets*, edition of 1801, II, 110–11.

4 Holden, S.M. 1925: *Fifty years of glorious oratory (1875–1925)*. Manchester: Weekly Advertiser Ltd, 97, 103, 186, 193, 201.

5 Estienne, Henri 1883: *Deux dialogues du nouveau langage François Italianizé et autrement desguizé, principalement entre les courtisans de ce temps*. Paris, Liseaux, I, 100 and 212; II, 99–100. [The first edition of the book saw its light in Geneva, in 1578.]

6 The last decade of the sixteenth century, and the first half of the seventeenth,

mark the period during which the formation of the 'société polie' and the 'préciosité' takes place. It is, it will be recalled, the period in which the French nobility, having already lost a great part of its political power, undergoes a process of social domestication under the influence of the rising middle class. The standards of vigorous emotionality of the 'gentilhomme d'épée' fall into temporary discredit, and are superseded by a new set of affective and bodily norms ('grace', 'mesure', 'raison', etc.), proper of the new type of model-man which the middle class sets forth as its ideal: the 'honête homme'. D'Urfé's *Astrée*, the *Hotel de Rambouillet*, and, a few years later, Mlle de Scudery's 'ruelle', her *Grand Cyrus*, and her *Clélie*, are landmarks in the history in this change in the standards of emotional demeanour and bodily conduct of the upper strata of early seventeenth-century French society. The *mot d'ordre* of the 'honête homme' is *self-control* (maitrise de soi-même), always and everywhere. This standard pervades most of the writings – literary, moralistic, religious, and philosophical – of that period. It is found in the pastoral novel, from Montreux to D'Urfé; in the treatises of 'civilité', from Menage to Somaize; in the historical novel, from Scudery to La Caprenède; in Corneille's tragedies; in Camus's, François de Sales's and Vincent de Paul's religious treatises; in Descartes's *Les Passions de l'Ame* and in his letters. To give just one example among hundreds, the primacy of 'raison' in emotional behaviour is very seldom questioned by D'Urfé's characters. In fact, they are eager to declare again and again the rational character of their affective reactions. Symptomatic of this attitude are certain recurring expressions in their vocabulary, such as the word 'coldly': '. . . Je vous parle froidement . . ., c'est pour vous fair entendre que la passion ne me transporte pas' (Astrée, I, 536). 'Ne croye pas, Hylas, repondit *froidement* Thamyra . . .' (*ibid.*, IV, 382). '. . . le Druide luy repondit *froidement*' (*ibid.*, I, 25). 'Je voy bien, repondit *froidement* Hylas' (*ibid.*, I, 70). 'Je ne scay, repondit *froidement* Sylvandre' (*ibid.*, I, 269); etc., etc. 'Maitrise de soi-même' finds a concrete application in the realm of expressive bodily conduct, in general, and particularly in that of gestural behaviour. The manifestation of feeling and thought is reduced to a minimum in the circles of the 'société polie'. An energetic play of features, a fiery glance, a vehement gesture, a loud tone of voice, are considered to be a violence to the spirit of 'bienséance', or, as Sarasin, one of the famous habitués of the Hotel de Rambouillet, used to say, things proper of 'the heap' (la tourbe), which is not rational enough to control its passions.

The two following statements are illustrative of the strong abhorrence that the 'société polié' felt for the unrestrained expression of the emotions. They represent the reactions of two of its prominent members to the vigorous affectivity of the Elizabethan stage which they witnessed in England. The statements are an interesting comment on the theory of 'racial' calmness of the Anglo-Saxon versus 'racial' excitability of the Frenchman. We see here Englishmen of the middle of the seventeenth century behaving like 'warm-blooded Mediterraneans' and Frenchmen of the same period reacting like 'cool Nordics'.

Our poets, who know the tastes of gentlemen, do not bloody our stage and never show violent acts. By contrast, the English poets, playing to the appetites of their audiences, always have the stage awash with blood and never fail to decorate their plays with catastrophes. . . . (lePays *Lettre de l'Angleterre*, in *Lettres*, III.)

[English tragedies are] a jumble of confused events with no regard for propriety. Eyes greedy for the cruelty of the spectacle are keen to see murders and bleeding bodies. To avoid the horror of it by means of narration, as is done in France. . . . (Saint Evremond, *Sur les Tragédies*, 1677). For standards of self-restraint of the 'société polié', cf. Henri Magendie, *La Politesse Mondaine et les Théories de l'Honnêteté.*

(Editors' translation)

III 19: Introduction to the presentation of self in everyday life (Erving Goffman)

Notes

1 Gustav Ichheiser, 'Misunderstandings in Human Relations', Supplement to *The American Journal of Sociology* LV (September 1949), pp. 6–7.
2 Quoted in E.H. Volkart (ed.), *Social behaviour and personality*, contributions of W.I. Thomas to Theory and Social Research (New York: Social Science Research Council, 1951), p. 5.
3 Here I owe much to an unpublished paper by Tom Burns of the University of Edinburgh. He presents the argument that in all interaction a basic underlying theme is the desire of each participant to guide and control the responses made by the others present. A similar argument has been advanced by Jay Haley in a recent unpublished paper, but in regard to a special kind of control, that having to do with defining the nature of the relationship of those involved in the interaction.
4 Willard Waller, 'The Rating and Dating Complex', *American Sociology Review* II, p. 730.
5 William Sansom, *A contest of ladies* (London: Hogarth, 1956), pp. 230–2.
6 The widely read and rather sound writings of Stephen Potter are concerned in part with signs that can be engineered to give a shrewd observer the apparently incidental cues he needs to discover concealed virtues the gamesman does not in fact possess.
7 An interaction can be purposely set up as a time and place for voicing differences in opinion, but in such cases participants must be careful to agree not to disagree on the proper tone of voice, vocabulary, and degree of seriousness in which all arguments are to be phrased, and upon the mutual respect which disagreeing participants must carefully continue to express towards one another. This debaters' or academic definition of the situation may also be invoked suddenly and judiciously as a way of translating a serious conflict of views into one that can be handled within a framework acceptable to all present.
8 W.F. Whyte, 'When Workers and Customers Meet', chap. vii, *Industry and society*, edited by W.F. Whyte (New York: McGraw-Hill, 1946), pp. 132–3.
9 Teacher interview quoted by Howard S. Becker, 'Social Class Variations in the Teacher–Pupil Relationship', *Journal of Educational Sociology* XXV, p. 459.

10 Harold Taxel, 'Authority Structure in a Mental Hospital Ward' (unpublished Master's thesis, Department of Sociology, University of Chicago, 1953).

11 This role of the witness in limiting what it is the individual can be has been stressed by the Existentialists, who see it as a basic threat to individual freedom. See Jean-Paul Sartre, *Being and nothingness* (London: Methuen, 1957).

12 Goffman, 'Communication Conduct in an Island Community', pp. 319–27.

13 Peter Blau, 'Dynamics of Bureaucracy' (PhD dissertation, Department of Sociology, Columbia University, University of Chicago Press, 1955), pp. 127–9.

14 Walter M. Beattie, Jr, 'The Merchant Seaman' (unpublished MA Report, Department of Sociology, University of Chicago, 1950), p. 35.

15 Sir Frederick Ponsonby, *Recollections of three reigns* (London: Eyre & Spottiswoode, 1951).

16 For comments on the importance of distinguishing between a routine of interaction and any particular instance when this routine is played through, see John von Neumann and Oscar Morgenstern, *The theory of games and economic behaviour* (second edition; Princeton University Press, 1947), p. 49.

III 20: Interaction between text and reader (Wolfgang Iser)

Notes

1 See Ingarden, Roman, *The literary work of art*, trans. Grabowicz, George G. (Evanston, Ill.: Northwestern University Press, 1973, 276 ff.).

2 Laing, R.D., Phillipson, H. and Lee, A.R. *Interpersonal perception: a theory and a method of research* (New York: Springer, 1966).

3 Ibid. 4.

4 Laing, R.D., *The politics of experience* (Harmondsworth: Penguin Books, 1968, 16). Laing's italics.

5 Ibid., 34.

6 Ibid.

7 See also Goffman, E., *Interaction ritual: essays on face-to-face behaviour.* (New York: Doubleday, 1967).

8 Woolf, Virginia, *The common reader: first series* (London: Hogarth Press, 1957, 174). In this context, it is well worth considering Virginia Woolf's comments on the composition of her own fictional characters. She remarks in her diary: 'I'm thinking furiously about Reading and Writing. I have no time to describe my plans. I should say a good deal about *The Hours* and my discovery: how I dig out beautiful caves behind my characters: I think that gives exactly what I want; humanity, humour, depth. The idea is that the caves shall connect and each comes to daylight at the present moment.' *A writer's diary: being extracts from the diary of Virginia Woolf*, Woolf, Leonard (ed.), (London: Hogarth Press, 1953, 60). The suggestive effect of the 'beautiful caves' is continued in her work through what she leaves out. On this subject, T.S. Eliot once observed: 'Her observation, which operates in a continuous way, implies a vast and sustained work of organization. She does not illumine with sudden bright flashes but diffuses a soft and placid light. Instead of looking for the primitive,

she looks rather for the civilized, the highly civilized, where nevertheless something is found to be *left out*. And this something is deliberately left out, by what could be called a moral effort of the will. And, being left out, this something is, in a sense, in a melancholy sense, present.' 'T.S. Eliot "places" Virginia Woolf for French readers', in Majumdar, Robin and McLaurin, Allen (eds.), *Virginia Woolf: the critical heritage*, (London: Routledge and Kegan Paul 1975, 192).

III 22: The flower dream (Sigmund Freud)

References

Ferenczi, S. 1917: Träume der Ahnungslosen. *Int. Z. ärztl. Psychoanal.* 4(208), 498.
[Translator's note: Dreams of the unsuspecting. *Further contributions to the theory and technique of psycho-analysis*. London, 1926, chapter LVI].
Freud, S. 1905a: *Jokes and their relation to the unconscious. Standard edition of the complete psychological works of Sigmund Freud* vol. 8. London: Hogarth Press, 1953–74.
Freud, S. 1905b: Fragment of an analysis of a case of hysteria. *Standard edition* vol. 7.
Freud, S. 1909: Notes upon a case of obsessional neurosis. *Standard edition* vol. 10.

IV 24: The production context of *Coronation Street* (Richard Paterson)

Notes

1 By this I mean the particular way in which all the signs (both visual and aural) are used to create meaning in the narrative.
2 The JICTAR national ratings show that in 1975 *Coronation Street* had fallen from its usual position as one of the top ten audience pullers. Thus in the week ending Sunday 19 October 1975, the Monday episode was 12th in the weekly ratings with an estimated audience of 7.3 million homes, and the Wednesday episode 20th with 6.35 million homes viewing. However by the week ending Sunday 15 October 1978 the Monday episode was first in JICTAR national ratings, and the Wednesday episode seventh, with an estimated 17.8 million and 15.05 million individual viewers respectively. These 'national' figures conceal regional differences in the programme's popularity and also don't indicate the demographic breakdown of the audience. While these in themselves could form the basis of another paper, it is possible to discern broad trends in the change of audience composition between 1975 and 1980, from the figures which JICTAR supply to their subscribers. In the North West (Granadaland) there was an increase in the proportion of available homes tuned in, with a small increase in the proportion of housewives and women viewing (they are classified separately), a static but quite high male viewership, but a substantial increase in the child audience.
3 Cf. 'How the backroom boys kept Stan Ogden out of jail', *TV Times* 85.46, 4 November 1976, p. 30.

4 *Editors' note* This is to be found in *Screen Education* 20, which contains a number of articles on this popular TV series.
5 *Editors' note* Susi Hush was a producer of *Coronation Street* in the 1970s. Her quoted comments appear in Thornber, R. Why Coronation Street will never be the Susi Hush show, *The Guardian*, 16 December 1974.

References

Alvarado, M. and Buscombe, E. 1978: *Hazell: the making of a TV series*. London: British Film Institute/Latimer.
Annan, Lord (Chairman) 1977: *Report of the committee on the future of broadcasting*. Cmnd. 6753. London: HMSO
Black, P. 1972: *The mirror in the corner*. London: Hutchinson.
Chanan, M. 1976: *Labour power in the British film industry*. London: British Film Institute.
Edmondson, M. and Rounds, D. 1973: *The soaps: daytime serials of radio and TV* New York: Stein and Day.
Goldie, G.W. 1977: *Facing the nation: television and politics 1936–1976*. London: Bodley Head.
Goodhardt, G.J., Ehrenburg, A.S.C. and Collins, M.A. 1975: *The television audience: patterns of viewing*. Farnborough: Saxon House.
Gordon, N. 1975: *My life at 'Crossroads'*. London: Star Books.
Paterson, R. 1980: 'Planning the family: the art of the television schedule', in *Screen Education 35*.
Scannell, P. 1980: 'The social eye of television, 1946–1955' in *Media, Culture and Society* 1.1
Seglow, P. 1978: *Trade unionism in television*. Aldershot: Saxon House.
Stedman, R.W. 1977: *The serial*. Norman, U.S.A.: University of Oklahoma Press.

IV 25: *Dallas* between reality and fiction (Ien Ang).

Notes

1 For a foundation of this semiological approach to television programmes, see *inter alia* U. Eco, 'Towards a semiotic inquiry into the television message', *Working Papers in Cultural Studies 2*, 1972; and S. Hall, 'Encoding and decoding in the television discourse', C.C.C.S. Occasional Stencilled Papers, University of Birmingham, 1973.
2 See also R.C. Allen, 'On reading soaps: a semiotic primer', in E. Ann Kaplan (ed.), *Regarding television*, Los Angeles: American Film Institute, 1983.
3 D. Morley, *The 'nationwide' audience*, London: British Film Institute, 1980, 10.
4 J-M Piemme, *La propagande inavoué*, Paris: Union Generale d'Editions, 1975.
5 *ibid.*, 176.
6 *ibid.*, 114.
7 'Empiricist' because the basic premise is used that reality can be gathered from the manifestation of the world. Cf. C. MacCabe, 'Theory and film: principles of realism and pleasure', *Screen 17.3*, 1976, 9–11.

8 R. Williams, *Marxism and literature*, Oxford: OUP, 1977, 97.

9 Piemme, *La propagande inavoué*, 120–1.

10 See also Piemme, 170–1.

11 For a critique of the theory of the classic-realist text, see *inter alia* T. Lovell, *Pictures of Reality*, pp 84–87; also D. Morley, 'Texts, readers, subjects', in S. Hall, D. Hobson, A. Lowe, P. Willis (eds.) *Culture, Media, Language*, Hutchinson, London, 1980, 163–73.

12 The distinction between denotation and connotation is made among others by Roland Barthes in his *Elements of Semiology*, Jonathan Cape, London 1967. Subsequently various semiologists have contested this distinction, because it suggests a hierarchy between 'literal' and 'figurative' meaning, which does not in fact exist. However, in his *S/Z*, Hill and Wang, New York, 1974/Jonathan Cape, London 1975, Barthes defends this distinction if it is a matter of the analysis of what he calls 'the classical text' (as opposed to the 'modern text'). It is in any case important to regard the distinction between denotation and connotation as an analytical difference. See also S. Hall, 'Encoding/Decoding', in Hall *et al.* (eds.), *Culture, Media, Language*.

13 The concept 'structure of feeling' comes from Raymond Williams. See for example his *Marxism and Literature*, 128–35.

IV 27: Vizualizing the news (R. V. Ericson, P. M. Baranek and J. B. Chan).

References

Gans, H. 1980: *Deciding what's news*. New York: Vintage.

GUMG (Glasgow University Media Group) 1976: *Bad news*. London: Routledge.

GUMG (Glasgow University Media Group) 1980: *More bad news*. London: Routledge.

Schlesinger, P. 1978: *Putting 'reality' together: BBC news*. London: Constable.

Williams, R. 1974: *Television: technology and cultural form*. London: Fontana.

Subject index